문학작품 속 실용영어

문학작품 속 실용영어

발행일	2021년 12월 15일

지은이	한상택		
펴낸이	손형국		
펴낸곳	(주)북랩		
편집인	선일영	편집	정두철, 배진용, 김현아, 박준, 장하영
디자인	이현수, 한수희, 김윤주, 허지혜, 안유경	제작	박기성, 황동현, 구성우, 권태련
마케팅	김회란, 박진관		
출판등록	2004. 12. 1(제2012-000051호)		
주소	서울특별시 금천구 가산디지털 1로 168, 우림라이온스밸리 B동 B113~114호, C동 B101호		
홈페이지	www.book.co.kr		
전화번호	(02)2026-5777	팩스	(02)2026-5747

ISBN   979-11-6836-066-2 03740 (종이책)   979-11-6836-067-9 05740 (전자책)

(주)북랩 성공출판의 파트너

북랩 홈페이지와 패밀리 사이트에서 다양한 출판 솔루션을 만나 보세요!

홈페이지 book.co.kr • **블로그** blog.naver.com/essaybook • **출판문의** book@book.co.kr

작가 연락처 문의 ▶ ask.book.co.kr

작가 연락처는 개인정보이므로 북랩에서 알려드릴 수 없습니다.

영문학이 영어를 만날 때

문학작품 속
실용영어

한상택 지음

북랩 book

　과거에는 문학과 언어를 물과 기름처럼 융해할 수 없는, 가령 수학적 도식에서 말하는 공집합 같은 것으로 생각했다. 그러나 1980년대에 들어서면서 미국이나 유럽에서는 문학과 언어가 서로 교류할 수 있는, 즉 상보적 관계에 있는 것으로 전제하고 이에 대한 많은 주장과 임상 실험들을 해왔다. 그 결과 두 영역이 공유하는 부분(interface)을 적절히 활용하여 문학과 언어 영역에 공히 상승효과(synergy)를 줄 수 있는 많은 활동이 제안되고 있다. 특히, EFL상황에서 언어학습을 위한 진정한 자료로서 언제 어디서나 손쉽게 구매 가능한 문학 텍스트의 활용 가치는 대단히 높다.

　언어학습 자원을 위한 문학 텍스트의 고유한 이점들은 언어의 4가지 기능을 고루 증진시킬 수 있다는 것이다. 특히, 산문으로 되어있는 문학 텍스트(소설이나 단편소설, 문학적 스토리 등)는 언어학습이나 습득에 필요한 '장면적 문맥(일명, 상황적 맥락: context of situation)'이 풍부하다. 즉, 실제 생활에서 의사소통 시 동원되는 제반 환경요소들이 문학 텍스트에도 그대로 녹아있기 때문에 좋은 언어학습 환경을 제공할 수가 있다.

　언어를 학습하는 데는 인지적인 면 외에도 정의적인 면이 중요하다. 문학은 특징상 여느 글과 달라 우선 정의적인 면에 많이 호소한다. 아울러 상상의 나래를 펴며 흥미를 자아내는 문학 텍스트는 계속적인 읽기 과정을 조장시킨다.

읽기 과업으로써 문학 텍스트가 언어학습에 일조한다는 가설은 이미 언급한 바와 같이 여러 학자의 임상실험을 통하여 증명된 바다. Clark & Cowan(1979)은 읽기 과업으로써 문학 텍스트의 독해 과정은 다른 능력-작문력, 구사력, 청취력 등-을 기르는 데도 도움이 된다고 피력한다. 일단 독해에 흥미를 갖게 되면 계속 읽음으로써 다양한 표현을 접하게 되고, 그 표현들은 작문 및 회화 과정에 응용이 되기 때문이다. Smith(1970) 또한 문학작품을 읽음으로써 회화 구사력과 작문력의 향상을 기를 수 있다고 한다. 그에 의하면 학생들은 문학을 독창적으로 읽는 과정에서 이중 효과를 거두는데, 그것은 스토리, 희곡, 시를 읽을 수 있을 뿐만 아니라 직접 스토리를 구술하며, 희곡을 무대에 올려보고, 시를 써보는 과정에서 언어를 송신하고 수신하는 능력을 기를 수 있다는 것이다.

위에서 언급한 여러 가지 이론을 바탕으로 문학 텍스트가 언어학습에 주는 구체적인 이점들은 다음과 같이 요약될 수 있다.

첫째, 문학 자체가 주는 즐거움으로 학습에 대한 흥미를 느낄 수 있다. 언어학습에 적극적이고도 지속적인 참여를 할 수 있는 동기유발을 할 수 있기 때문이다. 둘째, 어휘학습과 문법학습에 일조할 수 있다. 즉, 문맥을 통하여 모르는 어휘와 반복되는 다양한 문형을 자연스럽게 터득할 수 있다. 셋째, 문학은 많은 읽기를 요구하므로 많은 독서량으로 인한 독해능력을 향상할 수 있다. 아울러 독서 과정은 끊임없는 자기와의 대화 과정이기 때문에 자기 수양과 같은 교육적 가치가 있다. 넷째, 단순한 정보적 전달이 아닌 정의적 감화에 의해 장기 기억술에 도움이 되고, 창조적인 감정표현이나 사고능력을 가질 수 있다. 즉, 문학 텍스트의 구조 특성에 기인한 논리적인 전개 과정이나 추론능력을 기를 수 있다. 다섯째, 진정한 교재가 될 수 있다. 이를 통해 일부 외국어 교육을 위해 인위적으로 조작한 교재의 맹점을 어느 정도 해결 할 수 있다. 여섯째, 다양한 문학적 장치 등 텍스트에 나타난 제반 사항에 관한 토론 활동이 가능하고, 진정한 상황과 문화적 맥락에 의한 말의 여러 격식을 알수 있다. 이를 통해 의사소통능력 향상에 도움이 되는 것은 자명한 일이다. 일곱째, 간접체험에 의해 문화를 익힐 수 있다. 이는 목표 언어에 대한 스키마 형성에 이바지한다. 여덟째, 여러 가지 수사적 구조 및 비유적 표현을 익히는 과정에서 쓰기 능력을 향상할 수 있다. 글의 전개에 따른 상황적 맥락으로부터 나오는 대화 과정은 듣기 향상에도 이바지한다.

혼히 어떤 표현을 하고자 할 때 상황에 맞는 정확한 영어표현이 어떻게 되나 고심할 때가 있다. 문학 텍스트를 읽다 보면 그러한 표현을 발견할 수 있다. 이 책은 그러한 부분을 집중적으로 조명하여 문학 텍스트 속에 녹아있는 실생활에 적합한 표현을 발굴하여 제시하였다. 이 책은 어렸을 때부터 번역판으로 읽어왔거나, 대학 때 원서로 접했던 작품까지

약 100여 권의 정도의 문학 텍스트로부터 발췌한 일부분들을 수록하였다. 발췌된 장르는 모든 영역(소설, 단편소설, 에세이, 우화, 신화, 전설, 민담, 자전적 이야기, 일기, 전기, 서간문, 연설문 등)을 고루 다루었다. 이해를 돕기 위해 각각의 '예문(*로 시작되는 문장)' 아래에는 원문을 실었고, 더 완벽한 본문이해를 위해 'Note'를 더해 중요 표현에 대한 해설을 주었다.

끝으로 인용한 텍스트들은 축약된(abridged) 버전으로 원문(original)이 아닌 것도 일부 있으며 부득불 비영어권 작품이라서 영어로 번안한 작품들도 있다. 하지만 전문적인 원어민들에 의한 번역 작품으로 원문의 기본 뜻을 살리는 데는 별 지장이 없었다고 생각된다. 그렇지만 지면 할애 상 원문 전체를 기재하지 못하고 일부 필요한 부분을 제시하기 위해 텍스트 전체로부터 중간중간의 발췌로 본의 아니게 독해 과정상 흐름을 끊게 하여 문학 텍스트의 읽는 맛을 반감시켰다는 것에 대해 양해를 바라는 바다.

※ 본문에 115개의 문학 작품 제목하에 제시된 예문들은 실제로 각각의 작품 속에 나왔던 구어체 표현을 발췌하여 저자가 따로 만든 예문들이다. 따라서 제공된 문학 작품들을 감상하는 과정에서 아래의 예문들이 실제로 어떻게 표현되고 있는가 발견하는 기쁨을 갖게 될 것이다.

목차

여는 말 • *P.4*

001 *Daddy-Long Legs* - Jean Webster • *PP.14~25*

002 *Brother Griffith's Story of Mad Monkton* - Wilkie Collins • *PP.26~39*

003 *Brother Griffith's Story of the Family Secret* - Wilkie Collins • *PP.40~42*

004 *The Moonstone* - Wilkie Collins • *PP.43~45*

005 *To a Student in Uncertain Health* - Philip Gilbert Hamerton • *P.46*

006 *To a Student in Great Poverty* - Philip Gilbert Hamerton • *P.47*

007 *To a Friend Who Kindly Warned the Author of the Bad Effects of Solitude* - Philip Gilbert Hamerton • *P.48*

008 *Tom Brown's School Life* - Thomas Hughes • *PP.49~64*

009 *The Bottle Imp* - Robert Louis Stevenson • *PP.65~68*

010 *The Suicide Club* - Robert Louis Stevenson • *PP.69~74*

011 *Treasure Island* - Robert Louis Stevenson • *PP.75~85*

012 *The Life of Our Lord* - Charles Dickens • *P.86*

013 *A tale of Two Cities* - Charles Dickens • *PP.87~106*

014 *David Copperfield* - Charles Dickens • *PP.107~123*

015 *Oliver Twist* - Charles Dickens • *PP.124~132*

016 *Mrs Leicester's School* - Charles Lamb • *PP.133~135*

017 *Stories from Shakespeare* - Charles Lamb • *PP.136~141*

018 *Alice in Wonderland* - Lewis Carroll • *PP.142~147*

019 *The Adventure of King Arthur* - Howard Pyle • *PP.148~152*

020 *Woman's Wit(adapted)* - Howard Pyle • *PP.153~158*

021 *The Town Musician of Bremen* - J & W Grimm • *PP.159~160*

022 *The Sleeping Beauty* - J & W Grimm • *PP.161~162*

023 *'The Elves and the Shoemaker' in Grimm's Fairy Tales(adapted)*
  - J & W Grimm • *P.163*

024 *'The Wolf and the Seven Little Goats' in Grimm's Fairy Tales(adapted)*
  - J & W Grimm • *P.164*

025 *'The Frog Prince' in Grimm's Fairy Tales(adapted)* - J & W Grimm • *PP.165~166*

026 *'Rapunzel' in Grimm's Fairy Tales(adapted)* - J & W Grimm • *P.167*

027 *'Snow-White and Rose-Red' in Grimm's Fairy Tales(adapted)*
  - J & W Grimm • *P.168*

028 *Little Snow White(adapted)* - J & W Grimm • *PP.169~170*

029 *The Twelve Dancing Princesses(adapted)* - J & W Grimm • *P.171*

030 *Hansel and Gretel(adapted)* - J & W Grimm • *P.172*

031 *The Adventures of Sindbad the Sailor(adapted)* - J & W Grimm • *PP.173~174*

032 *Little Red-Cap(adapted)* - J & W Grimm • *P.175*

033 *Doctor Know-All(adapted)* - J & W Grimm • *P.176*

034 *The Stars* - Alphonse Daudet • *P.177*

035 *A Woman of Arles* - Alphonse Daudet • *P.178*

036 *To M Pierre Gringoire, Lyric Poet in Paris* - Alphonse Daudet • *P.179*

037 *The Fall of the House of Usher* - Edgar Allen Poe • *PP.180~182*

038 *A Descent into the Malestrome* - Edgar Allen Poe • *PP.183~185*

039 *The Purloined Letter* - Edgar Allen Poe • *PP.186~187*

040 *The Gold Bug* - Edgar Allen Poe • *PP.188~195*

041 *The Murders in the Rue Morgue* - Edgar Allan Poe • *PP.196~199*

042 *Up from Slavery* - Booker T Washington • *PP.200~205*

043 *Black Beauty* - Anna Sewell • *PP.206~211*

044 *The Golden Touch in a Wonder-Book for Boys and Girls*
- Nathaniel Hawthorne • *PP.212~213*

045 *The Three Golden Apples in a Wonder-book for Boys and Girls*
- Nathaniel Hawthorne • *PP.214~215*

046 *The Scarlet Letter* - Nathaniel Hawthorne • *PP.216~220*

047 *David Swan* - Nathaniel Hawthorne • *P.221*

048 *The Great Stone Face* - Nathaniel Hawthorne • *P.222*

049 *Sir Isaac Newton* - Nathaniel Hawthorne • *PP.223~226*

050 *Biographical Stories* - Nathaniel Hawthorne • *PP.227~228*

051 *The Bible Story* - Nathaniel Hawthorne • *PP.229~231*

052 *Little Woman* - Louisa May Alcott • *PP.232~234*

053 *After Twenty Years* - O Henry • *PP.235~236*

054 *A Retrieved Reformation* - O Henry • *P.237*

055 *The Cop and the Anthem* - O Henry • *P.238*

056 *The Sketch Book* - Washington Irving • *PP.239~243*

057 *The Necklace(adapted)* - Maupassant • *PP.244~247*

058 *Boule de Suif(adapted)* - Maupassant • *PP.248~253*

059 *God Sees the Truth, but Waits(adapted)* - Leo Nikolaevich Tolstoy • *PP.254~255*

060 *What Man Lives(adapted)* - Leo Nikolaevich Tolstoy • *PP.256~259*

061 *The Story of Ivan the Fool(adapted)* - Leo Nikolaevich Tolstoy • *PP.260~262*

062 *Darling(adapted)* - Anton Chekhov • *PP.263~265*

063 *The Bet(adapted)* - Anton Chekhov • *P.266*

064 *Once a Year(adapted)* - Anton Chekhov • *PP.267~268*

065 *Gusev(adapted)* - Anton Chekhov • *P.269*

066 *The Call of the Wild* - Jack London • *PP.270~274*

067 *Daisy Miller* - Henry James • *PP.275~276*

068 *Wuthering Height* - Emily Bronte • *PP.277~280*

069 *The King of the Golden River* - John Ruskin • *PP.281~284*

070 *Abraham Lincoln(adapted)* - Autobiography • *PP.285~287*

071 *Tom Sawyer Detective* - Mark Twain • *PP.288~294*

072 *The Prince and the Pauper* - Mark Twain • *PP.295~296*

073 *The Adventures of Huckleberry Finn* - Mark Twain • *PP.297~299*

074 *The Adventures of Tom Sawyer* - Mark Twain • *PP.300~305*

075 *Don Quixote* - Miguel De Cervantes • *PP.306~312*

076 *The Story of My Life* - Benjamin Franklin • *PP.313~314*

077 *Jane Eyre* - Charlotte Bronte • *PP.315~318*

078 *Silas Marner* - George Eliot • *PP.319~322*

079 *The Fir Tree(adapted)* - Hans Christian Andersen • *PP.323*

080 *Tom Thumb* - Hans Christian Andersen • *PP.324~325*

081 *The Little Match-girl* - Hans Christian Andersen • *P.326*

082 *The Red Shoes* - Hans Christian Andersen • *P.327*

083 *The Three Musketeers(adapted)* - Alexandre Dumas • *PP.328~330*

084 *Peter Pan* - James Matthew Barrie • *P.331*

085 *Ivanhoe* - Sir Walter Scott • *PP.332~333*

086 *Robinson Crusoe* - Daniel Defoe • *PP.334~337*

087 *Gulliver's Travel(Brobdingnag)* - Jonathan Swift • *PP.338~341*

088 *Gulliver's Travels(Lilliput)* - Jonathan Swift • *PP.342~345*

089 *The Happy Prince* - Oscar Wilde • *PP.346~348*

090 *King Alfred and the Cakes(adapted)* - James Baldwin • *PP.349~350*

091 *Androclus and the Lion(adapted)* - James Baldwin • *P.351*

092 *The King and His Hawk(adapted)* - James Baldwin • *P.352*

093 *Grace Darling(adapted)* - James Baldwin • *PP.353~354*

094 *The Story of William Tell(adapted)* - James Baldwin • *P.355*

095 *The bell of Atri(adapted)* - James Baldwin • *PP.356~357*

096 *Cornelia's Jewels(adapted)* - J & W Baldwin • *P.358*

097 *Story of Frankenstein* - Mary Shelley • *PP.359~365*

098 *The Bride Comes to Yellow Sky* - Stephen Crane • *PP.366~370*

099 *Ali Baba and the Forty Thieves(adapted)* • *PP.371~372*

100 *Aladdin and the Wonderful Lamp(adapted)* • *PP.373~377*

101 *The Terrible Iron Bed(adapted) from Greek Myth* • *P.378*

102 *The Monster of Crete(adapted) from Greek Myth* • *P.379*

103 *Noncooperation with Nonviolence* - Mohandas Karamchand Gandhi • *P.380*

104 *Franklin D Roosevelt's Declaration of War* - Franklin Delano Roosevelt • *P.381*

105 *An Iron Curtain Has Descended* - Winston Churchill • *PP.382~384*

106 *Against Hunger, Desperation, and Chaos* - George C Marshal • *PP.385~386*

107 *Decline to Accept the End of Man* - William Faulkner • *P.387*

108 *I have a Dream* - Martin Luther King • *P.388*

109 *The Speech in the Mass for Peace* - Pope Paul VI • *P.389*

110 *Nixon's Inaugural Address* - Richard Nixon • *P.390*

111 *Carter's Inaugural Address* - Jimmy Carter • *PP.391~393*

112 *Reagan's 1st Inaugural Address* - Ronald Wilson Reagan • *P.394*

113 *The Key to Progress is Freedom* - Ronald Wilson Reagan • *P.395*

114 *Solzhenitsyn's Speech of Acceptance of His 1970 Nobel Prize*
    - Alexander Solzhenitsyn • *PP.396~397*

115 *The Solitude of Latin America* - Gabriel Garcia Marquez • *PP.398~399*

Daddy–Long Legs

- Jean Webster

작품 소개: 고아 소녀, 제루샤 애벗(Jerusha Abbott)이 후원가의 도움으로 대학에 진학하고, 이름 모를 후원가, 일명 '키다리 아저씨(Daddy-Long Legs)'에게 보내는 편지글에 대한 책이다.

작가 소개: 미국의 소설가이며, 마크 트웨인의 조카로 영문학과 경제학을 전공하였으며 사회 문제에 많은 관심을 보였다. 대표작으로는 「키다리 아저씨」, 「키다리 아저씨 그 후 이야기」 등이 있다.

Smith <u>poked</u> his money <u>in</u> his pocket.
: Smith는 주머니 <u>속에</u> 그의 돈을 <u>찔러 넣었다.</u>

I don't think (in) that way.
: 저는 <u>그런 식으로</u> 생각하지 않습니다.

» **원문**

… <u>Sallie Mcbride just poked her head in at my door.</u> This is what she said: 'I'm so homesick that I simply can't stand it. <u>Do you feel that way?'</u> …

» **Note**

☐ poke A in B=A를 B에 집어넣다
☐ at...: ...을 향하여('목표', '겨냥'의 뜻)
☐ (in) that way: 그런 식으로('장소'나 '방법', '때'의 부사구에서는 종종 전치사를 생략한다.)

The soldiers went <u>out of</u> the house and <u>to</u> the field.

: 병정들은 집<u>으로부터</u> 나와 들판<u>으로</u> 들어갔다.

» **원문**

… Do you want to know something? I have three pairs of kid gloves. I've had kid mittens before from the Christmas tree, but never real kid gloves with five fingers. I take them out and try them on every little while. <u>It's all I can do not to wear them to classes.</u> …

» **Note**

☐ to classes의 'to'는 '...으로, …향하여,'의 뜻

   ex» I go <u>to</u> the school.: 나는 학교에[로] 간다.

☐ back <u>to</u> the future.: 미래로 다시 돌아가게 되어

Even if I drink a little, I feel <u>up high</u>.

: 비록 약간의 술을 마셔도, 나는 기분이 <u>위로 높이 올라가는 것처럼</u> 느낀다 [기분이 좋아진다].

» **원문**

… <u>The windows are up high</u>; you can't look out from an ordinary seat. But I unscrewed the looking-glass from the back of the bureau, upholstered the top and moved it up against the window. It's just the right height for a window seat. You pull out the drawers like steps and walk up. Very comfortable! …

  □ 부사와 전치사, 전치사와 부사, 부사와 부사, 형용사와 형용사 등 여러 가지
   품사들이 이웃해서 쓰며 하나의 숙어를 형성하는 경우가 많다.
   ex)) down right here, up there, upper right-hand corner, etc.
  □ Come <u>on in</u>.: 안으로 계속 들어오세요.
  □ Get <u>off of</u> the chair!: 의자로부터 떨어져요!

Our ship <u>was stuck in</u> the big iceberg on the way to South pole.
: 우리의 배는 남극으로 가는 도중에 커다란 빙산<u>에 걸려 꼼짝 못했다.</u>

» **원문**

… Are you bald? I have it planned exactly what you look like - very satisfactorily - until I reach the top of your head, and then <u>I am stuck</u>. I can't decide whether you have white hair or black hair or <u>sort of sprinklingly grey hair</u> or maybe none at all. …

» **Note**

  □ in[out of] stuck: 곤경에 빠져[으로부터 벗어나]
   ex)) I'm stuck in mud.: 나는 진흙에 빠졌어.
  □ sort of: 다소
  □ sprinklingly=sparsely(성긴)↔densely(빽빽한)

Don't <u>stick out</u> your tongue when you are giving a speech.
: 연설할 때 혀를 내밀지 말라.

Smith is a poor thing.
: Smith는 불쌍한 놈입니다.

» 원문

... They're grey, and <u>your eyebrows stick out like a porch roof</u>(beetling, they're called in novels), and your mouth is a straight line with a tendency to turn down at the corners. Oh, you see, I know! <u>You're a snappy old thing with a temper.</u> ...

» Note

□ stick out...: ...을 내밀다
□ thing: <비아냥하거나 경멸적으로>사람, 존재

There is a <u>shade of meaning</u> in the speech.

: 말속에는 <u>어감(nuance)</u> 이라는 것이 있습니다.

The native people should be treated <u>as such</u>.

: 원주민들은 <u>그 자체로</u> 대우받아야 한다.

» 원문

... And now, shall I tell you about my vacation, or are you only interested in my education <u>as such</u>? I hope you appreciate <u>the delicate shade of meaning</u> in 'such as'. It is the latest addition to my vocabulary. ...

» Note

□ as such: (1)그러한 것[사람]으로서, 그와 같은 자격으로서 (2)있는 그대로, 그 자체로
□ shade of meaning=nuance: 어감[말의 미묘한 차이]

17

Mary is about the (same) size of Susan
: Mary는 Susan과 <u>거의 크기가 같다.</u>

» 원문

... The kitchen is huge, with copper pots and kettles hanging <u>in rows</u> on the stone wall-the littlest <u>casserole</u> among them <u>about the size of a wash boiler.</u> ...

» Note

- □ in rows: 줄지어
- □ casserole: 요리한 채 식탁에 놓는 자루 달린 냄비
- □ about the size of...: ...와 거의 같은 크기(의)

The brand-new cosmetics will <u>come on</u> the next Friday.
: 그 신품 화장품들은 다음 금요일에 <u>나올 것이다.</u>

» 원문

... Good-bye, and thank you for thinking of me-I should be perfectly happy except for one little threatening cloud on the horizon. <u>Examinations come in February.</u> ...

» Note

- □ 'There are Examinations on Friday.'처럼 표현하려고 하는 것이 일반적인 발상 이지만 'come'을 글자 그대로 원 뜻을 살려 'Examinations come on friday.'처 럼 표현하는 경우가 많이 있다.
- □ come in: 출시하다, 물건이 (시장에) 나오다

Prepare your manuscript <u>till after</u> the meeting.
: 회의 <u>후까지</u> 원고를 준비하시오.

» **원문**

… We've forgotten we ever had a vacation. Fifty-seven irregular verbs have I introduced to my brain in the past four days-I'm only hoping they'll stay <u>till after examinations</u>. …

» **Note**

□ 흔히 '전치사' 다음에는 '명사'나 '동명사'만 오는 줄 알기 쉬운 데, 위의 예문처럼 '전치사구', '부사(구)', 등 다양한 구문이 올 수 있다.

I have a pet puppy (which is) <u>two years and seven months old.</u>
: 저는 <u>2년 7개월 나이가 된</u> 애완견을 가지고 있습니다.

» **원문**

… I'm learning to skate, and can glide about quite respectably all by myself. Also I've learned how to slide down a rope from the roof of gymnasium, and <u>I can vault a bar three feet and six inches high</u>-I hope shortly to pull <u>up to</u> four feet. …

» **Note**

□ 'I have a two year and seven month pet puppy.'라고 표현하는 것이 정도이지만 'I have a pet puppy (which is) two years and seven months old.' 처럼 뒤로 돌려 앞의 명사(a pet puppy)를 수식하는 형태를 취할 수가 있다. 즉, 우선 '일반적이고 큰 것'을 언급하고, 나중에 '구체적이고 세밀한 것'을 부연 설명하는 것이 영어의 한 표현 형태다.
  ex» I caught <u>her by the sleeve.</u>: <u>나는 그녀의 소매를 잡았다.</u>

19

Please, forgive me **this once.**

: 부디, <u>이번 한번만</u> 용서해 주세요.

» 원문

... So you see, Daddy, I'm much more intelligent than if I'd just stuck to Latin. Will you forgive me <u>this once</u> if I promise never to fail again? Yours in sackcloth. Judy ...

» Note

☐ this once: 이번 한번만

Don't take it seriously. That is just <u>a rhetorical question.</u>

: 그것을 너무 진지하게 받아들이지 마세요. 그것은 단지 <u>수사적 질문</u>에 불과해요.

The weather doesn't <u>count</u>, but our physical strength matters.

: 날씨는 <u>중요치</u> 않아요, 우리의 체력이 <u>문제입니다.</u>[중요합니다.]

» 원문

... Did you ever see this campus? (<u>That is merely a rhetorical question</u>. Don't let it annoy you.) ...

... Everybody is joyous and care-free, for vacation's coming, and with that to look forward to, <u>examinations don't count</u>. ...

» **Note**
- a rhetorical question(수사적 질문)=답을 요구하지 않고 답이 긍정(yes), 부정(No)이라는 것을 뻔히 알고 한번 해보는 말
- count=matter: 중요시되다, 문제가 되다

That's the way life goes.
: 인생은 다 그런 거야.

That's the way with everybody.
: 그것은 모든 사람에게도 해당되는 거야.

» **원문**

… Oh, I'm developing a beautiful character! It droops a bit under cold and frost, but it does grow fast when the sun shines. That's the way with everybody. I don't agree with the theory that adversity and sorrow and disappointment develop moral strength. …

» **Note**
- That's the way (how) we could solve the problem.: 그것이 우리가 그 문제를 해결한 방식입니다. 또는, 그런 식으로 해서 우리는 그 문제를 해결했습니다.(후자가 더 적절한 번역방식임.)

Anne walked on to the platform, where she met her teacher by chance.
: Anne는 플랫폼으로 계속 걸어갔다. 그리고 거기에서 그녀는 우연히 그녀의 선생님을 만났다.

... You just <u>tumbled on to</u> the Board <u>by chance</u>. The Trustee, <u>as such</u>, is fat and pompous and benevolent. He pats one in the head and wears a gold watch and chain. ...

☐ tumble: (우연히) 마주치다, 구르다, 넘어지다
  ex) tumble on to...: (우연히)...에 끼어들다, 관여하다
☐ by chance: 우연히
☐ as such: 그 자체(가)

The brave citizen <u>delivered</u> the thief <u>to</u> the police.
: 그 용감한 시민은 그 도둑을 경찰에게 넘겼다.

... So Julia dashed into my room and begged me to walk him about the campus <u>and then deliver him to her when the seventh hour was over</u>. ...

☐ 'walk'은 타동사로서 '...를 걷게 하다'의 뜻
☐ deliver (A) to (B): (A)를 (B)에게 넘기다

We spent our time <u>out in the field</u> when the girls were cooking in the house.
: 우리는 소녀들이 집안에서 요리를 하고 있을 때 밖에 있는 들판에서 우리의 시간을 보냈다.

» **원문**

… He's tall and thinnish with a dark face all over lines, and the funniest underneath smile that never quite comes through but just wrinkles up the corners of his mouth. And he had a way of making you feel right off as though you'd known him a long time. He's very companionable.

… So we just ran away and had tea and muffins and marmalade and ice-cream and cake at a nice little table <u>out on the balcony</u>. …

» **Note**

☐ out on the balcony: 밖의 발코니에 있는('막연한 지칭'으로부터 '구체적인 지칭'으로 어순을 정렬하는 것이 영어의 표현 방식이다.)

I don't mind. Do you mind?
: 저는 신경 쓰지 않아요. 괜찮겠어요?

» **원문**

… <u>I don't have to mind any one this summer,</u> do I? Your nominal authority doesn't <u>annoy</u> me <u>in the least</u>; you are too far away to do any harm. …

» **Note**

☐ mind: (1)…신경 쓰다 (2)〈의문문/부정문〉…싫어하다
   ex》 Would you mind opening the window?: 창문 좀 열어드리겠습니까? … Of course not: 괜찮습니다, 열어드리죠.
☐ not … in the least: 절대 …않은

To do it justice, it is not my type.
: 그것을 공평히 평가한다면, 그것은 나의 취향이 아니야.

» 원문

… It has a veranda on the side which I can't draw and a sweet porch in front. The picture really doesn't do it justice-those things that look like feather dusters are maple trees, and the prickly ones that border the drive are murmuring pines and hemlocks. …

» Note

☐ do+목적어(A)+justice=do justice to+(A)=(A)를 공평하게 평가하다 또는, (A)를 실물대로 나타내다[표현하다]

Look at the sky with your arms folded
: 팔짱을 낀 채로 하늘을 보아라.

Don't go out with your light off.
: 불을 끈 채로 나가지 말라.

» 원문

… The light one who is laughing is Sallie, and the tall one with her nose in the air is Julia, and the little one with the hair blowing across her face is Judy-she is really more beautiful than that, but the sun was in her eyes. …

24

» **Note**

  □ with+목적어(A)+목적보어(B)=(A)가 (B)한 채로[하고, 하며], (B)하는 (A)와 함께[더불어](즉, '부대상황'의 뜻)

I cried out his name to his face because he was hard of hearing.

: 나는 그의 면전에서 그의 이름을 소리쳤다. 왜냐하면 그는 귀가 잘 안 들리기 때문이다.

» **원문**

… I called him 'Master Jervie' to his face, but he didn't appear to be insulted. Julia says she has never seen him so amiable; he's usually pretty unapproachable. …

» **Note**

  □ to one's face=in front of one: …의 앞[면전]에서
  □ 'amiable'은 'him'의 '목적보어'다.

Brother Griffith's Story
of Mad Monkton

- Wilkie Collins

작품 소개: 콜린즈의 소설은 평이하고 명쾌한 문장으로 쓰여 있으면서도 스토리는 변화무쌍하여 한번 읽기 시작하면 결코 그칠 수 없는 재미가 있다. 이 작품은 파란만장한 사건과 면밀한 구성을 자랑하는 수작이며, 다양한 영어 표현과 명료한 문체가 특징이다.

작가 소개: 20세기의 심리파, 사회파 미스터리 작가의 원조라고 할 수 있는 영국의 소설가다. 멜로드라마적인 줄거리와 탁월한 묘사력으로 유명하며, 대표작은 「The Woman in White」(1860)와 「The Moonstone(월장석)」(1868)이다.

I am not related to the Mafia member at all.

: 저는 저 마피아원과 전혀 연관이 없어요.[친척관계가 아니에요.]

We've become so attached to each other since we lived here.

: 우리는 여기에 함께 산 이후로 서로에게 매우 정이 들었어요.

The twins are almost the same in appearance, but so different in character.

: 그 쌍둥이들은 외모는 거의 똑같지만 성격은 매우 다르다.

Eagles are nearly the equals of hawks in appearance

: 독수리들은 외모 상으로 거의 매들과 똑같은 부류다.

… My father had been an old school and college friend of Mr. Monkton, and accident had brought them so much together in later life, that their continued intimacy at Wincot was quite intelligible. …

… Her late husband had been distantly related to Mrs. Monkton, and my father was her daughter's guardian. … Mr. Monkton's son and Mrs. Elmslie's daughter became attached to each other. …

… I only remember her at that time as a delicate, gentle, lovable girl, the very opposite in appearance, and apparently in character also, to Alfred Monkton. … In all essential points, except that of wealth, the Elmslies were nearly the equals of the Monktons, and want of money in a bride was of no consequence to the heir of Wincot. …

» **Note**

- □ be related to…: …와 친척인[관계가 있는]
- □ attached: 정이 든
- □ opposite to…: …에 반대인
- □ of {no} consequence={not} important
- □ the equals of…: …와 동등한 자격물[상응물]
   cf) equivalent to…: …에 대한 상응물[등가물]

As he grows older, my father is failing.
: 나이를 먹어감에 따라 <u>나의 아버지는 기력이 쇠약해지고 있다.</u>

» 원문

… For some months past my father's health had been failing, and just at the time of which I am now writing …

27

When the public are very angry, the statesman usually holds his tongue

: 대중이 흥분되어있을 때, 그 정치가는 보통 <u>그의 말을 아낀다.</u>

» **원문**

... The few indoor servants had all been long enough in the family to have learnt <u>to hold tongues in public</u> as a regular habit. ...

... Others had heard odd noises in the uninhabited parts of the Abbey, had looked up, and had seen him forcing open the windows, as if to let light and air into rooms supposed to have been shut close for years and years ...

» **Note**

□ hold one's tongue: 말을 삼가다
□ force open: 무리한 힘을 가하여 열다
  cf) push open: 밀어 열다

Don't idle away your time when you are young.

: 젊을 때 너의 시간을 <u>헛되게 보내지 말라.</u>

» **원문**

… I was idling away the time one morning with my friend the attache, in the garden of the Villa Reale, when we were passed by a young man, walking alone, who exchanged bows with my friend. …

… "No; and he never ought to be. He has gone the way of the rest of the family; or, in plainer words, he has gone mad." …

» **Note**

□ idle away: 시간을 허비하다

□ exchange bows: 인사를 교환하다

□ go the way of...: ...의 전철을 밟다

As soon as the police saw him, the thief took to flight.

: 경찰이 그를 보자마자, 그 도둑은 도망쳤다.

I have nothing to do with her.

: 나는 그녀와 아무런 관계가 없다.

» **원문**

… The seconds and the Frenchman(who was unhurt) took to flight in different directions, as it is supposed. …

… "But what has all this to do with Alfred?" …

» **Note**

□ take to+명사=begin to 동원=...하기 시작하다

□ (A) have (B) to do with (C): A는 (C)와 (B)한 관계에 있다

   ex) I have something(a little, much) with the scandal.: 나는 그 스캔들과 중요한(약간, 많은) 관계가 있다. I have nothing(little) with the scandal.: 나는 그 스캔들과 아무것도(거의) 관계가 없다.

   rf) 위의 표현 "But what has all this to do with Alfred?"은 "But all this has what to do with Alfred."가 의문문이 된 형태다.

Don't assign your fault to others
: 당신의 잘못을 다른 사람에게 전가하지 말라.

Don't laugh him out of his mistake.
: 그의 실수를 웃음으로 얼버무려 넘기게 하지 말라.

Don't reason him out of his mistake.
: 그의 실수를 논리적으로 따져 아닌 것처럼 하지 말게 하라.

» 원문

... He will not assign to anybody the smallest motive for his conduct. You can't laugh him out of it, or reason him out of it. ...

» Note

☐ assign A to B=B에게 A를 할당[지정]하다 or A를 B의 탓으로 돌리다
☐ laugh 사람(A) out of (B)=(A)에게 웃게 하여 (B)를 그만두게[버리게, 잊게]하다
☐ reason 사람(A) out of (B)=(A)에게 논리적으로 따져 (B)를 그만두게[버리게, 잊게]하다

He humors his boss.
: 그는 그의 사장의 비위를 잘 맞춘다.

» 원문

... She humors his insanity, declares he gave her a good reason, in secret, for going away; says she could always make him happy when they were together in the old Abbey. ...

Note

□ humor: 맞장구치다, 비위를 맞추다(flatter)

Be ware of your icy walk. It's so slippery.

: 꽁꽁 얼어붙은 길을 조심하세요. 매우 미끄러워요.

You're more than welcomed to this party.

: 당신이 이 파티에 온 것에 대해 환영 이상입니다.[정말 파티에 잘 오셨습니다.]

» 원문

… But be ware of following up the subject after you have answered him, unless you want to make sure that he is out of his senses. In that case, only talk of his uncle, and the result will rather more than satisfy you. …

» Note

□ be ware of…: …을 조심하다[경계하다]
□ out of one's senses: 제정신이 아닌, 미친
□ more than…: …이상인(이 경우 'more than' 다음에는 '단어', '어구', '절'이 다 올 수 있다.)

His glance wandered from me to her.

: 그의 시선은 나로부터 그녀 쪽으로 이리저리 옮겨 다녔다.[두리번거렸다.]

... Instead of looking into my face as they had looked hitherto, his eyes wandered away, and fixed themselves intensely, almost fiercely, either on the perfectly empty wall at our side, or on the vacant space between the wall and ourselves-it was impossible to say which. ...

» Note
- □ wander: 〈눈, 시선 등을〉두리번거리다, 배회하다
- □ hitherto: (고어)지금까지

You should have called me perfect.
: 당신은 나를 완벽하다고 불렀어야만 했어.

I am inclined to go for a walk.
: 산책하고 싶다.

» 원문

... He was so shy, so quiet, so composed and gentle in all his actions, that at times I should have been almost inclined to call him effeminate. ...

» Note
- □ be inclined to 동원: ...하고 싶다, ...하는 경향이 있다
- □ should have p.p: ...해야했다
- □ effeminate: 여자같은, 나약한

You don't mean it!

: 설마![농담이겠지!]

Upon my honour, I am honest.

: 맹세코, 저는 정직합니다.

Mark my words, he's coming to attack us.

: 자 내 말을 잘 들으시오, 그는 우리를 공격하기 위해 다가오고 있소.

» 원문

… "You don't mean it! Upon my honour, you're a bold fellow to trust yourself alone with 'Mad Monkton' when moon is at the full." "He is ill, poor fellow. Besides, I don't think him half as mad as you do." "We won't dispute about that; but mark my words, he has not asked you to go where no visitor has been admitted before, without a special purpose. …

» Note

☐ I mean it!=I'm serious!=I'm not kidding!: 진정이야!

☐ Upon my honour!: 맹세코!, 정말로!

☐ Mark my words!: 자 명심하시오!

I am at your service.

: 분부대로 하겠습니다.

I'm John Smith at your service.

: 전 John Smith라고 해요. 말씀만 하세요.[기꺼이 도와드리겠습니다.]

» 원문

... I tried to set him at his ease by assuring him that if my assistance or advice could be of any use, <u>I was ready to place myself and my time heartily and unreservedly at his service.</u> ...

» Note

□ at one's service: ...의 마음대로[분부대로]
□ be ready to...: 기꺼이 ...하다, ...할 준비가 되어있다

<u>Take</u> your hat <u>off</u> your sweat suit.

: 체육복[운동복]<u>으로부터</u> 당신의 모자를 떼어 내시오.

» 원문

... By his direction <u>I took the shade off the reading lamp</u>, after I had lit the other lamp and the four candles. ...

» Note

□ take off: ...을 벗다
    cf) take ... off...: ...로부터 ...을 벗겨내다. (이처럼 문맥에 따라 다르게 쓰일 수 있다)

Please, come in. In a few minutes, we'll <u>resume</u> our sessions.

: 들어오세요. 잠시 후에, 우리의 회의를 <u>재개하겠습니다.</u>

» **원문**

… I resumed my chair, and said that I would stay with him as long as he wished. "Thank you a thousand times! You are patience and kindness itself," he said, going back to his former place, and resuming his former gentleness of manner. …

» **Note**

☐ resume: '다시 …하다'라고 표현할 때 요긴하게 쓰이는 말
  ex)) I resumed my chair.: 나는 다시 의자에 앉았다.
☐ a thousand times: 대단히(일종의 '강조어'다.)
  추상명사+itself=very+형용사
  ex)) You are patience and kindness itself.=You are very patient and kind.:
  당신은 매우 참을성이 있고 친절합니다.

Do you follow me?
: 당신은 (나의 말을) 이해하시나요?

» **원문**

… "And then it seemed to merge into the eager curiosity which had begun to grow on me rather before that time, about the origin of the ancient prophecy predicting the extinction of our race. Are you following me?" "I follow every word with the closest attention."…

» **Note**

☐ merge into…: …와 병합하다
☐ origin: 혈통, 기원
☐ follow: 따르다, 이해하다, 지키다

Mathematics is not to my taste.
: 수학은 나의 기호에 맞지 않는다.

» **원문**

… "Did you ever pass a day alone in the long-deserted chambers of an ancient house?" "Never; such solitude as that is not at all to my taste." …

» **Note**

☐ pass=spend: 소비하다
☐ to one's taste: …기호[취향]에 맞아
  ex) She is not to my taste.=She is not my type.: 그녀는 나의 취향이 아니야.

I have taught them English ever since.
: 나는 그때 이후로 쭉 그들에게 영어를 가르쳐왔다.

» **원문**

… Sometimes these discoveries were associated with particular parts of the Abbey, which have had a horrible interest of their own for me ever since. …

» **Note**

☐ part=area: 지역
☐ ever since: 그때 이후로 쭉

After taking some pills, I came to my senses soon.

: 약간의 알약을 먹은 후에 나는 곧 제정신이 들었다.

My lovable Mary happened to sit opposite to me in class.

: 나의 사랑하는 Mary가 우연히 수업 중에 나의 반대쪽에 앉았다.

Do it at this very moment.

: 바로 이 순간[지금]에 당장 그것을 하라.

» **원문**

… "It was not fainting, for I did not fall to the ground, did not move an inch from my place. …

… Then I came to my senses again; and then, when I opened my eyes, there was the apparition of Stephen Monkton standing opposite to me, faintly luminous, just as it stands opposite me at this very moment by your side." …

» **Note**

☐ come to one's senses: …제정신이 들다

☐ come to life: 소생하다. 활기를 띠다(자동사)

　cf) bring … to life: …소생시키다(타동사)

☐ opposite to…: …의 반대쪽에

　cf) on the opposite side: 반대쪽에

☐ at this very moment: 바로 이 순간에

　cf) This is the very man I tried to look for.: 이 사람이 내가 찾고자 하던 바로 그 사람이다.

As time goes by, he began to betray himself.
: 시간이 지남에 따라, 그는 서서히 본심을 드러냈다.

It will avail you little or nothing.
: 그것은 네게 거의 아무 소용이 없을 것이다.

> » 원문

> ... "I soon schooled myself to hide from others that I was looking at it, except on rare occasions-when I have perhaps betrayed myself to you. But my self-possession availed me nothing with Ada." ...

> » Note

> □ betray oneself: 본의 아니게 자기의 본심을 드러내다
> □ avail: 〈부정, 의문문에서〉...도움이 되다
> cf) avail oneself of...: ...을 이용하다
> □ to no avail=without avail: 무익하게, 쓸모없이

My pride got the better of me when my friend tried to help me with my difficult homework.
: 나의 친구가 나의 어려운 숙제를 도와주고자 했을 때, 나의 자존심이 나를 이겼다.(즉, 나는 허락했다.)

> » 원문

> ... My pity for him got the better of my prudence at that moment, and without thinking of responsibilities, I promised at once to do for him whatever he asked. ...

» Note

   ☐ get[have] the better of…=(1)overcome: …이겨내다 (2)defeat…: …에 이기다

The caravans <u>set</u> the camels <u>going</u> to the desert field.

: 그 대상들은 낙타들로 <u>하여금</u> 사막평원을 <u>가게끔 시켰다</u>.

Now morning has broken. Hurry up and <u>get</u> your travelling stuff <u>ready</u>.

: 이제 동이 텄다. 서둘러라 그리고 여러분들의 여행소지품들을 <u>준비하라</u>.

» 원문

  … <u>This set me thinking about the extent of his madness</u>, or, <u>to speak more mildly and more correctly</u>, of his delusion. …
  … In two days' time <u>I had got everything ready</u>, and had ordered the travelling carriage to the door some hours earlier than we had originally settled. …

» Note

   ☐ set+목적어(A)+…ing: (A)가 …하도록 시키다. 여기의 'set'는 일종의 준사역동사임
   ☐ ready: 준비된
     ex) ready money: 현금
     ex) get ready for…=get … ready: …을 준비시키다

003

Brother Griffith's Story of the Family Secret

- Wilkie Collins

작품 소개: Wincot Abbey의 모튼스 집안은 사교성이 부족한 사람들이었다. 그들은 결코 다른 사람들의 집에 가지 않았다. 그들 모두가 확실히 거만할지라도 그것은 자긍심이 아니고, 무서움이었다. 그리고 이것은 그들을 그들의 이웃과 떨어진 상태로 있게 했다. 그 가족은 유전적인 정신병의 고통으로 수세대에 걸쳐 고통을 겪고 있었다.

It's not on my own account, rather it's because of you.

: 그것은 나 자신 때문에[나 자신을 위해서가] 아니다. 오히려 그것은 당신 때문이다.

When I saw the poisonous spider, a shudder of horror ran through me.

: 내가 그 독거미를 보았을 때, 공포의 떨림이 나를 스쳤다.

» **원문**

... If I seem to speak particularly about them here, it is not on my own account. I can honestly say that, with all my heart and soul. ...

... Even Uncle George, who had never been allowed a holiday to come and see me, but who had hitherto often written, and begged me to write to him, broke off our correspondence. ...

... How well I remember the shudder of horror that ran through me at the vague idea of this deadly "something!" ...

» **Note**

☐ on one's own account: 자기 부담[비용]으로, 자기 책임 아래, 자기의 이익을 위해서

☐ with all one's heart and soul: 진심으로; 충심으로; 정성을 기울여

☐ broke off...: (서신이나 교제 따위를) 끊다

☐ run through...: ...을 꿰뚫다

She slipped out in the classroom and made a phone call to her friend.

: 그녀는 교실로부터 살며시 빠져 나왔다. 그리고 그녀의 친구에게 전화를 했다.

I stole to my room not to wake my father.

: 나는 나의 아버지를 깨우지 않기 위해 살금살금 방으로 들어갔다.

Never mind, I can understand your saying.

: 신경 꺼, 나는 당신의 말 을 이해할 수가 있어.

Their win in the championship was out of the question

: 그들의 우승은 불가능했다.

» **원문**

… I knew where the post-office was, and slipped out in the morning unobserved, and dropped my letter into the box. I stole home again by garden, and climbed in at the window of a back parlour on the ground floor. …

… "Never mind; don't talk about it any more. It was only a mischievous trick to frighten you, I dare say. Forget about it, my dear." …

… They lived far away, and never came to see us - and the idea of writing to them, at my age and in my position, was out of the question. …

- □ slip out: 살며시 빠져나가다
- □ steal: 살며시 다가가다
- □ Never mind.: 신경 쓰지 마.
- □ I dare say.: 아마 그럴 거야.
- □ at my age and in my position: 내 나이로 보나 내 위치로 보나
- □ out of the question: 불가능한

I leave for LA to <u>pay my respects to</u> my in-laws
: 나는 인척에 <u>문안드리기 위해</u> LA로 떠났다.

<u>Whatever</u> you do and <u>wherever</u> you go, I will welcome you.
: 당신이 <u>무엇을 하든 어디를 가든</u> 나는 환영할 것입니다.

» **원문**

... Determined not to be discouraged even yet, I undertook a journey to <u>pay respects to my father's family</u>, with the secret intention of trying what I could learn from them on the subject of Uncle George. ...

... But, <u>whatever I did, and wherever I went</u>, the memory of Uncle George, and the desire to penetrate the mystery of his disappearance, <u>haunted</u> me. ...

... Tears came into my eyes as the recollections of past days <u>crowded back on me</u>. ...

... "It is useless to shock you by <u>going into particulars</u>," said the priest, considerately. "Let it be enough if I say that your uncle's fortitude failed to support him when he wanted it most. ...

» **Note**

- □ go into particulars: 상세히 설명하다
- □ crowd back on...: ...에게 엄습해오다

004

The Moonstone

- Wilkie Collins

작품 소개: "월장석(The Moonstone)"(1868)은 서간체 형식의 소설로 영문학사에 있어서 최초의 추리소설이다. 다양한 서술자를 통해 사건이 진행됨으로써 지속적인 긴장감을 주는 것과 동시에 다양한 상징적인 소재를 통해 영국의 제국주의적 시각을 잘 보여주는 작품이다.

She was cheated on by her husband, and then she shut herself up in her bedroom.

: 그녀는 그녀의 남편에게 속았다. 그런 다음 그녀는 침실로부터 두문 분출 했다.

She set her heart on the position.

: 그녀는 그 지위를 탐냈다.

> **원문**

… This was a fine of man to recover Miss Rachel's diamond and to track down the thief! …

… She turned away and shut herself up again in her bedroom. I heard he burst out crying as soon as she was alone again. …

… "If I must see him, I must," she said. "But I can't see him alone. Bring him in, Gabriel, and stay here as long as she stays." …

… Out of pity for the girl I told the Sergeant what my daughter, Penelop, had once told me-that Rosanna was mad enough to set her heart on Mr. Franklin Blake. …

    ☐ turn away: 돌아서 가버리다

    ☐ shut oneself up: 자신을 감금하다, 외부와 교제를 끊다

    ☐ bring in : 데려가다[오다], 불러 들이다

    ☐ set one's heart on...=long for...: ...희망을 걸다, 탐내다, 열중하다, 사랑하다

The mountains run down to the southern part of Korea.

: 이 산맥은 한국의 남부로 쭉 뻗어있었다.

Two rocks jut out of the deep valley.

: 두 개의 바위들이 깊은 계곡으로부터 돌출해 있다.

I invited my student's confidence.

: 나는 나의 학생으로 하여금 비밀을 터놓도록 유도했다.

» **원문**

... The sand hills here ran down to the sea and ended in two spits of rock jutting out opposite to each other, till you lost sight of them in the water. ...

... She answered, 'Yes, if I dare.' I confess it made me uncomfortable. I had no wish to invite the girl's confidence. ...

... It ran as follows: "You have often forgiven me, Mr. Betteredge, in the past times. ...

» **Note**

    ☐ run down: 아래로 뻗어있다

    ☐ jut out: 돌출하다

    ☐ opposite to...: ...로부터 반대쪽에

    ☐ if I dare: 감히 해야 한다면[할 수 있다면]

    ☐ invite one's confidence: ...의 비밀을 터놓도록 유도하다

      rf) confidence: (1)자신감 (2)비밀

      cf) confidential: 친전

    ☐ run: ...라고 써있다. <동의어>It says...: 그것은 ...라고 써있다

What does the icon refer to?

: 이 아이콘은 무엇을 지칭합니까?

Sure, I would help them to the best of my abilities.

: 좋고말고요, 힘 닿는 데까지 나는 그들을 돕겠습니다.

As soon as she received a letter from his boy friend, she began to break the seal.

: 그녀가 남자 친구로부터 편지를 받자마자, 그녀는 밀봉된 부분을 뜯기 시작했다.

» **원문**

… "Do you refer to my daughter?" my lady said. "I do," Sergeant Cuff said. "You suspect Miss Verinder of deceiving us all, by secreting the diamond for purpose of her own? Is that true? …

… What makes you speak so rudely to me, Lucy? Rosanna always thought kindly of me, poor soul," I said; "and, to the best of my abilities, I always tried to act kindly by her." …

… The address was written as follows: "For Franklin Blake, Esq. To be given into his own hands (and not to be trusted to anyone else) by Lucy Yolland." He broke the seal. The envelope contained a letter ; and this, in its turn, contained a slip of paper. He read the letter first …

» **Note**

☐ refer to…: (1)언급하다 (2)지칭하다 (3)참고하다
☐ to the best of one's ability: …의 힘이 다하는데까지
☐ break the seal: (편지)겉봉을 뜯다
☐ in one's turn: 이번에는

To a Student in Uncertain Health

- Philip Gilbert Hamerton

작품 소개: '지적 생활'이라는 말을 처음으로 사용한 빅토리아시대의 지성 필립 길버트 해머튼이 지적 생활을 택했으면서도 지적 즐거움을 맛보지 못하는 이 시대의 지친 지적 노동자와 전 계층의 사람들에게 지적 생활의 본질을 일깨워줌으로써, 진정한 지적 즐거움으로 이끌어주는 책이다.

작가 소개: 다수의 수필집과 전기를 저술하였다. 1896년에는 필립 길버트 해머튼 자서전과 부인이 전하는 회고록이 출판되었으며, 그의 대표작인 「지적 생활(The Intellectual Life)」은 인생 철학의 명저로 구미의 지성인들로부터 꾸준히 호응 받고 있다.

The starving tribes will <u>stand in need of</u> many necessaries right now.

: 그 굶주린 부족들은 지금 당장 많은 생필품을 <u>필요로 할 것이다.</u>

Please lock the door <u>from without</u> pushing the knob.

: 손잡이를 누름으로써 <u>밖으로부터</u> 그 문을 잠그세요.

» **원문**

... We should have felt, that however agreeable this opinion might have been to the philosopher who held it, his private satisfaction <u>stood in need of</u> confirmation <u>from without</u> ...

» **Note**

☐ should have pp: ...했어야만 했다
☐ be[stand] in need of...: ...을 필요로 하다
☐ from without: 밖[외부]으로부터
☐ from within: 안[내부]으로부터

To a Student in Great Poverty

- Philip Gilbert Hamerton

Many responsibilities will be needed in proportion to many rights.

: 많은 책임이 많은 권리에 비례하여 필요 될 것이다.

This rule is not without exception.

: 이 규칙에도 예외가 없는 것이 아니다.

The hope is (the case) with them.

: 희망은 그들에게도 해당된다.

» **원문**

... Between these extremes we have various grades of the middle classes in which culture usually increases very much in proportion to the expenditure. The rule is not without its exception ...

... A rich man may sit down to an enormous banquet, but he can only make a good use of the little that he is able to digest. So it is with the splendid intellectual banquet that is spread before the rich man's eyes. ...

» **Note**

- ☐ in proportion to...: ...와 비례하여
- ☐ not without...: ...이 없는 것이 아닌(이중부정)
  cf) with no=without
- ☐ with...: (1)〈관계, 입장〉...에 관하여 (2)...관계하는 (3)...의 경우의
  ex) Such is the case with me.: 나도 그와 같은 경우다.

To a Friend Who Kindly Warned the Author of the Bad Effects of Solitude

- Philip Gilbert Hamerton

I <u>take in</u> New York Times by installments.
: 나는 할부제로 New York Times를 <u>구독한다.</u>

I can not <u>enter into</u> his wit.
: 나는 그의 재치를 <u>이해할 수가 없다.</u>

» **원문**

... He wore nothing but old cloths, read only a few old books, <u>without the least regard to the opinions of the learned,</u> and <u>did not take in</u> a newspaper. ...

... though he cherished a few tried friendships, and was grateful to those who loved him and could <u>enter into</u> his humor. ...

» **Note**

- □ with{without} regard to...: ...에 관해서는{관계없이}
- □ the+형용사=(1)복수보통명사 (2)단수추상명사
  ex) the poor=(1)poor people (2)poverty
- □ take in: 구독하다, (구어체)구경하다
- □ enter into: 시작하다, 가담하다, ...(재미 등)을 이해하다

008

Tom Brown's School Life

- **Thomas Hughes**

작품 소개: 공립 남학교 럭비 스쿨에서 일어난 일을 소설화한 1857년 작품이다.

작가 소개: 럭비 학교에서 교육을 받았다. 교장 토머스 아널드에 대한 그의 애정과 놀이를 즐기고 소년다운 진취적 기상을 펴던 그의 럭비 학교의 학창 시절이 1857년에 발간된 걸작 「톰 브라운의 학창 시절(Tom Brown's School Days)」에 잘 나타나 있다.

The boss looked over my official documents.
: 상사는 나의 공문서를 면밀히 검토하였다.

My dear[good] fellow, how have you been?
: 여보게, 어떻게 지냈나?

» **원문**

… One of the boys ran out from the rest, and after looking him over for a minute, began … "I say, you fellow, is your name Brown?" "Yes," said Tom, in considerable astonishment. "Ah, I thought so. You know my old aunt, Miss East?" …

» **Note**

☐ look over: 방관하다, 검토하다
☐ I say.: (구어)여보세요.
  ex) Say there.: 여보세요.

Don't sleep <u>with your light on</u>.

: 불을 켜놓은 채로 잠자지 말라.

» 원문

... "<u>This'll never do</u>. Haven't you got a hat? We never wear caps here. Bless you, if you were to go into the quadrangle <u>with that thing on</u>, I don't know what'd happen." ...

» Note

- ☐ That'll do.=That's enough.: 그만하면 충분해., 그만하면 됐어.
- ☐ with+목적어(A)+목적보어(B): (A)가 (B)한 채로[하고서], (B)하는 (A)와 함께 [더불어]('부대상황'의 뜻)

<u>Mind</u> your own job.

: 당신의 일에 <u>신경 써</u>.

They <u>played on</u> until the evening was coming near.

: 그들은 저녁이 다가올 때가지 <u>계속 경기를 했다.</u>

» 원문

... "No, nothing at all," said East, "only a little twist from that charge." "Well, <u>mind</u> and get all right for next Saturday."; and <u>the leader passed on</u>, leaving East better for those few words than all the medicine in England would have made him, and Tom ready to give one of his ears for as much notice. ...

50

» Note

☐ mind: (1)신경 쓰다 (2)〈부정문, 의문문〉싫어하다
☐ the leader passed on.: 그 상급생은 계속 지나쳤다.
☐ 동사+on=계속...하다. (이때의 'on'은 '계속'을 나타내는 부사)
　ex)) Walk on.=Keep (on) walking.=Go (on) walking.: 계속 걸어가라.

We can beat them.
: 우리는 그들을 물리칠 수[이길 수]가 있어.

Keep your pace up to the last.
: 마지막까지 너의 속도를 계속 유지해.

» 원문

... The School played splendidly too, I will say, and kept it up to the last. That last charge of theirs would have carried away a house. Well, but we beat'em. It's because we've union-(cheers). ...
... Depend on it, there's nothing that breaks up a house like bullying. ...

» Note

☐ I will say: 정말이야.
☐ Depend on it.: 맹세코., 틀림없어.
☐ break up: 해산하다, 헤어지다, (전쟁 등)이 발발하다, 파멸시키다

Let's drink a toast to king's health.
: 왕의 건강을 위해 건배합시다.

After we fought each other, our friendship bound us all together.
: 우리가 서로 싸운 후에 우정이 더욱 우리를 결속시켰다.

… But before I sit down I must give a toast to be drunk with three-times-three and all the honours. It's a toast which should bind us all together. …

» Note

□ drink a toast: 건배하다
□ propose a toast: 건배를 제의하다
□ three-times-three: 되풀이되는 세 번의 환호, 일종의 만세 삼창
□ to one's honour: 영예가 되어, 체면을 유지하게 되어
□ upon one's honour: 맹세코
□ with honours: 우등으로
□ bind 목적어(A) together: (A)를 결속시키다

They revealed[let on] their secrets against their will.
: 그들은 본의 아니게 그들의 비밀을 누설했다.

With an oath, the player kicked the opposite player.
: 욕설과 함께, 그 선수는 상대방 선수를 찼다.

We didn't let go of the rope setting our teeth.
: 우리는 이를 악물고 그 로프를 놓지 않았다.

» 원문

… "I'll be hanged if we'll toss anyone against their will. No more bullying. let him go, I say." Flashman, with an oath and a kick, released his prey, who rushed headlong under his bed again. …
… "No", said Tom, setting his teeth. "Come along then, boys" sang out Walker; and away they all went. …

» **Note**

- □ against one's will: 본의 아니게
- □ oath: 선서, 욕설
  ex) make an oath=take one's oath: 맹세하다 take[swear] (an) oath: 선서하다
- □ set[clench] one's teeth: 이를 악물다
  cf) between one's teeth: 목소리를 낮춰
- □ Come along!: (1)〈명령〉따라 오라!, 자 빨리!(Make haste!)
- □ sing out=cry out: 소리 지르다

We took part in the ceremony in honour of the king birthday.

: 우리는 왕의 생일을 기리기 위하여 그 의식에 참여했다.

» **원문**

… At Walker's suggestion all who were afraid were let off, in honour of Pater Brooke's speech. …

… "In with Scud; quick! there's no time to lose. Once, twice, thrice, and away!" Up he went like a shuttlecock, but not quite up to the ceiling. …

… They were in good wind now, and sent him right up to the ceiling first time, against which his knees came rather sharply. …

» **Note**

- □ in honour of…: … 경의를 표하여, 축하하여
- □ let off: 풀어주다, 면제하다
- □ in with: 〈명령문으로〉들어가라, 넣어라
- □ Away with him!: 그를 쫓아내라!
- □ Off with your hat!: 모자를 벗어라!
- □ in good wind: 완전히 몰래 진행되어
  cf) get wind of…: … 눈치 채다, … 소문을 알아내다

Suit yourself.
: 마음대로 하시오.

The enemy scattered back to their camp.
: 적들은 그들의 진지로 흩어 져 돌아갔다.

» 원문

... He and East, <u>having earned it</u>, stood now looking on. No catastrophe happened, as all the captives were <u>cool hands</u>, and didn't struggle. <u>This didn't suit Flashman.</u> ...

... But now there's cry that the praeposter of the room is coming; so the tossing stops, <u>and all scatter to their different rooms.</u> ...

» Note

☐ cool hand: 냉정하고 침착한 (사람)

☐ suit: 어울리게 하다, 만족시키다

    ex) Do these gloves suit you fine?: 그 장갑들은 당신에게 잘 어울립니까?

☐ scatter: 흩뿌리다, 흩어지다

Don't break in when older people are talking to each other.
: 연장자들이 말하고 계실 때 <u>끼어들지[참견하지]</u> 말라.

» 원문

… While matters were in this state, East and Tom were one evening sitting in their study. "I've made up mind," <u>broke in</u> Tom, "that I won't <u>fag</u> except for the sixth." …

… And soon a lot of the fags crept out <u>in league</u>, and Flashman excited his associates to join him <u>bringing</u> the young vagabonds <u>to their senses</u>. …

… One by one most of the other rebels <u>fell away from</u> them, while Flashman's cause prospered, and several other <u>fifth-form</u> boys began to <u>look black at</u> them and ill-treat them as they passed about the house. <u>Derby Day fell on a Saturday during this half</u>. …

… Tom groans and struggles. "<u>I say, Flashey, he has had enough</u>," says one boy, dropping the arm holds. …

» **Note**

- □ break in: 끼어들다, 참견하다
- □ fag: 상급생의 심부름 노릇을 하다. 또는 그런 하급생
- □ in league: 집단으로
- □ bring 목적어(A) to senses: (A)를 제정신이 들게 하다
- □ fall away from: …흩어지다
- □ fifth-form: 5학년
- □ fall on: 〈날짜가〉…에 해당하다
- □ had enough: 충분히 경험하다

The boy <u>held his ground</u> to persuade his parents.

: 그 소년은 자기의 양친을 설득시키기 위해 <u>그의 입장을 고수했다</u>.

55

… She examines his clothes, and looks up inquiringly. The boys are silent. "<u>How did he come so?</u>" …

… The boy who <u>held his ground</u> is soon among the rest, who are all in fear of their lives. Did he peach? …

» **Note**

- ☐ come...: ...한 상태가 되다, ...으로 판명되다
- ☐ hold[stand, keep, maintain] one's ground: 자기의 지반[입장, 주장]을 고수하다

What did you come to this island for?
: 무엇 때문에 당신은 이 섬에 왔느냐?

The public went in at the politicians.
: 국민들은 그 정치가들을 맹렬히 공격했다.

» **원문**

… "<u>What's that for?</u>" growled the assaulted one. "Because I choose. <u>You've no business here.</u>" "I say, you two," said Diggs from the end of the hall, "You'll never get rid of that fellow till you lick him. <u>Go in at him,</u> both of you. I'll see fair play." <u>Flashman was taken aback,</u> and retreated two steps. …

» **Note**

- ☐ What ... for?=Why...?=How come...?: 왜...?
- ☐ You have no business.=It's none of your business.: 네가 알 바 아냐.
- ☐ lick: (1)핥다 (2)때리다(whip) (3)쉽게 이기다
- ☐ go in at...: ...을 맹렬히 공격하다
- ☐ take back: 철회하다, 돌아가다

56

What is it to you?
: 그것이 당신과 무슨 관계가 있니?

Time is up.
: 시간이 다 되었어.

» 원문

… "What is it to you?" faltered Flashman, who began to lose heart. "I'm going to see fair, I tell you," said Diggs, with a grin, and snapping his great red fingers; "It isn't fair for you to be fighting one of them at a time-Are you ready, Brown? Time's up." …

» Note

□ be related to…: …와 관련이 있다
□ lose heart: 풀이 꺾이다
□ I (can) tell you.=Let me tell you.: 실제로, 정말로, 알았니?(확신을 나타냄) at a time: 한번에
□ Time is up[over].: 시간이 다 되었다.[시간이 끝났다.]

Get off the table, she is so busy now.
: 테이블로부터 떨어져라, 그녀는 지금 너무 바빠.

» 원문

… "Not he," said Diggs, getting leisurely off the table; It's all sham; he's only afraid to fight it out." …
… "Hang your sorrow!" answered Flashman, holding his handkerchief to the place; "you shall pay for this, I can tell you, both of you." And he walked out of the hall. …

- [ ] get off...: ...로부터 떨어지다
- [ ] sham: 가짜
- [ ] hang one's sorrow!: 뭐가 미안하다 말이야! (이 녀석아!)
- [ ] Hang you!: 망할 자식
- [ ] I can tell you.: 정말로, 틀림없어(확신을 나타낸다.)

Tom <u>burst in</u> when we're talking about our own things in secret.

: 우리가 비밀리에 우리 문제에 관해 말하고 있을 때 Tom이 <u>끼어들었다.</u>

<u>With something like a smile at the effort</u>, she tried to give a speech before the public people.

: <u>억지로 미소같은 것을 띤 채,</u> 그녀는 대중 앞에서 연설을 하고자 노력했다.

» **원문**

... "Well, well," <u>burst in</u> Tom, <u>with something like a sigh at the effort</u>, "I suppose I must give up East.-Come along, young un." ...

» **Note**

- [ ] burst in: 갑자기 말에 참견하다
- [ ] something like: ...다소 ..., 대략..., 굉장한
- [ ] Come along.: <명령문>따라 오라. 자, 빨리빨리.(Make haste)
- [ ] un=one: 사람(guy)

The politician will get into scrape when he is for the war.

: 전쟁에 대해 찬성할 때 그 정치가는 곤경에 처할 것이다.

Tom's cup is full.

: Tom의 행복은 극에 달했다.

» **원문**

… How frank, and kind, and manly was his greeting to the party by the fire! And Tom's cup was full when his master turned to him with a warm shake of the hand, and, seemingly oblivious of all the late scrapes which he had been getting into, said, "Ah, Brown here, you here! I hope you left your father and all well at home?" …

» **Note**

□ one's cup is full: …의 행복은 최고다

□ get into a scrape=get in trouble: 곤경에 처하다

That's why I love her.

: 그것이 내가 그녀를 사랑하는 이유다.[그 때문에 나는 그녀를 사랑한다.]

"Nope! you cannot swim in here." Tom struck in

: "안 돼! 당신은 여기에서 수영을 할 수가 없어." Tom이 갑자기 입을 열었다.

Sunday two weeks, I'll marry.

: 이주 후 일요일, 나는 결혼할 것이다.

... My eyes! cried East. "Oh! so that's why you didn't come to supper." ...

... The poor boy was trembling and hesitating. Tom struck in-"Shut up, Tadpole. He'll have to sing, whether he can or not, Saturday twelve weeks, and that's long enough off yet." ...

» Note

- □ My eye(s)!: 수상한데!, (어머나) 깜짝이야!
- □ strike in: 갑자기 입을 열다, 별안간 뛰어들다, 방해하다
- □ Friday week: 내주(또는 지난주)의 금요일

When she was teased by other children, Mary looked ready to burst in tears.

: 다른 아이들한테 놀림을 받았을 때, Mary는 눈물이 와락 쏟아지려고 하는 모습이었다.

What's that for?

: 그것은 왜냐? 왜 그러한가?

» 원문

... Poor little Arthur looked ready to cry. "But, please," said he, "mayn't I talk about-about home to you?" ...

... He then looked round more nervously than ever. Two or three of the little boys were already in bed, sitting up with their chins on their knees. ...

... Then two or three boys laughed and sneered, and a big, brutal fellow who was standing in the middle of the room, picked up a slipper, and shied it at the kneeling boy, calling him a sniveling young ass. ...

... "Confound you, Brown! what's that for?" roared he, stamping with pain. ...

» **Note**

- □ than ever: 여느 때 보다
- □ sitting up with their chins on their knees: 그들의 턱을 무릎에 괸 채로 앉아 있으며
- □ shy at...: ...을 내던지다
- □ (God) confound!=Compound it[you]!: 망할 놈!(가벼운 욕설)
- □ What...for?=Why...?: 왜?
- □ stamp: 발을 구르다

He'll betake himself to his philosophy study to get a good grade.
: 그는 좋은 등급을 받기 위해 철학공부에 전념할 것이다.

Beat time to the music with your feet.
: 너의 바로 가지고 음악에 박자를 맞춰라.

» **원문**

... Next moment he is reassured by the spirited tone in which Arthur begins construing, and betakes himself to drawing dogs's heads in his notebook, while the master, evidently enjoying the change, stands before Arthur, beating a sort of time with his hand and foot, and saying, "Yes, yes" "Very well", as Arthur goes on. ...
... Arthur can hardly get on at all. What can it be? ...

» **Note**

- □ betake oneself to ...: ...에 가다, 할 수 없이 ...하다, ...에 전념하다
- □ beat time to...: ...에 박자를 맞추다
- □ get on: 나아가다
- □ What can it be?: 도대체 무슨 일일까?

The gesture of the comedian <u>called the netizens'</u> <u>attention.</u>

: 그 코미디언의 동작은 <u>네티즌들의 주위를 끌었다.</u>

The soccer player <u>bottled up his anger</u> even if he was charged by the opposite player.

: 그 축구 선수는 비록 그가 상대방 선수에게 공격을 받았을 지라도 <u>그의 화 를 참았다.</u>

» 원문

... "No, you shan't," said Tom. "Hullo!" exclaimed Williams, looking at Tom, and then giving him a sudden dig in the ribs with his elbow, which sent Tom's books flying on to the floor, and <u>called the attention</u> of the master, who turned suddenly round, and said ...

... Another hour was occupied in preparing and saying fourth lesson, during which <u>William was bottling up his wrath</u>; and when five struck, and the lessons for the day were over, he prepared to take summary vengeance on the innocent cause of his misfortune. ...

» **Note**

☐ call the attention: 주의를 끌다
☐ bottle up...: ...을 참다

When you work for your company, <u>suit the action to the word.</u>

: 직장에서 일할 때, 행동과 말을 일치시켜라.

» 원문

… "I," said Tom; and <u>suiting the action to the word</u>, he struck the arm which held Arthur's arm so sharply that the Slogger dropped it with a startle, and turned the full current of his wrath on Tom. …

… <u>The news ran like wildfire about</u>, and many boys who were on their way to tea at their several houses turned back, and sought the back of the chapel, where the fights <u>come off</u>. …

» **Note**

- □ suit the action to the word: 언행을 일치시키다, 〈특히, 협박 등에서〉말한 바를 곧 실행에 옮기다
- □ run like wildfire about: 요원의 불처럼 번져나가다
  ex) Ill news runs apace.: 추문은 빨리[멀리] 퍼진다.
- □ come off: 빠지다, 벗어지다, 실행하다
- □ Your buttons came off.: 너의 단추가 떨어졌다.

I hope we will meet again some time later. Take it easy, Buddy. Good luck.

: 나는 우리가 조만간 다시 만나기를 바래. <u>안녕</u>, 친구. 행운을 빈다.

Take it easy, man. Why are you in a hurry?

: <u>마음 편히 가지라고</u>. 왜 그렇게 급히 하려고 하는 거야?

» 원문

… The time keeper is chosen, a large ring made, and <u>the two stand up opposite one another for a moment</u>. …

… "<u>Take it easy, take it easy ; keep away</u> ; let him come after you," implores East …

… <u>Tom goes in a twinkling</u>, and hits two heavy body blows, and <u>gets away</u> again before <u>the Slogger can catch his wind</u>. …

   □ take it easy: (1)마음 편히 가지다 (2)안녕
   □ go in: 뛰어 들어가다, 참가하다
       cfi go in at　=attack　; 공격하다
   □ keep away: 가까이 하지 않다, 피하다, 떨어지다
   □ catch one's wind: 숨을 잇다, 낌새를 알다

The Traditional Culture Festival is in full swing.

: 그 전통 문화 축제가 지금 한창이다.

I'll see (to it) that they can sleep well in spite of the bad weather.

: 나는 사나운 날씨에도 불구하고 그들이 잘 수가 있도록 조치[주의]를 취할 거야.

» **원문**

… The fight is in full swing, when suddenly young Brooke appears and approaches the ring. …

… It is grim earnest now, and no mistake. Both boys feel this, and summon every power of head, hand, and eye to their aid. …

… This fight is not to go on," said the Doctor; "you'll see to that. And I expect you to stop all fights in future at once." …

» **Note**

   □ in full swing: 한창(진행 중인), 신바람이 나서
   □ ring: 싸움장, 경기장
   □ see to...: ...에 주의하다, ...을 준비[조치]시키다
   □ see (to it) that...: ...하도록 주선하다, 꼭... 준비시키다

The Bottle Imp

- Robert Louis Stevenson

\# **작품 소개:** 1891년에 쓰인 단편소설로 최초로 New York Heral.d에 발표되었고(1891), 두 번째는 Black and White London(1891)에서 발간되었다. 주인공은 소원을 허용해주는 요정이 들어 있는 병을 구매한다. 그러나 그 병은 저주를 받고, 만약에 그 병을 가진 채로 세상을 뜬다면, 그 영혼은···

\# **작가 소개:** 인간 내면의 근원과 선악의 갈등을 탐구한 작가다. 대표작은 인간 내면에 잠재한 극단적 이중성을 다룬 대표작 「지킬 박사와 하이드 씨」, 첫 장편소설이자 해양 소설의 고전이 된 「보물섬」 등이 있다.

Jeju Island is 1,000㎞ south of this city

: 제주도는 이 시로부터 1,000킬로미터 남쪽에 있다.

The scandal between the famous musician and the handsome athlete went far and wide.

: 그 유명한 음악가와 그 잘생긴 운동선수 사이의 추문은 널리 퍼져 나갔다.

» **원문**

··· "No", said Keawe, "not in Kau

: they are on the mountain side-a little way south of Hookena." "These lands will now be yours?" asked Lopaka. "And so they will," says Keawe, and began again to lament for his relatives. ···

··· ··· ; but when any one came by they would go in and view the chambers and the pictures. And the fame of the house went far and wide; it was called Ka-Hale-Nui-the Great House-in all Kona ···

I had a word with my homeroom teacher for my future.
: 나는 나의 장래를 위하여 나의 담임선생님과 <u>몇 마디 나누었다</u>.

I have a thought in my mind to solve this tough problem.
: 나는 이 어려운 문제를 해결하기 위해 <u>좋은 생각을 가지고 있다</u>.

» **원문**

… and she was freshened with the bath, and her eyes shone and were kind. Now Keawe no sooner beheld her than he drew rein. …

… I will tell you who I am in a little," said Keawe, dismounting from his horse, "but not now. For I have a thought in my mind, and if you knew who I was, you might have heard of me, and would not give me a true answer. …

… The next day he had a word with Kiano, and found the girl alone. "Kokua," said he, "you made a mark of me all the evening; and it is still time to bid me go. …

» **Note**

☐ be freshened with…=freshen oneself with…: …으로 상쾌해지다
☐ draw rein[bit, bridle]: 고삐를 당겨 멈추다, 몸을 긴장시키다
☐ a thought: 의향, 생각
  ex) have a thought in one's mind: 좋은 생각을 가지고 있다
☐ have a word with…: …와 대화[몇 마디]하다
  cf) have words with…: …와 다투다
☐ make a mark of…: …에게 인상[감명]을 만들어 주다

When our team won the championship, I did not sleep a wink with excitement.

: 우리 팀이 우승을 했을 때, 나는 흥분 때문에 <u>한 잠도 못 잤다.</u>

When I happened to touch the horrible spider, <u>ice ran in my veins.</u>

: 우연히 무서운 거미를 만졌을 때, <u>온몸이 오싹했다.</u>

» **원문**

… He went round to the back porch, and called to memory the day when the devil had looked forth; and at the thought ice ran in his veins. …

… <u>Never a wink could he sleep; the food stuck in his throat</u>; but he sent a letter a Kiano, and about the time when the steamer would be coming, …

… That none could see her without joy. <u>She was pleasant in her nature.</u> <u>She had the good word always.</u> Full of song she was, and went to and fro in the Bright House, the brightest thing in its three stories, caroling like the birds. …

» **Note**

☐ stick in…: …에 틀어박히다, …걸리다

☐ in the(one's) nature: 천성적으로

☐ have a good word: 말이 늘 부드럽다, 듣기 좋게 하는 말을 한다, 비위를 맞추는 말을 한다

The company struggled to gain ground abroad.

: 그 회사는 해외로부터 기반을 확보하기 위해 몸부림 쳤다.

The thief was caught in the act of stealing.

: 그 도둑은 도둑질하는 현장으로부터 붙잡혔다.

» 원문

... So far from gaining ground, these two began to find they were avoided in the town. Depression fell upon their spirits. ...

..."Why else should she be so cast down at my release? But I will show her I am not the man to be fooled. I will catch her in the act." ...

» Note

□ cast down: ⟨눈을 어떤 방향으로⟩향하다, 쓰러뜨리다, ⟨보통 수동태⟩낙담 시키다

□ gain ground: 단단한 기반을 얻다, 신용을 얻다

□ catch+목적어(A)+in the act: 부정한 현장을 잡다

010

The Suicide Club
- Robert Louis Stevenson

작품 소개: 보헤미아의 왕자 플로리즐이 단짝이자 충복인 제럴딘 대령과 함께 목숨을 놓고 도박을 벌이는 클럽에 연루되어 겪는 기이한 모험 이야기다.

He was in low spirits all day long because he had a low grade in the SAT.
: 대학 수학능력시험에서 낮은 점수를 받았기 때문에 그는 하루 종일 기분이 언짢았다.

Will you honour a complete stranger?
: 잘 부탁드립니다.

» **원문**

… Once on a while when he was in low spirits, when there were no interesting plays to see in any of the London theaters, and when it was not the season for those field sports in which nobody could beat him, he would call for his confidant and cavalry commander, Colonel Geraldine, …

… "Will you honour a complete stranger? I have eaten 27 of these tarts since five o'clock, so I know they are good."

» **Note**

☐ in low spirits: 풀이 꺾어, 기분이 언짢아
☐ honour: 예우하다
 ex) Will you honour a complete stranger?: 전혀 모르는 사람[나]에게 경의를 표현해 주실 수 있겠습니까?, 아직 서로 모르고 있습니다만 잘 부탁합니다.
☐ tart: 타트, 파이

69

The dressed-up girl is suited to my taste.
: 저 말쑥한 소녀는 나의 취향에 맞다.

The action speaks for itself.
: 행동을 보면 안다.

... With these words he crushed the nine remaining tarts into his mouth, and swallowed each of them at a single gulp. ...

... Their conversation was light. The young man was gay and talkative, but he laughed louder than was natural for an educated person. ...

... "I've had all sorts of advantages, including a duel over nothing. Just a couple of months ago I met a young lady exactly suited to my taste in wit and appearance. ...

... Who but a ruined man would throw his notes into the fire? The action speaks for itself."

» Note

- ☐ Suit yourself.: 마음대로 하시오.
- ☐ to my taste: 나의 취향에 맞게
- ☐ The action speaks for itself.: 행동을 보면 알게 된다.

I now repeat it.
: 다시 한 번 말하겠다.

Lead on.
: 계속하여 안내하라.

Your laughter does you good.
: 당신의 웃음은 당신에게 이익[도움]을 준다.

» **원문**

… Remember that under no circumstances are you to tell any one who I am without my special permission. <u>This was my command and I now repeat it.</u> …

… "<u>Lead on</u>, sir," said the Prince. "I am not the man to go back." "<u>Your calmness does me good</u>," replied their guide. …

… There was little furniture, and <u>the coverings were worn to the thread.</u> There was nothing movable except a handbell in the centre of a round table and the hats and coats of a fairly large group <u>hung round the wall on hooks.</u>

» **Note**

☐ I repeat it.: 반복하겠다.(명령할 때 쓰는 말이다.)

☐ worn to the thread: 헤져 가지고 실밥이 나왔다(이때의 'to'는 '결과'를 나타낸다.)

☐ hang round: 이리저리 배회하다, 이리저리 걸려있다

When I was walking in the park, a stranger who seemed to be <u>a man of fitty or more</u> came near to me.

: 내가 공원에서 산보하고 있는 동안에, <u>약 50세가량의 남자가</u> 내 가까이에 왔다.

<u>With no sign of autumn</u>, the leaves of the trees began to fall.

: <u>가을에 대한 어떠한 신호도 없이</u> 나뭇잎들이 떨어지기 시작했다.

… The president was a man of fifty or more. He walked in larger relaxed steps. …

… He was dressed in light tweeds, with his neck very open in a striped shirt collar, and he carried a notebook under one arm. …

… I can understand gentlemen who get merry drinking; but that's enough of this. …

… He rose from his seat and sat down again, with no sign of his paralysis. It was the ace of spades. The honorary member had trifled once too often with his terrors.

» Note

- □ but that's enough of this.: 하지만 그것은 이 정도면 충분하다.
  - *cf)* Enough is as good as a feast.: (속담)배부름은 진수성찬이나 마찬가지다.
- □ No more!=Enough of it!: 이젠 됐어!
- □ Enough is enough.: 이 정도로 충분하다, 더 이상은 안 된다
- □ spade: 카드의 한 종류(삽 모양으로 되어있음)
- □ ace: 카드의 최고의 패 중 하나
- □ an ace of spades: 〈경멸적〉(피부가 검은) 흑인

When I finished the hard work, so much sweat ran down my face.
: 내가 그 어려운 일을 끝냈을 때, 많은 땀이 나의 얼굴로부터 흘러내렸다.

I looked into my exam paper with some show of worry.
: 나는 근심의 표정으로 나의 시험지를 들여다보았다.

When I take some medicine, I am easily helped.
: 약을 먹을 때, 나는 쉽게 도움을 받아요[약 효과가 좋다].

I am my own man again.
: 나는 본래의 내 모습을 찾았어요.

» **원문**

… "I can easily imagine that you sympathize with Mr. Malthus," replied the Prince. "<u>He struck me as being a man of a very original disposition</u>." …

… When Prince Florizel saw his fate on the table in front of him, his heart stood still. He was a brave man, but <u>the sweat ran down his face</u>. …

… "You feel a little sick?" asked the President <u>with some show of worry</u>. "Most people do. How about a little brandy?" …

… <u>I am more easily helped</u>," said the Prince, a good deal revived," <u>I am my own man again</u>, as you see. …

» **Note**

☐ strike: …로서 생각되다
☐ run down: (1)지치다 (2)흘러내리다
☐ with some show of worry: 약간의 걱정의 기색과 함께
☐ be helped=be of help: 힘이 되다, 도움이 되다
☐ be one's own one: 자기의 모습으로 들어오다

A cup of cool water <u>brought</u> him <u>to himself</u>.
: 시원한 한 컵의 물이 그를 제정신 들게 했다.

As soon as her child got back home safely, the mother <u>threw herself upon her child</u>.
: 그녀의 아이가 안전하게 집으로 돌아왔을 때, <u>그 아이의 어머니는 아이를 와락 안았다.</u>

... The sight of the street lamps and <u>the darkness brought him to himself</u>. "Come, come, I must be a man," he thought, "and <u>tear myself away</u>." ...

... <u>The Prince threw himself upon the Colonel's neck</u>. ...

... I would be unworthy of my rank <u>if I did not show my gratitude</u>. Choose any reward you like." ...

» **Note**

☐ bring ... to oneself: ...제정신 들게 하다

☐ tear oneself away: 뿌리치다

☐ throw+(A)+ upon(B): (A)를 (B)로 던지다(or (A)가 (B)를 와락 안다)

☐ show one's gratitude: ...의 사의를 표시하다

011

Treasure Island

- Robert Louis Stevenson

작품 소개: '보물'이라는 엄청난 행운을 손에 넣으려는 사람들이 노골적으로 드러내는 계략과 배반, 자멸의 과정을 세밀하게 담아내고 있다. 빅토리아 시대의 꿈과 낭만을 담은 이 작품은 한 소년이 모험을 통해 성장해 가는 성장소설인 동시에 선악의 경계를 아슬아슬하게 넘나드는 인간의 욕망을 적나라하게 그리고 있다.

The enemy is coming nearer. Let's get away from here.

: 적이 점점 더 가까워지고 있다. 여기로부터 빠져나가자.

The drunkard was sleeping lying full length upon the floor.

: 술 취한 주정뱅이는 마루 바닥에 큰 대자로 누워 잠자고 있었다.

My close friend sometimes gives my arms a wrench for fun.

: 나의 친구는 때때로 재미 삼아 나의 팔을 비튼다.

» **원문**

… "Are you hurt?" I said. "Rum," he said. "Bring me rum. I must get away from here." I ran to fetch it, when I heard a loud fall in the parlor. Running in, I saw the captain lying full length upon the floor. He was breathing loud and hard; but his eyes were closed and his face a horrible colour. …

… The captain opened his eyes and looked mistily about him. …

… "Oh," he sneered, "take me in straight, or I'll break your arm." And he gave it, as he spoke, a wrench that made me cry. …

75

» Note
- □ get away from...: ...로부터 빠져나가다
- □ lie full length upon...: ...위에 큰 대자로 누워있다
- □ look mistily about...: ...주위를 흐릿하게 쳐다보다
- □ give (A) a wrench: (A)에게 비틀음을 주다, 즉, (A)를 비틀다

An unknown dark shadow was coming nearer and so we held our breath.

: 어떤 어두운 그림자가 가까이 다가오고 있었다. 그러므로 우리는 숨을 크게 쉬지 못했다.

The weather man says the cloud will clear away this afternoon.

: 예보관은 오늘 오후에 구름이 걷힐 것이라고 말하고 있다.

Scatter and look for the hidden treasures.

: 뿔뿔이 흩어져라 그리고 숨겨진 보물을 찾아라.

When I fell over the fence, I was none the worse for the surprise.

: 내가 울타리에서 넘어졌을 때, 나는 놀란 것 외에는 별일이 없었다.

» 원문

... It drew nearer and nearer, while we sat holding our breath. Then it struck sharp on the door, and we could hear the handle being turned and the bolt rattling. But at last the tapping began again and soon ceased to be heard. ...

... The moon was shinning brightly, and the fog was rapidly clearing away. The sound of several footsteps running came to our ears. ...

... "That's Dirk!" one said. "Twice! We must get away at once!" "Dirk is a fool and a coward." Pew cried out. "Scatter and look for the boy!" ...

... My mother was none the worse for her terror, though she was still sorry about the balance of the money. ...

» **Note**

- ☐ draw near: 가까이 다가가다
- ☐ hold one's breath: 숨을 작게 내다
- ☐ clear away: 걷히다
- ☐ scatter: 흩어지다, 흩어지게 하다
- ☐ none the worse for...: ...에도 불구하고 아무렇지 않은[변함없는]

What she was in the wrong is <u>as clear as noonday</u>.

: 그녀가 틀린 것은 <u>명약관화한</u> 것이다.

I needed some water <u>to wet my throat</u> crossing the desert in the sun.

: 작렬하는 태양 아래에서 사막을 횡단하는 동안 <u>목을 축이기 위해</u> 나는 약간의 물이 필요했다.

I saw some camels crossing the desert <u>in a row</u>.

: 나는 <u>한 줄로</u> 사막을 횡단하고 있는 낙타 떼를 보았다.

» **원문**

... There was a date at one end of the line and at the other a sum of money, with a number of crosses between the two. "I can't understand it at all," Dr. Liversey said. "<u>It's as clear as noonday</u>," the squire cried out. "These crosses <u>stand for</u> the names of ships or towns they sank or plundered. The sum are his share." ...

... Well, when the time comes, I'll wring Trelawney's head off his body with these hands. Dick, jump up and get me an apple <u>to wet my throat</u>." ...

... There are three hills <u>in a row</u> running southward. The highest one is called the Spy-glass." ...

» **Note**

☐ as clear as noonday: 명약관화한

☐ stand for...: ...을 대신하다

☐ in a row: 한 줄로

Just wring the cap off the bottle.

: 단지 병으로부터 뚜껑을 비틀어 떼어내라.

Give some water to wet my throat.

: 나의 목을 축이게 물 좀 주소.

The acasia seeds lay about by the wind.

: 아카시아 씨들이 바람에 의해 이리저리 흩어졌다.

When the thief tried to cover his behavior up, the policeman stared at him with a black look.

: 도둑이 그의 행위를 은폐하고자 했을 때, 경찰은 못마땅한 표정으로 그를 노려보았다.

I tried to soothe and humor the defeated player but the man did not bat an eye.

: 내가 그 패한 선수를 달래고 기분을 맞춰주려고 했지만 그 선수는 눈 하나 꿈쩍도 하지 않았다.

I always think highly of my university professor in character and in ability.

: 나는 늘 나의 대학 은사님을 인격 면이나 능력 면에 있어 높이 평가하고 있다.

» 원문

… You're seamen, but you can't set a course. Well, when the time comes, I'll wring Trelaway's hea.d off his body with these hands. Dick, jump up and get me an apple to wet my throat."

… They lay about the deck growling together. The slightest order was received with a black look and was carelessly obeyed. Silver alone was anxious to soothe and humour them. …

… "Silver, sir" the captain answered. "He is anxious to cover the matter up. …

… "Tom," Silver was saying, "It's because I think highly of you. If I didn't take to you, do you think I'd have been here warning you? …

… Tom leaped at the sound, but Silver did not bat an eye. …

» Note

☐ wring (A) off: (A)를 비틀어 떼어내다
☐ wet one's throat: 목을 축이다
☐ lie about: 이리리 누워있다[산재해있다]
☐ with a black look: 못 마땅한 얼굴로
☐ soothe and humor: 달래주고 기분을 맞춰주다
☐ cover … up: …을 은폐하다

One of the runners in the second group began to head me off.

: 2위 그룹에 있던 달리기 선수들 중의 한 사람이 나를 앞지르기 시작했다.

I'll tell you what, Smith won the first prize unexpectedly.

: 있잖아, Smith가 기대하지 않게 일등상을 탔대.

Let's strike a tent. It is likely to be clear.

: 텐트를 걷자. 하늘이 개일 것 같다.

… Instantly the figure reappeared and began to head me off. …

… "I'll tell you what," he went on, "I was in Flint's ship when he buried the treasure, he and six strong seaman. They were ashore nearly a week, and we stood off and on in the old Walrus. …

… "Strike my colours!" the captain cried out. "No, sir, not I." All through the evening they kept thundering away. Ball after ball flew over or fell short or kicked up the sand in the enclosure. …

- head (A) off…: (A)를 앞지르다
- I'll tell you what.: 있잖아.[좋은 소식 있어.]
- Strike one's colours.: 기를 내려라.
  ex) Strike your tents.: 너의 텐트들을 걷어라.
- fall short: 부족하다, 못 미치다

She was a silent woman by birth but became a social woman by custom.

: 그녀는 태생은 조용한 여자였다 하지만 관습상 사교적인 여자가 되었다.

He was fired a few days ago and now he hangs round the town.

: 그는 며칠 전에 실직 당했다 그리고 지금 도시를 배회한다.

… He was a very silent man by custom. All day he hung round the cove, or stood upon the cliffs, with a telescope. All evening he sat in a corner of the parlour next the fire and drank very strong rum and water. …

» Note

□ by custom: 보통, 습관에 의해(즉, 언제나)

□ hang around(or about): 배회하다

I put my hand upon my student's arm and tried to encourage her.

: 나는 나의 손을 나의 학생의 팔위에 얹어 놓았다 그리고 그녀를 격려하고자 했다.

When some strange sound was heard outside of room we held our breath.

: 어떤 이상한 소리가 문밖으로부터 들렸을 때 우리는 숨소리를 크게 내지 못했다.

» 원문

… I suddenly put my hand upon her arm ; for I had heard the tapping of the blind man's stick upon the frozen roa.d. It drew nearer and neared, while we sat holding our breath. Then it struck sharp on the door, and we could hear the handle being turned and the bolt rattling. …

» Note

□ put 소유격(A) hand upon 소유격(B) arm: (A)의 팔을 (B)의 팔에 얹어 놓다 [잡았다]

□ hold 소유격(A) breath.: 숨소리를 크게 밖으로 내지 않다

Crawling on all fours, the damaged man cried out for help.

: 네발로 기면서, 그 다친 사람이 도움을 위해 소리쳤다.

I'll employ you as soon as possible, because I think highly of you in every way.

: 나는 당신을 바로 고용하겠다. 왜냐하면 모든 면에서 나는 당신을 높이 평가했기 때문이다.

Even when I tried to scare them away, the children did not bat an eye.

: 겁주어 쫓아내려고 했을 지라도, 그 아이들은 눈 깜짝도 하지 않았다.

» **원문**

... Another voice answered; and then the first voice, which I now recognize to be Silver's, began to talk. Crawling on all fours, I went slowly towards them, till at last I could see Silver and another of the crew standing face to face in conversation.

"Tom," Silver was saying, "It's because I think highly of you. If I hadn't taken to you, do you think I'd have been here warning you? ...

... Tom leaped at the sound, but Silver did not bat an eye. He stood where he was, resting lightly on his crutch ...

» **Note**

- □ craw on all fours: 네발로 기다
- □ stand face to face: 얼굴을 맞대고
- □ think highly of ...: ...을 높이 평가하다
- □ bat an eye: 눈을 깜작거리다
- □ rest on...: ...에 의지하다

The drunken sailor tumbled down the stairs and fainted.

: 그 술 취한 선원은 계단 아래로 굴러 떨어졌고 의식을 잃었다.

Load this boat with your belongings and sail to the island.

: 이 보트에 너의 소지품들을 실어라 그리고 그 섬으로 항해하라.

» 원문

… Instantly the figure reappeared and began to head me off. …

… "I'll tell you what," he went on. "I was in Flint's ship when he buried the treasure; he and six strong seaman. They were ashore nearly a week, and we stood off and on in the old Walrus. …

… The sailors were astonished and tumbled down the fore companion. Hunter brought the boat round. Joyce and I set to work loading her with powder tins, muskets, bags of biscuits, kegs of pork, a cask of cognac and my medicine chest. …

» Note

□ stand off and on…: …에 붙었다 떼었다하다

   ex) It has been raining on and off a week.: 비가 일주일 동안 오락가락해왔다.

□ tumble down: 굴러 넘어지다

□ set to work: 일하기 시작하다

□ load (A) with (A): (A)를 (B)로 싣다[장전하다]

Let's strike a tent. It looks like rain.

: 텐트를 걷자. 비가 올 것 같다.

His ball-throwing fell short, so the catcher didn't catch the ball.

: 그의 공 송구는 못 미쳤다 그러므로 포수는 그 공을 잡지 못했다.

Whatever they do in the area we mind it no more cricket.

: 그들이 이곳으로부터 무엇을 하든지 간에 우리는 눈곱만큼도 신경을 쓰지 않는다.

» 원문

... "It must be the flag they're aiming at. Wouldn't it be wiser to take it in?" "Strike my colours!" the captain cried out. "No. sir, not I." All through the evening they kept thundering away. Ball after ball flew over or fell short or kicked up the sand in the enclosure. We soon minded it no more than cricket. ...

» **Note**

- strike a flag: 기를 내리다
- fall short (of)...: ...에 못 미치다, 미달하다, 부족하다
- mind (A) no more than cricket: (A)에 눈곱만큼도 신경을 쓰지 않다

When I was alone in the dark in the foreign country, I was at my wit's end.

: 외국에 홀로 밤에 있었을 때, 나는 어찌할 줄 몰랐다.

As soon as I got back from my long job training, I was so exhausted and I slept like a log.

: 긴 직업 강습으로부터 돌아오자마자, 나는 녹초가 되었다 그리고 아무것도 모르고 푹 잠을 잤다.

The student slipped out of the room when his cellular phone rang up.

: 핸드폰이 울렸을 때 그 학생은 슬그머니 강의실로부터 빠져 나왔다.

» **원문**

… It appeared they were at their wit's end what to do. I was completely exhausted. When I got to sleep, I slept like a log. …

… We're outnumbered, but we fight in shelter. I have no doubt that we can defeat them, if you choose." …

… It was to go down the sandy spit and find Ben Gunn's boat. I made up my mind to slip out when nobody was watching. …

» **Note**

☐ at one's wit's end: 어찌할 줄 모르는
☐ sleep like a log: 푹 잠자다
☐ outnumbered: 수적으로 우세하다
☐ if you choose: 당신이 마음에 있다면
☐ slip out: 살그머니 빠져나가다

The Life of Our Lord

- **Charles Dickens**

작품 소개: 예수 그리스도의 인생에 관한 책이다. 소설 「David Copperfield」를 쓰고 있는 동안 그의 어린아이들을 위하여 1846년부터 1849년까지 이 작품을 썼다.

작가 소개: 19세기의 영국을 대표하는 소설가다. 풍자적 희극성과 감상주의적 휴머니즘이 풍성하게 어우러진 그의 작품들은 후기로 가면서 사회 비판의 성격을 강하게 띤다. 「올리버 트위스트」, 「데이비드 코퍼필드」, 「위대한 유산」, 「크리스마스 캐럴」을 비롯한 다수의 소설과 여러 산문 작품을 남겼다.

May I be healthy!
: 내가 건강해지길 (바란다)!

Be it so!
: 그렇게 될 지어다!

» **원문**

… Jesus, always full of compassion, stretched out his hand, and said "I will! <u>Be thou well</u>!" And his disease went away, immediately, and he was cured. …

… Then Jesus Christ, glad that the Centurion believed in him so truly, said "<u>Be it so</u>!" And the servant became well, from that moment. …

» **Note**

☐ Be thou well!: 네[그대]는 좋아질 지어다!
☐ Be it so!: 그렇게 될 지어다!

A tale of Two Cities

- Charles Dickens

작품 소개: 「두 도시 이야기」는 디킨스의 두 번째 역사소설이다. 토머스 칼라일(Tomas Carlyle)의 「프랑스 혁명(The French Revolution)」을 읽고 이에 영향을 받아 프랑스 혁명을 배경으로 쓴 작품이다.

The strong nations should not put their nose into the weak nations.

: 강대국은 약소국에 간섭하지 말아야한다.

When he went bankrupt, he was in his rich friend's debt. But because of his diligence he recovered his company and then he could pay him off clear.

: 그가 파산했을 때, 그는 그의 부자친구에게 빚을 지고 있었다. 하지만 근면성 때문에 그는 그의 회사를 회복시킬 수가 있었고 그 때문에 친구의 빚을 완전히 갚을 수가 있었다.

» **원문**

… "Nonsense, child! to be sure, I shouldn't. What do you talk so for? I would as soon have one of my own children sold. But really, Eliza, you are getting altogether too proud of that little fellow. A man can't put his nose into the door, but you think he must be coming to buy him." …

… "He hasn't done anything-it isn't for that. Master doesn't want to sell, and missis-she's always good. I heard her plead and beg for us : but he told her it was no use-that he was in this man's debt, and that this man had got the power over him-and that if he didn't pay him off clear, it would end in his having to sell the place and all the people and move off. …

» **Note**

□ what ...for?=why?: 무엇 때문에?
□ put one's nose into...: ...에 간섭하다
□ in one's debt: ...의 부채 속에 있는, 즉 ...에게 빚지고 있는
□ pay off: 청산하다, 상쇄하다

She is not to blame, rather they are to blame.

: 그녀는 비난받지 말아야 한다. 오히려 그들이 비난 받아야한다.

His friends pushed him to the very last standing places

: 그의 친구들은 그를 최후의 궁지로 몰아넣었다.

» **원문**

... "Master always found me on the spot-he always will. I never have broken trust, and I never will. It's better for me alone to go than to break up the place and sell all. Master isn't to blame, Chloe; and he'll take care of you and the poor ..." ...

... They have pushed him to the very last standing places, and he told me today that he was going to run away. Do try, if you can, get word of him. ...

... Her husband's suffering and dangers, and the danger of her child, all blended in her mind with a confused and stunning sense of the risk she was running, in leaving the only home she had ever known. ...

» **Note**

□ be to blame=be to be blamed: 비난받아야 한다
   cf) sell=be sold: 팔리다
□ take care of...: ...을 돌보다, 해결하다
□ push (A) to the very last standing places: (A)를 최후의 마지막까지 궁지에 몰아넣다
□ get word of (A): (A)에게 꼭 전해주다

She was weary and footsore, but still strong in her heart.

: 그녀는 지치고 발도 아팠다. 하지만 마음만은 여전히 강했다.

After heavy rain, the stream was swollen and flooded.

: 폭우 후에 시냇물이 불어 범람했다.

The ferry boat takes people over to opposite river bank every three hours.

: 그 나룻배는 매 세 시간마다 사람들을 반대쪽 강둑으로 건네다 준다.

» 원문

… An hour before sunset, Eliza entered the village of T-, by the Ohio River, weary and footsore, but still strong in her heart. Her first glance was at the river, which lay, like Jordan, between her and the Canaan of liberty on the other side.

It was now early spring, and the river was swollen and turbulent; great cakes of floating ice were swinging heavily to and fro in the turbid water. …

… "What is it?" she said. "Isn't there any ferry or boat, that takes people over to B-, now" she said. …

… In that dizzy moment her feet to her scarce seemed to touch the ground and a moment brought her to the water's edge. …

» Note

☐ in one's heart: 마음은
☐ swollen: 부푼
☐ take (A) over to (B): (A)를 (B)로 건네다 주다

The pattern of the new dress <u>was to her taste</u> and she choco it.

: 그 새 옷의 무늬는 <u>그녀의 취향에 맞았다.</u> 그러므로 그녀는 그것을 선택했다.

We are going to play the game on schedule <u>except on extreme occasions</u>.

: <u>특별한 경우들을 제외하고는</u> 우리는 예정대로 경기를 할 것이다.

The missing girl seemed to <u>be between five and six years of age</u>.

: 그 미아 소녀는 <u>나이가 다섯 살과 여섯 살 사이가 된</u> 것처럼 보였다.

» 원문

... The poor soul had expended all her little energies on this farewell feast-had kiiled and dressed her choicest chicken, and prepared her corn-cake with scrupulous exactness, <u>just to her husband's taste</u>, and brought out certain mysterious jars on the mantlepiece, some <u>preserves</u> that were never produced <u>except on extreme occasions</u>. ...

... Among the passengers on the boat was a young gentleman of fortune and family, resident in New Orleans, who bore the name of St. Clare. He had with him a daughter, <u>between five and six years of age</u>, together with a lady who seemed to claim relationship to both, and to have the little one especially <u>under charge</u>. ...

» **Note**

- □ to one's taste: ...의 취향에 맞게
- □ preserves: 잼
- □ except on extreme occasions: 특별한 경우를 제외하고
- □ between five and six years of age: 나이가 다섯 살 여섯 살 사이에 있는
- □ under charge: 책임 하에 있는[보호 하에 있는], 맡고 있는

I could recognize that she was my long forgotten sister at a glance.

: 나는 그녀가 나의 오랫동안 잊혀져 왔던 누이라는 것을 한 <u>첫눈에</u> 인식할 수가 있었다.

Hand in your report <u>in due form</u> by tomorrow.

: <u>적당한 형식으로</u> 내 일까지 리포트를 제출하시오.

» **원문**

… It was evident, <u>at a glance</u>, that the gentleman was Eva's father. He was listening with a good-humored, negligent air, half comic, half contemptuous, to Haley, who was very volubly expatiating on the quality of the article for which they were bargaining. …

… The fact was, that Tom's home-yearnings had become so strong, that he had begged a sheet of writing-paper of Eva; and <u>mustering up</u> all his small stock of literary attainment acquired by Master George's instructions, he conceived the bold idea of writing a letter …

… Tom's letter was written <u>in due form</u> for him that evening, and safely lodged in the post-office. …

» **Note**

☐ at a glance: 일견으로
☐ must up: 소집하다, 동원하다
☐ in due form: 적당한 형식[태](으)로
☐ lodge: 맡기다

What a story! You are to blame.
: 무슨 허튼 수작이야! 네가 비난 받아야해.

We tried my best to win the championship, but we lost the game. We couldn't help it. That's because at the beginning of the second half our physical strengths began to fail
: 우리는 결승전에서 이기려고 최선을 다했다. 그러나 졌다. 어찌할 수가 없었다. 그것은 후반전 시작부터 우리의 체력은 바닥나기 시작했기 때문이다.

» **원문**

… "Topsy, you naughty girl, don't tell me a lie! You stole that ribbon!" I didn't, missis; I never saw it <u>till this minute</u>." Miss Ophelia was so indignant at the barefaced lie that she caught the child and shook her. <u>The shake brought gloves on to the floor</u>, from the other sleeve. "There, you!" said Miss Ophelia, "will you tell me now you didn't steal the ribbon?" …
… "Burn up?-<u>What a story!</u> Go and get them, or I'll whip you." Topsy, with loud protestation, and tears, and groans, declared that she could not.
"<u>What did you burn them up for?</u>" said Miss Ophelia. "Because I'm wicked. I am, anyhow. <u>I can't help it</u>." …

» **Note**

□ till this minute: 지금 순간까지
□ The shake brought gloves on to the floor.: 그러한 동요[흔들림]가 장갑을 마루바닥에 떨어지게 했다.
□ What a story!: 무슨 엉터리 같은 수작이야!
□ What … for?=why?: 무엇 때문에?
□ I can't help it.: 어쩔 수가 없다.

I've had my new blouse on all day to show off in front of my classmates.

: 반 급우들 앞에서 자랑하기 위해 나는 하루 종일 <u>새 블라우스를 입고 있었다.</u>

The passers-by <u>bent over</u> the poor beggar and threw some coins into his coin bowl

: 지나가던 사람들이 불쌍한 거지를 <u>굽어보고</u> 동전 몇 잎을 동전사발에 던 저 넣었다.

» **원문**

… "Why, Eva, Where did you get your necklace?" said Miss Ophelia. "Get it? Why, <u>I've had it on all day</u>," said Eva. "Did you have it on yesterday?" Yes; and, what is funny, aunty, I had it on all night, I forgot to take it off when I went to bed." …

… She <u>laid her head down between her knees</u>, and wept, and sobbed; while the beautiful child, <u>bending over her</u>, <u>looked like the picture of</u> some bright angel stooping to reclaim a sinner. …

» **Note**

- □ have (A) on=wear (A): (A)를 입고[착용하고] 있다
- □ lay her head down between her knees: 무릎사이로 머리를 집어넣다
- □ bend over…: …위로 몸을 구부리다
- □ look like the picture of…: …의 상[모습]처럼 보이다

Familiarize yourself with the new circumstance and try to **succeed** in your life.

: 너 자신을 새로운 환경에 친숙화[적응]시켜라 그리고 성공하고자 노력하라.

As is often the case, he tease his fellow students without some special reasons.

: 흔히 있는 일이지만, 그는 특별한 이유 없이 그의 동료 학생들을 괴롭힌다.

» 원문

... He read his little Eva's Bible seriously and honestly; he thought more soberly and practically of his relations to his servants; and one thing he did, soon after his return to New Orleans, and that was to commerce the lega.l steps necessary to Tom's emancipation, which was to be perfected as soon as he could get through the necessary formalities. ...

... It took but a short time <u>to familiarize Tom with all</u> that was to be hoped or feared in his new way of life. He was an expert and efficient workman in whatever he undertook; and was, <u>both from habit and principle</u>, prompt and faithful. Legree <u>took silent note of</u> Tom's availability. He rated him as first-class hand; and yet he felt a secret dislike to him-the native antipathy of bad to good. He saw plainly that when, <u>as was often the case</u>, his violence and brutality fell on the helpless, Tom took notice of it ...

» Note

- □ familiarize (A) with (B): (A)를 (B)에 친숙화[적응]시키다
- □ both from habit and principle: 습관과 주의의 양면
- □ take note of...: ...을 주목하다
    cf) take a silent note of...=take a note of... silently
- □ as is often the case: 흔히 있는 일이지만

He yielded himself to a small light plane and flew over the Atlantic ocean.

: 그는 자신을 조그맣고 가벼운 비행기에 맡겼다 그리고 대서양 위를 날았다.

I used to be a handsome guy when I was young.

: 젊었을 때, 나는 잘생긴 사내였다.

» **원문**

… He yield himself to the rough, brutal grasp with which Cuimbo seize him. …

… Neither George nor Mrs. Shelby could be easy at this result; and, accordingly, some six months after, the former having business for his mother down the river, resolved to visit New Orleans in person, and push his inquiries in hopes of discovering Tom's whereabouts and resorting him. …

"He used to be on my father's place, and I came to see if I couldn't buy him back."

Legree's brow grew dark, and he broke out passionately. "Yes, I did buy such a fellow. The most rebellious, saucy, impudent dog! Set up my niggers to runaway, got off two girls worth eight hundred or a thousand dollars apiece. …

… Truly, those poor disciples had little to give-only the cup of cold water; but it was given with full hearts. …

» **Note**

- □ yield oneself to (A): 자신을 (A)에 맡기다
- □ in hope of…: …의 바람 속에서
- □ used to+동원: …하곤했다, … 였었다
- □ set up (A) to (B): (A)가 (B)하도록 주선하다[계도하다]
- □ (A) worth (B): (B)의 가격이[가치개]있는 (A)
- □ with full hearts: 완전한 기운을 가지고, 뿌듯함을 가지고

He was accused of stealing some necessaries.

: 그는 약간의 생활필수품을 훔쳤기 <u>때문에 고소되었다</u>

The young runner informed his country men of his country's victory.

: 그 젊은 주자는 <u>그의 동포들에게 나라의 승리를 알렸다</u>.

» 원문

... The prisoner was <u>a young man of about twenty-five</u> named Charles Darney. He appeared to be a gentleman. He was quite calm, bowed to the judge, and stood quiet. Silence in the court. <u>He was accused of</u> being a spy and of helping the French King, in his wars against the King of England. He was accused of coming and going between the two countries, and <u>informing the French of what forces</u> our King was preparing to send to Canada and North America. ...

» Note

- □ a young man of about twenty-five: 약 25세가량의 젊은 남자
- □ be accused of...: ... 때문에 고소[비난]받다
- □ inform (A) of (B): (A)에게 (B)를 알려주다

To my surprise, <u>my friend gave his witness against me.</u>

: 놀랍게도 <u>나의 친구는 나에게 불리한 증언을 했다.</u>

[A] <u>How do you say</u>, friend?

: 친구, <u>어떻게 생각하는가?</u>

[B] Nothing unusual.

: 특별한 것은 없네.

<u>She is very like me</u> so every body calls us twins.

: <u>그녀는 나와 매우 똑같다.</u> 그러므로 모든 사람들은 우리를 쌍둥이라고 부른다.

» **원문**

… First John Barsad, who was once the prisoner's friend, <u>testified to</u> the fact that the prisoner carried papers in his pockets on which there were lists of the English forces and their positions. Next came Roger Cly, the prisoner's servant. <u>He also gave his witness against the prisoner.</u> …

… "Have you ever seen anyone very like the prisoner?" "Not so like him that he could be mistaken." "Look well at that gentleman, my learned friend there," said Stryver, pointing to the man who had tossed him the paper. "<u>How do you say?</u> Isn't he very like the prisoner?" …

» **Note**

☐ testify to…: …증언하다
☐ give 소유격(A) witness against (B): (B)에게 불리하게 (A)의 증언을 하다
☐ How do you say?: 당신은 어떻게 생각하는가?
☐ be very like…: …와 매우 흡사하다[같다]

When I happened to see her, she sat in the bench <u>with her face turned away</u>.

: 내가 우연히 그녀를 만났을 때, 그녀는 <u>그녀의 얼굴을 외면한 채</u> 벤치에 앉아있었다.

I've never been at ease with her since I fought her.

: <u>그녀와 다툰 이후로 나는 결코 그녀와 편한 상태에 있는 적이 없다.</u>

» **원문**

... "Dear Dr. Manette, I love your daughter, deeply, dearly, devotedly. If there were love in the world, O love her." The doctor sat <u>with his face turned away</u>. Darney's words had brought a look of deep pain into his eyes. ...

One August day, Carton <u>called at</u> the Manette's house and found Lucie at her work alone. <u>She had never been quite at ease with him</u>. She received him with some embarrassment. Looking up at his face, she observed a change in it. ...

» **Note**

☐ with one's face turned away: ...의 얼굴을 외면한 채

☐ call at+장소(A): (A)를 방문하다

☐ be not at ease with...: ...와 편한 상태에 있지 않다[...와 심기가 불편하다]

98

There was some uneasiness in the city at that time.

: 그 당시에 그 도시는 불안한 상태[소요]가 있었다.

That country has a bad look now.

: 그 나라는 지금 정세가 좋지 않다.

I searched every nook and corner to catch the thief.

: 나는 그 도둑을 잡기 위해 모든 구석을 샅샅이 수색했다.

» **원문**

… "I began to think," he said, "there must be some uneasiness in Paris, because the people over there are putting their property in our hands and sending it to England in haste." "That has a bad look," said Darney. "Yes, but we don't know what reason there is in it." …

… "Monsieur, it is a room." "Show it me." It was the room where Dr. Manette was imprisoned. Defarge searched every nook and corner, even inside of the chimney. …

» **Note**

□ there is uneasiness in it.: 그것에는 불안한 기운이 있다
□ That has a bad look.: 그것은 정세가 좋지 않습니다.
□ Show it me.: 나에게 그것을 보여주시오[안내하세요].
□ search every nook and corner: 구석구석 수색하다[찾다]

99

I left her office half an hour before the time of closing.

: 나는 폐업 시간 반시간 전에 그녀의 사무실을 떠났다.

The tall man was smoking his pipe leaning on the big maple tree.

: 그 키 큰 사람은 커다란 단풍나무에 기대고 파이프 담배를 피우고 있었다.

The summary of his story is as follows.

: 그의 개인사를 요약하면 다음과 같다.

She is American now but she was Chinese by birth.

: 그녀는 지금 미국인이다 그러나 태생은 중국인이었다.

» 원문

... One summer afternoon in 1792, half an hour before the time of closing, Mr. Lorry was sitting at his desk in Tellson's Bank, and Charles Darney stood leaning on it, talking with him in a low voice. Mr. Lorry told him that he intended to go to Paris to look after the security of the branch of the bank there. ...

... "Then will you take charge of the letter?" said Mr. Lorry. "Do you know where to deliver it?" "I do." Very uneasy in his mind, he hurried out into a quiet place nearby, and opened the letter. It was as follows: ...

... You married in England? The President continued questioning. "True; but not an Englishwoman. A French woman by birth." "Her name and family?" "Lucie Manette, only daughter of Dr. Manette, the good doctor who sits there." ...

» Note

- □ half an hour before the time of closing: 영업시간 마감 반시간 전
- □ lean on…: …에 기대다
- □ as follows: 다음과 같은
- □ by birth: 태생은

I came back to bear witness for my friend in danger.

: 나는 위험 속에 처해 있는 나의 친구에게 증인이 되기 위해 돌아왔소.

Can it be a kind action in the eyes of the proud people?

: 그 자존심 강한 사람들의 눈엔 그것은 친절한 행위가 될 수가 있는가?

I left the tiger alone until he stopped growling of his own will.

: 나는 호랑이가 그 자신의 의지로 포효하는 것을 멈출 때까지 홀로 그것을 내버려두었다.

» 원문

… I came back to try to save a citizen's life, to bear witness for him at whatever personal danger. Is that a crime in the eyes of the Republic?" The Crowd shouted, "No!" and the President rang his bell to quiet them. But they continued crying "No," until they stopped of their own will. …

… He was always faithful and devoted to my daughter and to myself in England. He was far from being in favour with the aristocrat government there. …

- ☐ bear witness for (A): (A)에 증인이 되다
- ☐ in the eyes of (A): (A)의 눈으로 볼 때
- ☐ of one's own will: 자기 자신의 의지로
- ☐ far from...ing: 전혀...하지 않는
- ☐ in favor with...: ...을 지지하여

What I spat on the sidewalk in this city was <u>against the rule</u>.

: 내가 이 도시의 인도 위에 침을 뱉는 것은 <u>규칙에 위반</u>이었다.

The house breaker <u>was put to trial</u> as soon as he was caught.

: 잡히자마자 그 가택침입자는 <u>재판에 회부되었다</u>.

Is he punished <u>openly or secretly?</u>

: 그는 <u>공공연히</u> 벌 받는가 아니면 <u>비밀리에</u> 벌 받는가?

Gentlemen, <u>listen to what is to follow</u>.

: 신사양반들 이제부터 말씀 드리는 것에 귀를 기울이시오.

» **원문**

... On the evening of the same day that Darney was set free, the Manette family gathered round a fire, and the grandfather was telling a fairy tale to little Lucie. Suddenly a violent knock was heard on the door. ...

... "It is against the rule. But-well-he is accused by Citizen and Citizeness Defarge. And by one other. "What other?" "You will be answered tomorrow. He is to be put to trial tomorrow." ...

... "Charles Everemonde, called Darney, set free yesterday. Re-accused and taken back yesterday. Accused as an enemy of the Republic, a nobleman, a member of a family that mercilessly oppressed the people." "Is he accused openly or secretly?" asked the President. ...

... "President, I protest to you that this is a fraud. You know the accused to be the husband of my daughter. Who says that I accused the husband of my daughter?" "Citizen Manette, be calm. Listen to what is to follow. In the meanwhile, be silent!" ...

» **Note**

- □ gather round: ... 에 모이다
- □ against the rule: 규칙 위반인
- □ be put to trial: 재판에 회부되다
- □ openly or secretly: 공공연히 또는 비밀리에
- □ accuse (A) of (B): (A)를 (B) 때문에 고소하다[비난하다]
- □ listen to what is to follow: 말할 것에 귀를 기울이다

The champion boxer knocked the opponent down on the canvas, and then the referee began to count up to ten.

: 챔피언 복서가 도전자를 링 위에 때려 눕혔다. 그때 심판은 <u>열까지 셈을 하기 시작했다.</u>

The missing were <u>cute girls aged six at the most.</u>

: 그 행방불명자들은 <u>많아봤자 여섯 살 먹은 귀여운 소녀들</u>이었다.

» **원문**

… "My husband, my father, and my brother!" and then <u>counted up to twelve</u>, and said "Hush!" And she seemed to listen. Then she repeated the same words again and again. …

… On some hay on the ground lay <u>a handsome boy aged seventeen at the most</u>. His right hand was clenched on his breast. His glaring eyes were looking straight upward. …

» **Note**

   □ count up to...: ...까지 셈을 하다
   □ (A) aged (B): (B)나이의 (A)
   □ at the most: 많아봤자

Please put the medicine in the place <u>beyond the reach of</u> the children.

: 이 약을 <u>어린아이들이 미치지 못하는</u> 장소에 놓으시오.

When in danger, the man <u>drew his sword to defend himself.</u>

: 위험에 처하게 되었을 때, 그 사람은 <u>자기를 방어하기 위해 칼을 뽑았다.</u>

» 원문

… I took my younger sister to a place <u>beyond the reach of</u> this man. Then I followed the brother here, and last night I climbed into the house, a sword in hand. She heard me and ran in. Then he came. I struck at him with my sword <u>so as to</u> make him <u>draw his sword to defend himself.</u> …

… I supported him to sit up and stand up completely with all his remaining power. "Marquis," he said, "I call upon you and yours, to the last of your bad race, to pay for these things. …

» **Note**

☐ beyond the reach of…: …가 미치지 않는
☐ so as to+동원: …하기 위해
☐ draw one's sword…: …의 칼을 뽑다
☐ defend oneself: 자신을 옹호[방에]하다

We have a vague notion of the excuse that our team did not climb up to the mountain top on time.

: 우리는 우리의 팀이 제 시간에 산 정상에 도달하지 못한 변명에 대한 막연한 생각을 갖고 있다.

I'll study hard to make up for my youth when I spent without a special purpose.

: 나는 시간만 소비했던 청춘을 보상하기 위해 열심히 공부할 것이다.

» 원문

... The elder brother tried to offer me a bag of gold. "Please excuse me," I said. "In the circumstance, no." The bag of gold was left at my door the next morning, but I did not accept it. ...

... She had a vague notion of what her husband had done. She was a good, compassionate lady, and wanted to do what little she could to make up for her husband's wrong. ...

... "To whom do I address it" ...

... There was something in his hand. "What have you in your hand? A weapon." "No. I am not armed." ...

014

David Copperfield

- Charles Dickens

작품 소개: 1849~1850년에 발표됐다. 작가 자신의 어린 시절의 추억과 고난이 새겨져 있어서 주인공 데이비드는 작가의 분신으로 생각할 수 있는 작품이다.

The king who was deprived of his land tried to take revenge upon the enemy.

: 그의 땅을 빼앗긴 그 왕은 적을 복수하고자 했다.

The beautiful princess fell in love with the knight who caught her fancy.

: 그 아름다운 공주는 그녀의 마음을 빼앗은 그 기사와 사랑에 빠졌다.

» **원문**

… Whenever Hera heard of such an affair, she grew hot with rage. Sometimes she simply scolded him, but more often she tried to take revenge upon the person who caught his fancy.
The Greeks declared that in some cases Zeus assumed the form of an eagle. An old Greek picture shows Zeus as an eagle bearing a pretty maiden up to heaven. …

» **Note**

- □ take revenge on…: …에게 복수하다.
- □ catch(or strike, take) one's fancy: …의 마음을 빼앗다, …마음에 들다
  cf) The fancy seized me.: 나는 마음이 내켰다.

107

Since I was divorced from my ex, I vowed never to love any woman.

: 전 처와 이혼한 후에, 나는 어느 여자도 사랑하지 않겠다고 맹세했다.

The award was made in honour of his good conduct.

: 그 상은 그의 선행을 기리기 위해 제정되었다.

The new theme park was founded in memory of the missing during the civil war.

: 그 주제 공원은 내란 동안에 행방불명된 사람들을 기념하기 위해 건립되었다.

» 원문

... A story about Pan says that he fell in love with a nymph named Syrinx. She was a great beauty, but had vowed never to love any god or man. One day Pan met her and told her how charming she was. Not wishing to listen to compliments, she fled-with Pan in swift pursuit. ...

... So saying, he cut the reed into seven parts of unequal length and made the shepherd's pipe, which he called a Syrinx in honour of the nymph. Flutes are sometimes spoken of as "pipes of Pan," in memory of this myth. ...

... Hercules was supposed to have mighty muscles. At one time he was said to have wrestled with a lion and beaten it. At another time he "held the sky on his shoulders" while Atlas went off to fetch some golden apples. ...

» **Note**

☐ vow to...: ...을 하려고 맹세하다

☐ in honour(memory) of...: ...을 영예롭게 하기 위해, ...을 기리기 위해

☐ be supposed to+동원: (1)해야만 한다 (2)...하기로 되어있다 (3)...라고 생각 되다

☐ at some time: 한 때는

☐ at another time: 다른 때는

To prevent the damage of the seasonal heavy rain something must be done.

: 해마다 반복되는 그 계절적인 폭우의 피해를 예방하기 위해 <u>무슨 조치가 강구되어야만 한다</u>.

» **원문**

... "What have you left for man? asked Prometheus. "Alas! I have given away all the main things," returned the brother giant. "Something must be done," said Prometheus. "I'll try to get fire for him." ...

» **Note**

☐ give away...: ...을 〈무료로, 죄다〉주다

☐ do something: 어떤 조치를 강구하다

All of you are supposed to be worn out after taking such a hard training, and we had no special afternoon schedule to do, so you may <u>sleep on</u> until this evening.

: 당신들 모두는 그렇게 심한 고된 훈련 후에 무척 피곤함에 틀림이 없다. 그리고 지금 우리는 특별한 오후 일정이 없다. 그러니 여러분들은 오늘 오후까지 <u>계속 잠자도</u> 좋다.

» 원문

... So there in a cave, on Mount Latmus, Endymion <u>sleeps on to this day</u>; and his wonderful beauty had not faded in the smallest degree, but is a joy still to all who can climb those lofty heights. ...

» Note

☐ sleep on...: ...계속 자다
☐ to this day: 오늘[오늘날]까지

The shy girl <u>was peeping out</u> from her window with her cheeks blushed.

: 그 수줍은 소녀는 얼굴을 붉힌 채로 창문을 통해 <u>살짝 밖을 쳐다보고</u> 있었다.

» **원문**

... As she <u>was peeping out</u> shyly from cave or <u>from behind a great tree</u>, Echo often saw Narcissus and she admired him very much. ...
... After this, Echo never came out and <u>allowed herself to be seen</u> again, and <u>in time</u> she fade away till she became only a voice. ...

» **Note**

- □ peep out: 살짝 밖을 내다보다
- □ from behind a great tree: 큰 나무 뒤로부터
- □ allow (A) to 동원: (A)가 ...하도록 허락하다
  ex) allowed herself to be seen: 그녀 자신을 눈에 띄도록 허락하다 (즉, 위에서는 눈에 보이지 않았다의 뜻임)

The enemy <u>laid siege to</u> our castle.

: 적이 우리의 <u>성을 포위했다</u>.

<u>All told</u>, we have twelve bottles of water left.

: <u>전부 합하여</u>, 우리는 12개의 물병을 가지고 있다.

» **원문**

... The "Ilia" tells of an army of Greeks who <u>laid siege to</u> the City of Troy. The Greeks <u>were supposed to</u> be trying to <u>take revenge upon</u> a Trojan prince who had carried away the wife of the king of Sparta. ...
... <u>All told</u>, there were nine cities. One was built by Romans and was known as "Ilium." From that comes the name of the poem of the Iliad. ...
... The Chief Poems <u>Credited to</u> Homer are the "Iliad" and the "Odyssey." ...

111

» **Note**

    ☐ lay siege to...: ...를 포위하다

    ☐ be supposed to+동원: ...하기로 되어있다

    ☐ all told: 모두 합하여

    ☐ be credited to...: ...으로 공을 돌리다

My parents opposed the marriage between me and her on the ground that she was not only a foreigner.

: 나의 양친들께서는 그녀가 단지 외국인이 아니라는 이유로 나와 그녀의 결혼을 반대하셨다.

The bridegroom's age is double the bride's age.

: 신랑의 나이는 신부 나이의 두 배다.

The state of affairs was still good.

: 사태는 여전히 좋았다.

» **원문**

... My father had once been a favorite of hers, I believe; but she was bitterly offended by his marriage, on the ground that my mother was 'a wax doll.' She had never seen my mother, but she knew her to be not yet twenty. My father and Miss Betsey never met again. He was double my mother's age when he married, and of a delicate constitution. ...

... This was the state of affairs on the afternoon of that important Friday. Yet I can make no claim to have known, at that time, how things stood; or to have any remembrance, founded on the evidence of my own senses, of the following. ...

» **Note**

- □ on ground that...: ...라는 이유 때문에[...라는 이유로]
- □ double of my mother's age: 나의 어머니의 나이의 두 배
- □ the state of affairs: 일의 사태[정세]
- □ at that time: 그 당시에

My success <u>was indebted to</u> his efforts in some aspects.

: 나의 성공 은 일부 면에서 그의 노력에 빚지고 있다.[그의 노력 때문이다.]

She <u>made a frown</u> in the dazzling sun light.

: 그녀는 현란한 햇빛 속에 서 얼굴을 찡그렸다.

I <u>was accustomed to</u> following a foreign culture.

: 나는 외국 문화를 따르는 데 익숙해 있었다.

» **원문**

... She gave my mother such a shock, that I have always been convinced I <u>am indebted to</u> Miss Betsey for having been born on a Friday. My mother had left her chair in her agitation, and gone behind it in the corner. Miss Betsey, looking round the room, slowly and inquiringly, began on the other side, and carried her eyes on, until they reached my mother. Then she <u>made a frown</u> and a gesture to my mother, like one who <u>was accustomed to</u> be obeyed, to come and open the door. ...

» **Note**

- □ be indebted to...: ...에 빚을 지고 있다
- □ make a frown: 얼굴을 찡그리다
- □ be accustomed to+동원: ...하는데 익숙해있다
- □ be accustomed to+명사: ...에 익숙하다

My friends say I look ill, but I think it's nothing but fancy

: 나의 친구들은 내가 아픈 것처럼 보인다고 말한다. 하지만 그것은 단지 기분 탓이라고 나는 생각한다.

The doctor took pains to help the poor.

: 그 의사는 가난한 사람들을 돕고자 노력했다.[애썼다.]

» 원문

… "Of course, it will, said Miss Betsey. "It's nothing but fancy. What do you call your girl?" "I don't know that it will be a girl yet, Ma'am," said my mother, innocently. …

… Having been upstairs and come down again, and having satisfied himself, I suppose, that there was a probability of this unknown lady and himself having to sit there, face to face, for some hours, the doctor took pains to be polite and social. He was the meekest of his sex, the mildest of little men. He sidled in and out of a room, to take up the less space. …

» Note

□ It's nothing but fancy.: 그것은 단지 기분 탓 때문이다.
□ face to face: 얼굴을 맞대고
□ take pains: 애쓰다 배려하다
  cf take pains to…: …하려고 애쓰다
□ sidle: 옆걸음질 치다, 옆으로 걷다

Our team could not beat our opposite team unexpectedly, so I lost my presence of mind.

: 우리의 팀은 예상치 않게 상대팀을 물리치지 못했다. 그러므로 나는 마음의 평정을 잃었다.

His tumor was progressing badly.

: 그의 종양이 악화되고 있다.

» 원문

… Mr. Chillip, looking mildly at my aunt with his head on one side, and making her a little bow, said, in allusion to the jewellers' cotton, as he softly touched his left ear:
"Some local irritation, ma'am" "What!" replied my aunt, pulling the cotton out one ear like cork. Mr. Chillip was so alarmed by her abruptness-as he told my mother afterwards-that it was a mercy he didn't lose his presence of mind. But he repeated sweetly:
"Some local irritation, ma'am"…
…"Well, ma'am," returned Mr. Chillip, "we are-we are progressing slowly, ma'am." …

» **Note**

- with his head on one side: 그의 고개를 한쪽으로 기울이고
- local irritation: 국부적인 통증
- presence of mind: 마음의 평정
- progress: 발전하고 있다, 회복하고 있다, …한 상태로 진행되고 있다

We can not decide which one to take, that is just a matter of opinion.

: 우리는 어느 쪽을 택할 것인가 결정할 수가 없다. 그것은 단지 <u>견해상의 문제다.</u>

Before we got married, my wife <u>had been so short with me.</u>

: 내가 결혼하기 전에, 나의 아내는 나에게 너무 퉁명스러웠었다.

» **원문**

... then you may marry another person, mayn't you, Peggotty"

"You May," said Peggotty, "if you choose, my dear. <u>That's a matter of opinion."</u>

"But what is your opinion, Peggotty" said I. I asked her, and looked intently at her, because she looked so curiously at me. ...

... <u>You aren't cross</u>, I suppose, Peggotty, are you?" said I, after sitting quiet for a minute.

I really thought she was, <u>she had been so short with me</u>; but I was quite mistaken: for she <u>laid aside</u> her work (which was a stocking of her own), and opening her arms wide, took my curly head within them, and gave it a good squeeze. ...

» **Note**

□ a matter of opinion: 견해상의 문제
  cf) a matter of (A): (A)의 문제
□ cross: 뿌루퉁한, 시무룩한
□ be short with...: ...에 퉁명스럽다
□ lay aside...: ...을 옆에 두다, 비축하다, 치우다

Put away your stuff and get your study ready right now.

: 너의 소지품을 치워라 그리고 즉시 공부를 준비하라.

The child was crying out keeping her stuffed doll close to her chest.

: 그 아이는 그녀의 봉제 인형을 가슴가까이 유지하고 큰소리로 울기 시작했다.

» **원문**

… He patted me on the head; but somehow, I didn't like him or his deep voice, and I was jealous that his hand should touch my mother's in touching me-which it did. I put it away as well as I could.

"Oh, Davy!" remonstrated my mother. "Dear boy!" said the gentleman. "I cannot wonder at his devotion!" …

… She gently chid me for being rude; and, keeping me close to her shawl, turned to thank the gentleman for taking so much trouble as to bring her home. She put out her hand to him as she spoke, and, as he met it with his own, she glanced, I thought, at me. …

» **Note**

- □ put … away: …을 치우다
- □ keep (A) close to (B): (B)가까이로 (A)를 유지하다
- □ take so much trouble as to…: 일부러[수고스럽게]…하다
- □ put out: (1)내밀다 (2)(불을) 끄다

We messed up our plans at one time that we had made for almost ten years. What are we to do now?

: 우리는 거의 십 년 동안 만들어 왔던 계획들을 단 한 번에 망쳤다. 지금 무엇을 우리는 해야만 하는가?

They took their failure in their exam to heart.

: 그들은 그들의 시험 실패를 가슴 아파했다.

» 원문

... Peggotty continuing to stand motionless in the middle of the room, and my mother resuming her singing, I fell asleep, though I was not so sound asleep that I could not hear voices, without hearing what they said. ...

... You talk of admiring love. What am I to do?, If people are so silly as to indulge the sentiment, is it my fault?, What am I to do?, I ask you ...

... Peggotty seemed to take this aspersion very much to heart, I thought. "And my dear boy," cried my mother, coming to the elbow-chair in which I was, and caressing me, "my own little Davy! Is it to be hinted to me that I am wanting in affection for my precious treasure, the dearest little fellow that ever was!" ...

» Note

- □ in the middle: ...한 중간에, 한 복판에, ...하는 와중에
- □ resume...: ...을 재개하다, 다시 시작하다
- □ What am I (supposed) to do?=What should I do?: 나는 어떻게 해야만 하는가?
- □ take (A) to heart: (A)를 가슴아파하다
- □ hint: 넌지시 비추다

118

We had an unbelievable family reunion since we had parted with each other for last ten years.

: 우리는 지난 10년 동안 서로 <u>헤어진</u> 이후로 꿈만 같은 가족 재회를 가졌다.

The glass-made vase fell down on the floor and <u>fell to pieces</u>.

: 그 유리로 만든 꽃병이 마루 바닥에 넘어졌다. 그리고 <u>산산조각</u> 났다.

In this situation, you <u>as good as</u> gave up the game.

: 이러한 상황 하에, 너는 <u>사실상</u> 그 경기를 포기한 <u>것과 같다</u>.

» **원문**

… She begged him to choose it for himself, but he refused to do that-I could not understand why-so she plucked it for him, and gave it into his hand. He said he would never, never <u>part with it</u> any more; and I thought he must be quite a fool not to know that it would <u>fall to pieces</u> in a day or two. …

… Peggotty meant her nephew Ham. I was excited her summary of delights, and replied that it would indeed be <u>a treat</u>, but what would my mother say!

"Why, then <u>I'll as good as bet a guinea</u>," said Peggotty, intent upon my face, "that she'll let us go. I'll ask her, if you like, as soon as ever she comes home. <u>There now!</u>" …

… "I say! Peggotty! She can't live <u>by herself</u>, you know." "Oh, bless you! said Peggotty, looking at me again at last. Don't you know! She's going to stay fortnight with Mrs. Grayper. Mrs. Grayper's going to have a lot of company." …

- part with...: ...와 헤어지다, ...을 떼어놓다
- fall to pieces: 산산조각 나다
- a treat: 즐거움
- as good as=practically the same as: 사실상...와 같은, ...에 충실한
- bless you!: 어머나[당치도 않다]!
- There now!: 자아, 어서(결단을 하는 말[촉구])

The cute girl gave her grandma a hearty smack on the cheek.
: 그 귀여운 소녀는 그녀의 할머니에게 볼에다 애정 어린 뽀뽀를 했다.

We have much in common with each other.
: 우리는 서로 많은 공통점을 가지고 있다.

» **원문**

... One thing I particularly noticed in this delightful house, was the smell of fish: which was so piercing that when I took out my pocket handkerchief to wipe my nose, I found it smelt exactly as if it had wrapped up a lobster. ...

... As he called Peggotty 'Lass,' and gave her a hearty smack on the cheek, I had no doubt that he was her brother; and so he turned out-being presently introduced to me as Mr. Peggotty, the master of the house. ...

... He soon returned, greatly improved in appearance; but so rubicund, that I couldn't help thinking his face had this in common with the lobster, crabs, and crawfish-that it went into the hot water very black and came out very red. ...

» Note

- □ piercing: 통렬한, 따끔한
- □ as if...: 마치 ...인 양(가정법)
- □ give (A) a heart smack on the cheek: (A)에게 볼에다 애정 어린 뽀뽀를 주다
- □ can not help ...ing: ...하지 않을 수가 없다
- □ have (A) in common with...: ...와 공통으로 (A)를 가지고 있다

We decided to <u>have</u> the deep-rooted problem <u>out with</u> them.

: 우리는 깊이 뿌리박힌 문제를 그들과 <u>결말 짓기로</u> 결심했다.

We must <u>get to bottom of</u> the problem.

: 우리는 그 문제를 <u>철저하게 규명해야만</u> 한다.

» 원문

... I was very much surprised that Mr. Peggotty was not Ham's father, and began to wonder whether I was mistaken about his relationship to anybody else there. I was so curious to know, that I made up my mind to <u>have it out with</u> Mr. Peggotty. ...

... "Drowned," said Mr. Peggotty. I felt the difficulty of resuming the subject, but had not <u>got to the bottom of</u> it yet, and must get to the bottom somehow. ...

» Note

- □ have (A) out with (B): (B)와 (A)를 결말짓다
- □ get to the bottom of...: ...의 진상을 규명하다

121

He was <u>such</u> an able man <u>that</u> he can solve any problem

: 그는 <u>대단히</u> 능력이 뛰어난 사람이므로 어떤 문제도 해결할 수가 있다.

<u>No sooner</u> had he seen me <u>than</u> he hid himself.

: 그는 나를 보<u>자마자</u> 숨어버렸다.

» **원문**

... But <u>at this point</u> Peggotty-I mean my own Peggotty-made <u>such</u> impressive motions to me not to ask any more question, <u>that</u> I could only sit and look at all the silent company, until <u>it was time to go to bed</u>. ...

... Now, all the time I had been on my visit, I had been ungrateful to my home, and had thought little or nothing about it. But I was <u>no sooner</u> turned towards it, <u>than</u> my reproachful young conscience seemed to point that way with a steady finger; and felt, <u>all the more for</u> the sinking of my spirits, that it was my nest, and that my mother was my comforter and friend. ...

» **Note**

- □ at this point: 바로 이때
- □ such ... that...: 너무 ...하여 ...하다
- □ it was time to 동원: ...할 시간이다
- □ no sooner (A) than (B): (A)하자마자 (B)하다
- □ (all) the more (...) for[because, (in) that] ...: ...이므로 한 층 더 ...

Honey, good news! I'll tell you something.

: 여보, 좋은 소식이야, <u>말할 것이 있어</u>.

Control yourself and try it again. You can do it.

: <u>냉정해</u> 그리고 다시 시도해봐. 너는 할 수 있어.

» **원문**

… The door opened, and I looked, <u>half laughing</u> and <u>half crying</u> in my pleasant agitation, for my mother. It was not she, but a strange servant. "Why, Peggotty!" I said, ruefully, "isn't she come home?" "Yes, yes, Master Davy," said Peggotty. "She's come home. Wait a bit, Master Davy, and I'll-<u>I'll tell you something</u>." …

… "Now, Clara, my dear," said Mr. Murdstone. "<u>Recollect! control yourself</u>, always control yourself! Davy boy, how do you do …

» **Note**

- □ I'll tell you something.: (중요한)할말이 있어요.
- □ recollect: 마음을 가라앉히다
- □ control oneself: 마음을 냉정하게 하다

015

Oliver Twist

- Charles Dickens

작품 소개: 19세기 영국 린던의 뒷골목을 배경으로 올리버 트위스트라는 고아 소년이 겪는 파란 많은 인생 여정을 통해 영국 사회의 불평등한 계층화와 산업화의 폐해를 날카롭게 비판했다. 디킨스 특유의 생생한 인물 묘사와 예리한 시대비판 정신으로 대중의 큰 사랑을 받은 작품이다.

He ate <u>nothing but</u> a pack of milk all day.

: 그는 하루 종일 <u>단지</u> 우유 한 각만을 먹었다.

He walked <u>no more than</u> two miles, but his feet <u>were</u> <u>sore</u>.

: 그는 <u>단지</u> 2마일만을 걸었다. 하지만 그의 발은 <u>쓰렸다</u>.

I <u>exchanged</u> my remaining money <u>for</u> some <u>pieces</u> of cake.

: 나는 나의 나머지 돈을 케익의 일부<u>와 교환했다</u>.

He <u>was left behind</u> the rest group.

: 그는 나머지 무리 <u>뒤로 뒤처졌다</u>.

… He walked twenty miles that day. He tasted <u>nothing but</u> a crust of dry bread and a few draughts of water, which he begged at the cottage by the roadside. …

… When he got up next morning, he <u>exchanged</u> the last penny <u>for</u> a small loaf in the first village through which he passed.

When the night closed in again, he had walked <u>no more than</u> twenty miles. <u>His feet</u> <u>were sore</u>, and his legs were so weak that they trembled beneath him. When he set off again next morning, he could hardly crawl along. …

… Poor Oliver tried to <u>keep up with</u> the coach a little way, but he was so exhausted and his feet were sore that <u>he was soon left behind</u>. They laughed and gave him nothing. …

… He had been crouching on a doorstep for some time, when a boy, who had passed him some minutes before, returned and looked at him curiously. Oliver raised his head and returned his steady look. …

» **Note**

□ nothing but=only: 단지
□ exchange (A) for (B): (A)를 (B)와 교환하다
□ no more than=only: 단지
□ sore: 쓰린, 벗겨진, 아픈
□ keep[catch] up with…: …을 따라 잡다
□ leave behind…: …뒤에 처지다

Some bad students were smoking and drinking <u>with the air of men</u> in secret.

: 일부 나쁜 학생들이 몰래 <u>어른 티를 내며</u> 담배를 피우고 술을 마시고 있었다.

<u>They're putting on an arrogant air</u> coming out of the concert hall.

: 그들은 공연장으로부터 나오며 <u>거만한 표정을 띠고</u> 있었다.

» 원문

… Don't worry," the boy said. "I know a respectable old gentleman, who will give you lodgings <u>for nothing</u>, If I introduce you." …

… The walls and ceiling of the room were black <u>with age</u> and dirt. There was a rough wooden table in front of the fire. Seated round the table were four or five boys, <u>none older than</u> the Dodger, smoking and drinking <u>with the air of men</u>. …

… Then it happened that his bright, dark eyes fell on Oliver's face. The boy's eyes were fixed on his in curiosity. …

… <u>At one moment</u> Fagin looked fierce, but <u>at another</u> he <u>put on an obliging air</u> and said, "Don't worry my dear. I only tried to frighten you. You're a brave boy. Ha! ha!" …

» **Note**

- □ for nothing: 무료로
- □ with age: 세월과 함께
- □ none older than…: …보다 더 나이든 사람이 없는
- □ with the air of men: 어른들 티를 내고
- □ at one moment: 한 순간에는
- □ at another (moment): 다른 순간에는
- □ put on an obliging air: 친절한 태도를 띠다

The volunteers began to help the villagers damaged by the flood with their shirt-sleeves tucked up.

: 자원 봉사자들은 홍수에 의해 피해를 입은 마을 사람들을 옷소매를 걷어 올린 채로 돕기 시작했다.

Stand aside and make room for the president.

: 옆으로 비켜 그 회장을 위해 자리를 양보하시오.

» 원문

… The Dodger went with his coat-sleeves tucked up and his hat cocked as usual; Bates with his hands in his pockets; and Oliver between them, wondering where they were going and what kind of business he would learn. …

… "He'll do," the Dodger said. Oliver looked from one to the other with the greatest surprise, for the two boys walked stealthily across the roa.d and slunk close behind the old gentleman." …

… "Stand aside!" "Where's the gentleman?" "Here he is, coming down the stree.t." "Make room for the gentleman!" "Is this the boy, sir?" "Yes." …

» **Note**

- □ with his coat-sleeves tucked up: 그의 코트 소매를 걷어 올린 채로
- □ stand aside: 비켜 있다
- □ make room for the gentleman: 그 신사를 위해 자리를 양보하다

It's no use trying it on them, because they are so stubborn.

: 그들에게 그것을 시도해봤다 아무 소용이 없다, 왜냐하면 그들은 너무나 고집이 세기 때문이야.

The old king began to take fancy to the little lass.

: 그 왕은 그 작은 아가씨가 마음에 들기 시작했다.

» **원문**

… "I say no!" Fagin said. "Betty will go to the police and find out how the matter stands." "I say no!" Betty exclaimed. "Well, Nancy my dear," Fagin said in a soothing manner, turning to the other girl. "What do you say?" "I say that it won't do. It's no use trying it on me, Fagin," Nancy replied. …

… Oliver was too weak to tell his personal history to Mr. Brownlow; but the old gentlemen took a fancy to the boy and gave him a new suit, a new cap and a new pair of shoes. …

… He buttoned up the bank note in his jacket pocket and made a respectful bow. Mrs. Bedwin, the housekeeper, gave him many directions about the nearest way, the name of the bookseller and the name of the stre.et. …

» **Note**

☐ I say no!: 정말 아니야!, 안 돼!

☐ how the matter stands: 일이 어떻게 진행되다

☐ what do you say?: 당신은 어때?[어떻게 생각하는가?]

☐ It won't do: 그건 도움이 안 될 것이다.

☐ it is no use…ing: …하는 것은 소용이 없어요

☐ take fancy to…: …를 마음에 놓다[…가 마음에 들다]

The beggar accepted the offer with mock humility.

: 그 거지는 <u>거짓으로 겸손한 채하며</u> 그 제의를 받아들였다.

We fought against our enemy setting our teeth.

: 우리는 <u>우리의 이를 악물고</u> 적과 대항하여 싸웠다.

Keep off the desk.

: 책상<u>으로부터 떨어져라</u>.

» **원문**

… "Delighted to see you looking so well, my dear," Fagin said, bowing <u>with mock humility</u>. "The artful Dodger will give you another suit, my dear, <u>for fear</u> you <u>might spoil</u> that Sunday one." …

… "Fair or not fair," Sikes retorted, "hand it over, I tell you. Do you think Nancy and <u>I have got nothing else to do with our time</u> but to spend it in scouting after and kidnapping a young boy! Give it here, you greedy old thief, give it here!". …

… "Shan't he!" Sikes said, <u>setting his teeth</u>. "It'll soon do that, <u>if you don't keep off</u>." The housebreaker flung the girl from him to the further end of the room, just as Fagin and the two boys returned, dragging Oliver with them. …

» **Note**

□ with mock humility: 거짓으로 겸손한 채하며
□ for fear (A) might+동원...: (A)가...하지 않도록 하기 위하여
   cf) for fear (that) (A) should+동원=est (A) should+동원:(A)가 ... 하지 않도록
□ I have got nothing else to do with our time but to 동원: ...하는 것 외에
   우리의 시간을 가지고 내가 해야 할 일은 아무것도 없다
□ set one's teeth: ...의 이를 악물다
□ if you don't keep off: 만약 당신이 떨어지지 않는다면
   cf) keep off: 멀리하다, 떨어지다

129

The policeman <u>took</u> the pistol <u>away from</u> the robber.

: 그 경찰관은 그 강도<u>로부터</u> 권총을 <u>빼앗았다</u>.

All of you did a good job, so you <u>deserve</u> the award.

: 당신들 모두는 훌륭한 일을 했어요, 그러므로 당신들은 그 상을 <u>받을 가치</u> <u>가 있어요</u>.

<u>Let</u> me <u>in</u> Sir, I'll never be late for school.

: 선생님 <u>들여보내 주세요</u>, 다시는 수업에 늦지 않겠습니다.

» **원문**

... Fagin <u>gave a strong blow on</u> Oliver's shoulders with the club, and was raising it for a second, when the girl, rushing forward, <u>took it away from his hand</u>. ...

... "<u>Civil words!</u>" the girl exclaimed. "Civil words, you villain! Yes, <u>you deserve them from me</u>. I thieved for you when I was a child not half as old as this boy! I have been in the same trade for twelve years. Don't you know it! <u>Speak out!</u> Don't you know it!" ...

... Now, Listen," Sikes whispered. "I'm going to put you through there. Take this light. Go softly up the steps straight before you, and along the hall, to the street-door. Unfasten it and <u>let us in</u>." ...

» **Note**

□ give a strong blow on...: ...에 강한 일격을 가하다
□ take (A) away from (B): (B)로부터 (A)를 빼앗다
□ civil words: 정중한 말씨
□ deserve: ...을 받을[할] 가치[자격]가 있다
  cf) worth...: ...을 받을[할]가치가 있는
□ speak out!: 터놓고 말해!
  cf) Speak up.: 큰 소리로 말해.
□ let (A) in: (A)를 들여보내다
  cf) let (A) out: (A)를 내보내다

Let's keep in touch with each other from now on.
: 지금부터 계속 연락을 계속 취하자.

I can't catch your words. Please speak in more plain words.
: 나는 당신의 말을 이해할 수가 없다. 좀 더 평이한 말로 말해주시오.

» 원문

… "It's of no use saying any. I tell you I must see her on urgent business." At last she was shown into a small antechamber. "Are you Miss Rose Maylie who offered food, clothing and shelter to poor Oliver?" the girl said to a young lady who entered the room with a light step. "Yes." "And have you come to London to get in touch with Mr. Brown? …

… "Oh, you haven't, eh?" Sikes said sternly and passed a pistol into a more convenient pocket. "Open your mouth and say in plain words what you've got to say. Out with it, you old cur!" Fagin stared hard at him and whispered, "Nancy!" "Nancy what?" …

» Note

☐ it is of no use …ing=it is useless to 동원: …해봤자 소용이 없다
☐ on urgent business: 긴급한 업무로
☐ food, clothing and shelter: 의식주
☐ get in touch with…=keep in touch with…: …와 연락을 계속 취하다
☐ in plain words: 이해하기 쉬운 평이한 말로
☐ Out with…: 〈보통 명령문〉 입밖에 내라, …쫓아내라, …때려내라
☐ Nancy what?: Nancy가 어떻다고?
  ex) The rumor what?: 풍문이 어떻다고?

The man returned home <u>with the sunken eyes and hollow cheeks.</u>

: 그 사람은 <u>가라앉은 눈과 움푹 들어간 볼</u>을 하고 집으로 돌아왔다.

Help yourself to the food, <u>if you please.</u>

: <u>원하신다면</u>, 마음껏 그 음식 을 드세요.

<u>At first</u> I could not recognize her, but little by little I got to know she was my long-forgotten sister later.

: <u>처음에는</u> 나는 그녀를 인식할 수 가 없었다. 그러나 후에 조금씩 그녀가 나의 오랫동안 잊었던 누이라는 것을 알게 되었다.

» **원문**

... Sikes was <u>so</u> much changed <u>that</u> the inmates of the house hardly recognized him. With <u>a pale face, sunken eyes, hollow checks, a beard of three days' growth</u>, <u>wasted flesh, a short thick breath</u>, it was the very ghos.t of Sikes. ...

... "There is somebody else who should not be forgotten," Mr. Brownlow said when he returned with Oliver. He rang the bell. "Send Mrs. Bedwin here, <u>if you please</u>."

The old housekeeper's eyes were now <u>so</u> dim with age <u>that</u> she <u>could not recognize</u> Oilver <u>at first</u>. ...

» **Note**

- □ so ... that...: 너무나 ...하여 ...하는
- □ a pale face: 창백한 얼굴
- □ sunken eyes: 가라앉은 눈
- □ hollow cheeks: 움푹 들어간 볼
- □ a beard of three days' growth: 3일 동안 자란 턱수염
- □ wasted flesh: 초췌해진 살
- □ a short thick breath: 짧고 둔탁한 숨소리
- □ the very: 바로 그
- □ if you please: 만약 좋으시다면
- □ so ... that can not+동원=너무나 ...하여 ...할 수가 없는
- □ at first: 처음에는

Mrs. Leicester's School

- Charles Lamb

작품 소개: 1809년에 내놓은 「레스터 부인의 학교(Mrs. Leicester's School)」는 허트퍼드셔 학교 학생들의 가상 이야기 모음이다.

작가 소개: 영국 수필가(1775~1834)다. 그의 작품 중 「엘리아의 수필」은 그의 신변 관찰을 멋진 유머와 페이소스(pathos)를 섞어가며 훌륭하게 문장화한 것으로, 영국 수필의 걸작으로 평가받고 있다.

The peacemakers take pains to supply the poor with some foods.

: 평화애호가들은 그 가난한 사람들에게 음식을 제공하느라 수고하고 있다.

Instead of leading an easy life, he tried to seek an adventurous life.

: 편안한 삶을 영위하고자 하는 대신에 그는 모험생활을 모색하고자 노력했다.

» **원문**

… Now I began justly to understand why he had taken such pains to keep my father from visiting my mother's grave,-that grave which I often stole privately to look at; but now never without awe and reverence, …

… I was introduced to the ladies at the Manor-house, instead of hanging down my head with shame, as I should have done before my uncle came, like a little village rustic, I tried to speak distinctly, with ease and modest gentleness, as my uncle had said my mother used to do …

» Note

    □ take pains to...: ...하느라 수고하다[고생하다]

    □ keep+목적어(A)+from+...ing(B): (A)가 (B)하는 것을 막다

    □ steal: 몰래가다

    □ instead of...: ...대신에

Look at that freezer. It works well now.

: 저 냉장실을 보아라. 그것은 지금 잘 작동한다.

When I and my younger brother fight each other, my mother always takes my brother's part.

: 나와 남동생이 싸울 때, 나의 엄마는 늘 남동생 편만 드신다.

» 원문

... My father was astonished; and he said, 'Is this the sullen Elinor? What has worked this miracle?' 'Ask no questions,' she replied, 'or you will disturb our new-born friendship. ...

... My aunt always took Sophia's part because she was so young, and she never suffered me to oppose Mary, or Elizabeth, because they were older than me. ...

... She said I had not one atom of affection in my disposition, for that no kindness ever made the least impression on me. ...

» Note

    □ work: 작동시키다(operate), 효과가 있다(take effect)

    □ take the part of...=take part with...: ...을 편들다

    □ suffer: (1)...으로부터 고통을 받다 (2)...하도록 허락하다(allow)

    □ not an atom of...: ...털끝만큼도 ...없는

Look at that <u>good-looking</u> girl. She is my old girl friend.

: 저 <u>아름답게 보이는</u> 소녀를 보아라. 그녀는 나의 옛 여자친구다.

<u>The moment</u> the girl met the boy, her heart began to beat fast.

: 그 소녀가 그 소년을 보<u>자마자,</u> 소녀의 심장은 빠르게 뛰기 시작했다.

» **원문**

… and I told him all my little troubles, for <u>he was such a good-natured-looking gentleman</u> that I prattled very freely to him. …

… <u>I could not say much for his beauty</u>, but I told him he was a much finer gentleman than my uncle, and that <u>I liked him the first moment I saw him</u>, because he looked so good-natured. …

» **Note**

□ good-natured-looking: 성격이 좋게 보이는
  ex) ill-smelling: 악취가 나는
□ well- educated: 교육을 잘 받은
□ for…: …에 비해
□ the first moment…: 첫 번째 …하자마자

Stories from Shakespeare

- Charles Lamb

작품 소개: 윌리엄 셰익스피어의 희곡을, 19세기 영국 수필가 찰스 램이 누이 메리 램과 함께 아이들을 위해 동화 형식으로 재구성한 것이다. 4대 비극과 5대 희극을 포함하여 20편에 달하는 셰익스피어 이야기를 통해 착하고 명예로운 생각과 행동뿐 아니라 예의, 자비, 관용, 박애 등을 배울 수 있다.

This door is locked from within.
: 이 문은 내부로부터 잠긴다.

I feel the strings of conscience whenever I am reminded of my youth-consuming idleness.
: 나는 젊은 시절의 낭비적인 게으름을 생각할 때마다 나는 양심의 가책을 느낀다.

Your face shows it.
: 너의 얼굴에 그것이 쓰여 있어.

» 원문

... From within the palace the sound of feasting was faintly heard. The watchers were talking about the coldness of the night, when suddenly Horatio whispered to Hamlet, "Look, my lord! look, it comes!" ...

... It warned him, however, never to do any violence against his mother, but to leave her to the stings of conscience. ...

... "I shall watch them closely and mark their conduct," he said to himself. "If their hearts are guilty, their faces will show it." ...

» Note

□ from within: 내부로부터

□ the stings of conscience: 양심의 가책

□ Their face will show it.: 그들의 얼굴들이 그것을 보여줄 것이다.

I bought some presents for my foreign friend <u>as a sign of goodwill.</u>

: 나는 <u>호의의 표시로써</u> 나의 외국 친구에게 약간의 선물을 사 주었다.

He is a near <u>relation to</u> the English Royal family.

: 그는 영국의 왕족<u>과</u> 가까운 <u>친척</u>이다.

It is easy to <u>lay</u> <u>the ungrounded guilt</u> <u>upon</u> the weak people.

: <u>약한 사람들에게 근거 없는 죄를 씌우는</u> 것은 쉬운 일이다.

» 원문

… He knew that both Hamlet and Laertes were skilful fencers, so he persuaded Laertes to challenge Hamlet to a friendly match of fencing. Hamlet accepted it <u>as a sign of goodwill.</u> …

… When King Duncan ruled over Scotland, there lived a great thane, or lord, named Macbeth. <u>He was a near relation to the king</u>, and he was much admired and respected at court for his courage and success in wars. …

… She persuaded him that it was very easy to <u>lay the guilt upon the drunken, sleeping servants.</u> And encouraged by her tongue, he got rid of his fear and taking the dagger in his hand, softly stole in the dark to the room where Duncan lay. …

When he met his wife after his long absence, his words stuck in his throat.

: 그가 오랫동안 부재 후에 그의 아내를 만났을 때, 그의 말이 <u>그의 목구멍에 걸렸다.</u>

Talk no more! I can not listen to the music.

: <u>더 이상 말하지 말라!</u> 음악을 들을 수가 없다.

The general passed his sword across the enemy's body and then he fell down on the ground.

: 장군이 그의 칼을 적의 몸을 <u>가로질러 휘둘렀다.</u> 그때 적은 땅위로 고꾸라졌다.

» **원문**

... Macbeth, who stood listening to them, tried to say "Amen," but, <u>the word stuck in his throat</u>, and he could not say it. Again he thought he heard a voice which cried, "<u>Sleep no more!</u> Macbeth does murder sleep." ...

... While she took his bloody dagger and <u>passed it across the cheeks of the still sleeping servants</u>, that it might appear as if they had committed the murder. ...

» Note

- □ stick in...: ...그대로 붙어있다
- □ sleep no more!: 더 이상 잠자지 말라!
- □ pass (A) across (B): (B)를 가로질러 (A)를 스치게 하다[휘두르다]

The cake took shape of a half moon.

: 그 케익은 반달 모양을 취했다.

The thief who told a lie and was released from the jail is suffering a remorse of conscience because of his fellow thieves who are still in jail.

: 동료 도둑을 감옥에 남겨놓고 자기만 거짓말해서 석방된 그 도둑은 양심의 가책을 느끼고 있다.

She broke up with her boyfriend and shuts herself up in her house.

: 그녀는 그녀의 남자친구와 헤어졌다 그리고 집에서 칩거생활을 하고 있다.

» 원문

… The third took shape of a crowned child with a tree in his hand, and said that Macbeth should never be overcome until Birnam Wood should come against him to his castle. …

… All this time Lady Macbeth was suffering the keenest remorse of conscience, and so troubled was her mind that she would rise in her sleep and begin rubbing her hands as if to take from them the bloody stai.n; …

… and that he was never to be beaten till Birnam Wood should come to his castle. So he shut himself up in his strong castle, and waited. …

» Note

□ take shape of...: ...의 형태를 취하다
□ all this time: 이 시간 내내
□ remorse of conscience: 양심의 가책
□ shut oneself up: 자신을 감금시키다, 두문불출하다

He pulled himself together and began to climb to the hilltop.

: 그는 기운을 다시 냈다. 그리고 정상을 향하여 올라가기 시작했다.

» 원문

... He began to be weary of living and wished his life at an end; yet he again pulled himself together, and went desperately out at the head of the few followers who remained faithful to him. ...

» Note

□ pull oneself together: 기운을 내다

He is under the suspect and walks around in disguise.

: 그는 혐의를 받고 있다. 그리고 위장하고 돌아다니고 있다.

» 원문

... A stranger came to him one day and begged to be taken into his service. He was the earl of Kent in disguise. Though banished by Lear, he chose to stay with him and be of service to him. ...

» Note

□ in disguise: 위장하여, 몰래

She set a cute friend of hers against the other friends.

: 그녀는 예쁜 친구 하나를 나머지 친구들로부터 이간시켰다.

Their neglects pierced them to the heart.

: 그들의 후회막심함이 마음속 깊이 사무쳤다.

The greedy hostess turned the poor beggar out beating him.

: 그 욕심 많은 안주인은 불쌍한 거지를 때리며 내쫓았다.

» 원문

… But the king was shocked to see in their company the hated Goneril, who had come to set her sister against her father. …

… But he was mistaken in expecting kinder treatment. …

… Their ingratitude pierced him to the heart. …

… Then Lear fell on his knees and begged pardon of his child. She told him that it did not become him to kneel, and she accused her two sisters, saying that they should be ashamed of themselves, to turn their old father out into the cold night. …

» Note

□ set 목적어(A) against (B): (A)를 (B)로부터 이간시키다
□ be mistaken: 잘못하다
□ pierce 목적어(A) to the heart: … 마음속 깊이 사무치다
□ turn out…: …내쫓다

Alice in Wonderland

- Lewis Carroll

작품 소개: 우연히 토끼 굴에 빠져진 엘리스는 기이한 생물들이 가득한 이상한 나라에서 길을 잃게 된다. 흰 토끼와 체셔 고양이도 만나고, 미치광이 모자장수와는 차 한 잔을, 하트여왕과는 크로케 한 판을 즐기는 상상의 나래를 펼친다.

작가 소개: 영국의 수학자이자 동화작가다. 「거울 나라의 앨리스(Through the Looking Glass) (1871)」 등의 작품을 썼고, 수학 분야의 저서로는 「유클리드와 그의 현대 경쟁자들(Euclid and His Modern Rivals)(1879)」가 유명하다.

What is the use of crying over the spilled milk?
: 엎질러진 우유에 대해 울어봤자 무슨 소용이 있느냐?

We didn't have the slight idea that we failed in the easy mid-term test.
: 우리는 우리가 그 쉬운 중간고사를 불합격한다는 생각을 전혀 생각지도 못 했다.

» 원문

... : once or twice she had peeped into the book her sister was reading, but it had pictures or conversations in it, "and what is the use of a book," thought Alice, "without pictures or conversations?" ...

... (Alice had not the slightest idea what Latitude was, or Longitude either, but she thought they were nice grand words to say.) ...

... : she tried the little golden key in the lock, and to her great delight it fitted! Alice opened the door and found that it led into a small passage, not much larger than a rat-hole. Through it she could see a lovely garden. ...

» **Note**

- □ peep into...: ...안을 들여다보다

  cf) peeping Tom: 호기심 많은 사람

- □ peep show: 은밀한 쇼

- □ What's the use of...?: ...하는 것은 무슨 소용이 있느냐?

- □ the slightest idea: 털끝만한 생각

- □ to one's(A)+추상명사=(A)가...하게도

  ex) to my disappointment: (내가) 실망스럽게도

Jump and catch hold of this rope

: 뛰어라 그리고 이 밧줄을 잡아라.

I am up to the ninth lesson

: 나는 9과까지 나가고 있다.

» **원문**

... And I declare it's too bad!" As she said these words her foot slipped, and in another moment, splash! she was up to her chin in salt-water. ...

... "Fetch the ladder, Bill!" "Catch hold of this rope-will the roof bear?" "Who's to go down the chimney?" "Bill's got to go down." ...

... "Why, they seem to put everything upon Bill! I wouldn't be in Bill's place for a good deal!: this fireplace is narrow, to be sure; but I think I can kick a little!" ...

... and a bright idea came into her head. "If I eat one of these cakes," she thought, "it must make me smaller, I suppose." ...

- □ up to...: 〈위치, 정도, 시점, 지위 등이〉...까지, ...에 이르게 되어
  cf) (부정문에서)...을 감당하여, 할 수 있는
  ~~ex) You are not up to the job.~~ 당신은 이 일을 감당할 능력이 없어.
- □ "Catch hold of this rope-will the roof bear?": "이 밧줄을 잡아라-그 지붕은 견디어 낼까?"
- □ they seem to put everything upon Bill!: 그들은 모든 것을 Bill에게 밀어주고 있어!
- □ in one's place: ...대신에
  cf) in place: 적절한
- □ It occurred to me that...: ...이 (나에게) 번득 떠올랐다
  cf) It strikes me that...: ...라는 생각이 들다
- □ An idea hits me.=I hit on an idea.: 생각이 나에게 떠올랐다.
- □ An idea flashes on me.: 생각이 나에게 번득였다.

I am so excited at the game, so I am not myself now.
: 나는 그 게임에 너무 흥분한 나머지 지금 <u>제정신이 아냐</u>.

I can't follow you. Please put it more clearly.
: 나는 당신을 이해할 수가 없어. 제발 <u>그것을 좀 더 분명히 표현해주세요.[설명해주세요.]</u>

» **원문**

... "What do you mean by that?" said the Caterpillar sternly. "Explain yourself!" "I can't explain myself, I'm afraid, Sir," said Alice, "because I'm not myself, you see." "I don't see," said the Caterpillar. "I'm afraid I can't put it more clearly," Alice replied very politely. ...

» Note

- ☐ What do you mean by that?: 당신은 그것에 의해 무엇을 의미하는가?
- ☐ explain oneself: 해명하다, 납득시키다
- ☐ I'm not myself.: 나는 제정신이 아니에요
- ☐ put it more clearly: 좀 더 명쾌하게 설명하다

Smith swallowed down his anger and broke up with his rival.

: Smith는 그의 분함을 삭혔다. 그리고 그의 라이벌과 화해를 했다.

I know you won the first place, but don't give yourself airs to others

: 나는 네가 우승을 했다는 것을 알고 있다. 그러나 다른 사람에게 잘났다고 우쭐하지 마라.

» 원문

… Alice felt a little irritated and drew herself up and said, very gravely, "I think you ought to tell me who you are, first." …

… This sounded promising, certainly. Alice turned and came back again. "Keep your temper," said the Caterpillar. "Is that all?" said Alice, swallowing down her anger as well as she could. …

… Pray, how did you manage to do it?" "In my youth," said his father, "I took to the law, …

… "I have answered three questions, and that is enough," said his father. "Don't give yourself airs! …

- □ draw up: 정렬시키다, 끌어올리다
- □ sound...: ...처럼 들리다[생각되다]
- □ swallow down one's anger: 분함을 삭히다
- □ manage to+동원: ...하는 데 (겨우) 성공하다
- □ give oneself airs: 뽐내다
- □ take to...: ...에 전념하다

Get down off your horse and walk to the house straight.

: 너의 말로부터 내려라 그리고 똑바로 곧장 집으로 걸어가라.

How is it I have never seen her even if we have lived in the same town?

: 비록 똑같은 마을에 살았을지라도 내가 그녀를 결코 본적이 없는 것은 어찌된 일이냐?

» **원문**

... In a minute or two the Caterpillar took the hookah out of its mouth, and yawned once or twice, and shook itself. Then it got down off the mushroom, and crawled away into the grass, merely remarking, as it went, "One side will make you grow taller, and the other side will make you grow shorter." ...

... "What can all that green stuff be?" said Alice. "And where have my shoulders got to? And oh, my poor hands, how is it I can't see you?" she was moving them about as she spoke ...

» **Note**

- □ get down: 내리다, 실망시키다
- □ crawled away into...: ...기어서 멀리 ...속으로 들어가다
- □ How is it...?: ...은 어찌된 일이냐? 즉, 왜냐?(why is it that...?)

Whether you like this dress or not does not matter.
: 당신이 이 옷을 좋아하는가 아니냐는 <u>문제가 안된다[중요하지 않다]</u>

» **원문**

... "You're looking for eggs, I know that well enough; and <u>what does it matter to me</u> whether you're a little girl or a serpent?" "<u>It matters a good deal to me</u>." said Alice hastily ...

» **Note**

- □ matter=count=be important: 중요하다

147

The Adventure of King Arthur - Howard Pyle

작품 소개: 6세기경 전설적인 왕의 모험을 그린 이야기다. 아서 왕은 잉글랜드의 왕으로, 원탁의 기사들과 함께 명검 엑스칼리버(Excalibur)를 휘두르며 수많은 무훈을 세웠다. 용감하고 위풍당당하며 다른 사람을 배려할 줄 알았던 아서 왕은 부하들뿐 아니라 온 백성의 존경과 사랑을 받았다.

작가 소개: 대부분 젊은이를 위한 책의 저자 겸 미국 삽화가(1853~1911)다. 1894년에 지금의 드렉셀대학교 전신인 드렉셀 예술, 과학, 산업 연구소에서 삽화를 가르치기 시작했다.

I saw some people moving their hands for help <u>in the distance</u>.

: 나는 <u>멀리서</u> 도움 때문에 손을 흔들고 있는 것을 보았다.

I would like to leave early for my travel <u>rather than</u> sleep in this camp site.

: 이 야영지에서 자는 것<u>보다 오히려</u> 나의 여행을 위해 오히려 일찍 떠나고 싶다.

» **원문**

… And <u>when they came out into the open fields</u>, King Arthur whistled and sang and jested and laughed and made merry. So <u>by and by</u> they came into the forest; …

… So Boisenard climbed a very tall tree and <u>from the top of the tree he saw a light in the distance</u>. He said, "Lord I see a light over there." …

… "Sir," said the porter, "if you know what is good for you, <u>you will sleep in the forest rather than come into this castle</u>, for this is not a very good place for knights to stop in."…

» **Note**

- □ come out into...: ...으로부터 나와 ...안으로 들어가다
- □ by and by: 이윽고
- □ in the distance: 멀리로부터
- □ rather than: ...보다는 오히려

They <u>burst out crying</u> out when they saw their famous athletic star.

: 그들의 유명한 스포츠 스타를 보았을 때 그들은 <u>갑자기 크게 소리를 지르기 시작했다.</u>

<u>Let's draw lots</u> about who will take the first to do the cleaning

: 청소를 누가 먼저 할 것인가 <u>제비뽑기를 합시다</u>.

» **원문**

... Now when King Arthur said this, <u>all those who were in the hall burst out laughing</u>. Then, when they became a little quiet, the knight said, "Sir, are you afraid of that sport?" ...

... So he said to the knight, "Sir, I am ready for that sport of which you spoke, but who is to strike that first blow and <u>how shall we draw lots for it</u>?" ... Then that knight stood up and laid aside his back robe, and <u>he opened the linen undergarment at the throat</u> and <u>turned down</u> the collar so as <u>to lay his neck bare to the blow</u>. ...

» **Note**

- □ burst out+...ing: 갑자기 ...하기 시작하다
- □ draw a lot: 제비를 뽑다
- □ open (A) at (B): (A)를 (B)를 향하여 열어젖히다
- □ turn down: 접어 내리다
- □ lay (A) bare to(B): (A)를 (B)에 벌거벗은[노출된] 채로 남겨두다

I really have enjoyed this visit <u>because of</u> you.

: 저는 당신 <u>때문에</u> 정말로 이번 방문을 즐겼습니다.

[A] <u>What brought you here?</u>

: <u>당신 이곳에 왜 오셨어요?</u>

[B] I came here on business.

: 사업상 여기 왔습니다.

» **원문**

… Then the knight said, "<u>Well, stand away a little distance</u> so that I may not strike you too close, and so lose the virtue of my blow." …

… <u>The knight smiled very sourly</u>, and he said, "I do not offer this to you because of mercy to you, but because I find pleasure in tormenting you. …

… Then King Arthur gave her greeting, and she gave the King greeting, and she said to him, "My lord King, where have you come from? <u>What has brought you here?</u>" …

» **Note**

☐ a little distance: 조금 떨어져서(이처럼 '부사구'에서는 종종 '전치사'를 생략한다.)

☐ sour: (맛이) 신, 못 마땅한

☐ What brings you here?: 〈직역하면〉무엇이 당신을 이곳에 데려왔는가?(이 말은 좀 더 정중하고 우언적으로 표현할 때 쓰인다.)

I gave the natives my sweater <u>in return for</u> their warm welcome.

: 나는 그들의 따뜻한 환영에 대한 <u>답례로</u> 나의 스웨터를 원주민들에게 주었다.

I'll <u>be willing to explain myself</u> in front of the public.

: 나는 대중 앞에서 <u>나 자신을 기꺼이 해명하겠다.</u>

» **원문**

… Then king Arthur was greatly astonished that she should know who he was, and he said, "<u>Who are you that seem to know me?</u>" …

… King Arthur was very glad to hear this, but he felt doubtful what she would ask of him; so he said, "<u>What is it you must have in return for that answer?</u>" …

… ; therefore the knight shrieked very loud, and <u>fell down upon</u> his knees and begged the king for mercy. …

… Queen Guinevere said, "Sir, what is this? <u>Have you a mind to play some merry jest</u> that you have brought here that old woman?" …

… Then King Arthur said to Sir Gawain, "Sir, <u>are you willing to fulfill my promise</u> to this old woman?" And Sir Gawain said, "Yes, lord, I will do <u>whatever you would like me to do.</u>" …

» **Note**

- 여기의 'that'은 관계대명사, 'that'은 선행사가 어떤 것이 와도 일반적으로 사용 가능하다.
- fall down on: …을 대고 떨어지다[무릎을 꿇다](여기의 'on'은 '부착', '지지'를 나타내는 '전치사')
- be willing to+동원=기꺼이 …하다
- whatever=no matter what: …이든지 간에, …일지라도('양보'를 나타내는 '복합관계사')

The enemy <u>shut</u> the light and water <u>off</u> from the citizens.

: 적은 불과 물을 시민<u>으로부터 막아버렸다.</u>

We <u>took the occasion to attack</u> the enemy taking advantage of darkness.

: 우리는 야음을 틈타 적을 <u>공격할</u> 좋은 기회를 잡았다.

020

Woman's Wit(adapted)

- Howard Pyle

작품 소개: 작가는 우리에게 다음처럼 말하고 있다. 남자의 힘이 쇠약해지는 곳에서[다하는 곳에 서], 여자의 지혜는 우세해진다[살아난다]. (Where man's strength fails, woman's wit prevails). 결국 여자의 지혜[본능적 통찰력]는 필요할 때 우월한 힘을 발휘한다고 주장하고 있다.

After having some coffee break, we <u>set our hands to work again.</u>

: 약간의 커피 먹는 휴식을 가진 후에, 우리는 <u>일꾼으로 하여금 다시 일하도 록 했다.</u>

Our advance party marched forward <u>putting some barriers out of the way.</u>

: 우리의 선발대는 장애물을 제거하며 계속 앞으로 나갔다.

» **원문**

... So King Solomon, who was so wise and knew so many potent spells that he had power over evil such as no man has had before or since, <u>set</u> himself <u>to work</u> to <u>put</u> those enemies of mankind <u>out of the way</u>. ...

» **Note**

☐ set 목적어(A) to 동원: (A)로 하여금 ...하게 하다
☐ put 목적어(A) out of the way: (A)를 제거하다

153

What do you say to going fishing?
: 낚시질 가는 것에 대해 어떻게 생각하십니까?

I wish I had loved the girl first, as it was, she loved me first.
: 내가 먼저 그녀를 사랑했기를 바랬다. 그러나 실제는, 그녀가 나를 먼저 사랑했다.

» **원문**

… What do you say to such an offer as that?" "I say yes!" said King Solomon, and, without another word, he stripped off his royal robes and stood bare-breasted, man to man with the other. …

… As it was, he scraped away the soil, and then he found a box of solid build, with a ring in the lid to lift it by. The Tailor clutched the ring and bent his back, and up came the box with the damp earth sticking to it. He cleaned away, and there he saw, written in red letters, these words: …

» **Note**

☐ What do you say to …?: …은 어떻습니까?
☐ as it was: 그런데 실제는(일반적으로 앞에 '가정법 문장'이 오는 것이 특징, '현재 사실'을 기술하는 경우에는 'as it is')

154

Turn the stopped bottle upside down and let the content out of it.

: 막힌 병을 거꾸로 하라. 그리고 내용물이 나오게 하라.

Break the seal and peer at the strange letter.

: 봉인을 뜯어 그 이상한 편지를 엿보아라.

The hungry children began to gather round at the sight of the rescue party.

: 굶주린 아이들은 구조대를 보자마자 몰려들기 시작했다.

» **원문**

… "And is this all?" said the little Tailor, turning the bottle upside down and shaking it, and peeping at it by the light of the lamp. "Well, since I have gone so far I might as well open it, as I have already opened the seven boxes." Soon he broke the seal that stoppered it. …

… Tailor's skin quivered and shrivelled, and his tongue cleaved to the roof of his mouth at the sight of it. …

» **Note**

☐ turn (A) upside down: (A)를 거꾸로 하다
☐ peep at…: …을 엿보다
☐ go so far: 정도를 넘다
☐ may as well+동.원(A): (A)하는 편이 낫다
☐ break the seal: 봉인을 뜯다
☐ at the sight of (A): (A)를 보자마자

You can do whatever you want, but there is one condition attached to it.

: 당신이 무엇을 원하든지 간에 할 수가 있습니다. 하지만 그것에 덧붙여진 하나의 조건이 있습니다.

I did my homework with my legs tucked up.

: 다리를 걷어 위로 한 채 나는 나의 숙제를 했다.

A **What kind of clothes do you want?** : 어떤 종류의 옷을 원합니까?

B **I want such and such a suit of clothes.**: 나는 그러그러한 옷을 원합니다.

» 원문

... Every morning at the seventh hour I will come to you, and I will perform for you whatever task you may command me. But there is one condition attached to the agreement, and woe be to you if that condition is broken. ...

... Now it happened that the Prime Minister of that country had left an order with the Tailor for a suit of clothes; so the next morning, when the Damon came, the little man set him to work on the bench, with his legs tucked up like a journeyman tailor. "I want," said he, "such and such a suit of clothes." ...

» **Note**

- □ attached to...: ...에 첨부된
- □ It happen that...: ...하는 일이 (우연히) 발생하다, 즉, 우연히... 하다
- □ with his legs tucked up: 그의 다리를 올린 채로
- □ such and such...: 그러그러한...

What you have done for our city can be <u>the talk of the town</u>.

: 당신이 우리의 도시를 위해 행해온 것은 <u>세상의 평판</u>이 될 수 있다.

He had been to the west and he <u>made a fortune</u>.

: 그는 서부에 갔다 왔다. 그리고 <u>큰돈을 벌었다</u>.

When I saw the wonderful scenery, <u>my heart seemed to stand till</u>.

: 내가 그 아름다운 광경을 보았을 때 <u>나의 심장은 정지하는 듯했다</u>.

» **원문**

… The Prime Minister wore the clothes to court that very day, and before evening they were <u>the talk of the town</u>. <u>All the world</u> ran to the Tailor and ordered clothes of him, and <u>his fortune was made</u>. …

… It was the first time that the Tailor had seen her, and when he saw her <u>his heart seemed to stand still</u> within him, and then began fluttering like a bird, for one so beautiful was not to be met with <u>in the four corners of the world</u>. Then she was gone. …

» **Note**

- □ the talk of the town: 세상의 평판
- □ all the world: 세상 사람들
- □ his heart stood still: 그의 심장이 멈췄다
  - *ex)* stand still: 정체하다
- □ in the four corners of the world: 세상의 모든 곳에서

She shall marry you.

: <u>그녀는 당신과 결혼하게 될 거다</u>. 즉, 나는 그녀가 당신과 결혼하게 만들 것이다.

… "Tell your master that <u>he shall have my daughter</u> for his wife if he will build over there a palace such as no man ever saw or no King ever lived in before."

… The next morning when the Damon appeared the Tailor <u>was ready for</u> him "Build me," said he, "such and such a palace in such and such a place. …

» Note

☐ shall: 2인칭이나 3인칭에 쓰이면 화자(speaker)의 '의지'를 나타낸다.

☐ be ready for...=be prepared for...: ...을 준비하다

To my mind, they were in the wrong.

: 내 의견으로는 그들이 틀렸다.

We are all in the wrong, not to speak of him.

: 그는 말할 것도 없이 우리 모두가 틀리다.

» 원문

… So ends the story, with only this to say: <u>Where man's strength fails, woman's wit prevails.</u> For, <u>to my mind</u>, the Princess-<u>not to speak of her husband</u> the little Tailor-did more with a single little hair and her woman's wit than King Solomon with all his wisdom. …

» Note

☐ to one's mind: ...의 의견으로는

☐ not to speak of (A): (A)는 말할 것도 없이

021

The Town Musician of Bremen - J & W Grimm

작품 소개: 농장에서 많은 세월을 보낸 당나귀, 개, 고양이 그리고 수탉은 주인에 의해 학대받고 버림받게 된다. 그들은 농장을 떠나 자유로운 땅, 브레멘으로 가서 음악가가 되기로 결심한다. 브레멘으로 가는 길에 그들은 빛이 흘러나오는 집을 보게 되고 그 안에 네 명의 도둑들이 자신들이 훔친 전리품을 감상하는 것을 목격한다. … 결국 도둑들은 집을 포기하고 동물들은 그곳에서 여생을 행복하게 보냈다.

작가 소개: Jakob Ludwig Karl, Grim.m(1785~1863)과 그의 동생 Wilhelm Karl, Grimm(1786~1859)은 독일의 언어학자, 민속학자다. 「그림 동화(1812~1815)」를 편집했다. 그림 형제는 "The Brothers Grimm"이라고 불린다.

After finishing the tough game, our physical strength began to fail.

: 힘든 경기 후에 우리 모두의 체력은 <u>딸리기 시작했다</u>.

Come with me to the sea to see a beautiful sunset

: 아름다운 일몰을 구경하기 위하여 <u>바다로 나와 함께 가자</u>.

I tried to roll the big rock to the side with all my might.

: 나는 <u>온 힘을 다해</u> 옆쪽으로 그 큰 바위를 굴리고자 노력했다.

The noise of the bomb was so loud that it almost split our ears.

: 그 폭탄의 소음이 너무나 커서 그것은 거의 우리의 <u>귀청이 떨어지게 했다</u>.

… A man had an ass, which for many years faithfully carried the sacks to the mail. At last, however, <u>his strength began to fail</u>, and he became more and more unfit for work. …
… <u>Come with us to Bremen</u>," said the ass. "You are good at serenading, so you can become a town musician." …
… Soon afterwards the three runaways came to a farmyard. A cock was sitting in front of the gate crowing <u>with all his might</u>. "<u>You're crying loud enough to spilt our ears</u>." said the ass. "What's the matter with you?" …

» Note

☐ fail: (기운 등이)약해지다
☐ come with...: ...을 따르다('명령문'의 형태를 띠어 '...하자'는 '청유'의 형태를 의미한다.)
☐ with all one's might: ...의 온힘을 다하여
☐ split one's ears: ...의 귀청이 떨어지게 하다

She <u>hit on[up]</u> a good idea.
: 그녀는 좋은 생각을 <u>떠올렸다.[좋은 생각이 났다.]</u>

The swimmer <u>coiled herself</u> and dived into the pool.
: 그 수영선수는 <u>몸을 웅크렸다.</u> 그리고 수영장으로 잠수했다.

» 원문

… Then the animals took counsel as to how to set about driving the robbers out. <u>At last they hit upon a plan.</u> …
… The ass lay down on a pile of straw; <u>the dog coiled himself</u> behind the door; the cat lay down on the hearth near the warm ashes …

» Note

☐ hit (up)on...: ...을 번뜩 생각해내다
☐ coil oneself: 웅크리다

022

The Sleeping Beauty

- J & W Grimm

작품 소개: 오랜 기다림 끝에 오로라 공주가 태어나고, 왕과 왕비는 축제를 연다. 이때 초대받지 못한 손님 말레피센트가 나타나 공주가 16세 생일에 물레에 찔려 죽게 될 것이라는 저주를 걸고 떠난다. 이에 요정들은 이 저주를 잠이 드는 것으로 바꿔주고, 진실한 첫 입맞춤만이 공주를 깨울 수 있다고 한다. 마침내 16세 생일이 되던 날 오로라 공주는 물레에 찔려 깊은 잠에 빠지게 된다.

The public was so crowded but I forced my way through a crowd into the gate.

: 군중들은 너무나 혼잡했다 그러나 나는 군중 속을 뚫고 문 속으로 들어갔다.

» **원문**

… Now the old fairy had come to revenge for not being invited to the feast, so she forced her way into the hall and, without greeting or looking at anyone, went straight up to the cradle. …

» **Note**

□ force oneself into…: …으로 비집고 들어가다

The scenery was so beautiful to the letter.

: 그 광경은 글자 그대로 너무 아름다웠다.

I have a mind to try this bet to make a fortune.

: 나는 돈을 벌기 위 해 이 도박을 할 의향이 있다.

» 원문

... Meanwhile, the promises of the fairies were fulfilled to the letter, for the young Princess grew up to be so beautiful, most, wise and kind that all who saw her loved her. ...

... When he heard this, the Prince's face brightened and showed that he had a good mind to try his luck. So the old man warned him ...

... The very next day, the Prince and the Princess were married in the chapel of the castle, and they lived happily together for the rest of their lives. ...

» **Note**

- □ to the letter: 글자그대로
- □ try one's luck: ... 요행을 쳐보다
- □ the very next day: 바로 그 다음 날

023

'The Elves and the Shoemaker' in Grimm's Fairy Tales(adapted)

- J & W Grimm

작품 소개: 제화공의 아내에게는 일감이 무척 많이 있었다. 라이벌 업자가 그들의 고객을 빼앗아가기 전까지 미래는 점점 불투명해지고 있었다. 그때 두 명의 요정이 도착했다. 그들만의 비밀 임무를 하기 위해서…

When they felt somebody peeping at them, the girls swimming in the pool slipped their clothes on.

: 누군가가 그들을 엿보고 있다는 것을 느꼈을 때, 수영장에서 수영하고 있던 그 소녀들은 그들의 옷을 <u>재빨리 입었다</u>.

» **원문**

… With the greatest swiftness they took up the pretty garments and <u>slipped them on</u>, singing, "What spruce and dandy boys are we! No longer cobblers we will be." …

» **Note**

□ slip on: 옷을 잽싸게 입다

cf) 'slip'는 '재빨리[살며시, 몰래]…하다'라는 뜻을 가지고 있다.

ex) slip in: 살며시 들어오다

163

'The Wolf and the Seven Little Goats' in Grimm's Fairy Tales(adapted)

- J & W Grimm

작품 소개: 계교를 꾸며 성공하려던 악한 자의 말로를 그린 작품이다.

Our rangers are <u>on their guard against</u> the enemy who disguise themselves.

: 우리의 특수요원들은 위장하고 있는 적들에 대항하여 경계 태세를 게을리 하고 있지 않다.

<u>Can it be that</u> the captives are still alive?

: 그 포로들이 여전히 살아 있는 것이 가능할 것인가?

» **원문**

... "Dear children," said she, "I am going out into the wood; and while I am gone, <u>be on your guard against the wolf</u>, for when he were once to get inside he would eat you up, skin, bones, and all. <u>The wretch often disguise himself</u>, ...

... "Dear me!" thought she. "<u>Can it be that my poor children that he devoured for his evening meal are still alive</u>?" ...

» **Note**

☐ be on one's guard against...: ...에 대항하여 경계대세를 갖춰라

☐ disguise oneself: 위장하다

☐ can it be that...?: ...그것은 가능할까?, ...하는 것은 있을 수가 있을까?

025

'The Frog Prince' in Grimm's Fairy Tales(adapted)

- J & W Grimm

작품 소개: 어느 날 한 나라의 공주가 황금공을 가지고 놀고 있었다. 놀다가 호수 앞을 지나면서 그 공을 떨어뜨리고 말았다. 공주는 호수 앞에서 어쩔 줄 몰라 하며 울고 있었다. 그런데 어디선가 개구리가 나타나 공주에게 공을 찾아 주겠다고 했다. 개구리와 잠을 자고 일어나니 개구리는 온데간데없고 왕자가 있었다.

You are <u>nothing but</u> a novice.

: 너는 <u>단지</u> 풋내기에 불과해.

» 원문

… And when she <u>looked to see</u> where the voice came from, <u>there was nothing but</u> a frog stretching his thick ugly head out of the water. …

» Note

- ☐ look to see…: …을 보기 위해 몸을 돌리다
- ☐ nothing but…: …에 아무것도 없는[아닌], 즉 단지…한[…있는]
   rf) nothing but=only

Let' me go home now, I do<u>n't</u> want to talk to you <u>any</u>
<u>more</u>.
: 집에 가게 해주세요, 나는 <u>더이상</u> 말하고 싶지 <u>않아요</u>.

If you keep our promise, I'll give <u>anything you like</u>.
: 네가 우리의 약속을 지킨다면 나는 너에게 <u>네가 원하는 어느 것이라도</u> 주
겠다.

» **원문**

... "<u>Don't cry any more</u>," said the frog. "I can help you. But what
you will give me, if I get back you toy for you?"
   "<u>I will give you anything you like</u>, dear frog," she said, "my clothes,
my jewels, or anything you like." ...

» **Note**

☐ not ... any more: 더 이상...하지 않는
☐ anything you like: 당신이 좋아하는 어느 것이라도(긍정문의 'any'는 '양보'의 뜻)

026
'Rapunzel'
in Grimm's Fairy Tales(adapted)

- J & W Grimm

작품 소개: 18년을 탑 안에서만 지낸 끈기 만점의 소녀 라푼젤이 어느 날 자신의 탑에 침입한 왕국 최고의 대도를 한방에 때려잡는다. 그리고 그를 협박해 꿈에도 그리던 집 밖으로의 모험을 단행한다. 점점 흥미진진한 사건들이 터지기 시작한다. 그러나 세상 물정 깜깜한 라푼젤은 자신 앞에 펼쳐진 스릴 넘치는 세상을 맘껏 즐기는데…

As she grows up, she pines away.
: 나이를 먹어감에 따라, 그녀는 초췌 해졌다.

I'll go up to the mountain top, cost what it will.
: 나는 어떠한 대가를 치르고라도 그 산을 정복할 것이다.

There are many kinds of fruits. Eat them to your heart's content.
: 많은 과일들이 있습니다. 마음껏 그것들을 드세요.

» 원문

... This went on for days, and she knew she could not get the rampion, she pined away, and grew pale and miserable. Then the man was uneasy, and asked "What is the matter, dear wife?" ...
... "Rather than lose my wife I will get some rampion, cost what it will." ...
... She made a salad of it at once, and ate of it to her heart's content. ...

» Note

☐ pine away: 초췌해지다
☐ cost what it will: 어떤 희생을 치르고라도 (이때 동사의 원형이 앞에 오고 비인칭 'it'를 쓴다는 것에 유의한다.)
☐ to one's heart's content: 실컷, 마음껏

Snow–White and Rose–Red' in Grimm's Fairy Tales(adapted)

- J & W Grimm

작품 소개: 「하얀 눈과 빨간 장미」는 유럽에서 구전되어 오던 이야기를 그림 형제가 수집하여 각색한 작품이다.

I all the time try to <u>take all the pains</u> to help other poor people.

: 나는 늘 다른 가난한 사람들을 돕고자 <u>모든 수고를 다하고자</u> 노력한다.

Bob, run and <u>fetch</u> the pail, I'll water the flower garden.

: Bob, 꽃밭에 물 주려고 하니 달려가 물주전자 좀 <u>가져오너라</u>.

» **원문**

… The children <u>took all the pains</u> they could to pull the Dwarf's beard out; but without success. "<u>I will run and fetch some help</u>," cried Rose-Red at length. …

» **Note**

☐ take pains: 수고하다
☐ fetch: 가지고 오다

028

Little Snow White(adapted)   - J & W Grimm

작품 소개: 옛날, 한겨울에 눈이 펑펑 내리고 있었을 때, 한 여왕이 좋은 검은 흑단으로 만들어진 창가에 앉아서 일하고 있었다. 그녀는 바느질을 하는 동안 때때로 눈을 향해 밖을 쳐다보다 갑자기 자신의 손가락을 찔렀고 세 방울의 피가 눈 위에 떨어졌다. 후에 곧 그녀는 눈처럼 하얀 피부를, 피처럼 붉은 볼을, 그리고 흑단처럼 검은 머리를 가진 아이를 갖게 되었고, 아이는 백설 공주라 불리게 되었다.

Your jacket becomes you very well.
: 너의 재킷은 너와 매우 잘 어울린다.

When the comb ran through her hair, the actress found some portion of it turned grey.
: 빗질을 하였을 때, 그 여배우는 그의 머리카락의 일부가 희색으로 변한 것을 발견했다.

Take back your money, I don't need any money.
: 너의 돈을 다시 가져가라, 나는 어떤 돈도 필요하지 않다.

» **원문**

… This answer so frightened the Queen that she became yellow and green with envy. …
… At length she sent for a huntsman and said, "Take the child away into the forest; I will look never upon her again. …
… "You can't think, my dear, how it becomes you!" exclaimed the old woman. "Come, let me lace it up for you. …
… But as soon as the comb ran through the hair, the poison began to work, and the maiden soon fell down senseless. …
… "That is hard on me," said the old woman, "for I must take back my apples, but here is one which I will give you." …

- ☐ yellow and green=yellow-green: 황록색의
- ☐ with envy: 시샘[부러움] 때문에
  cf) jealousy; 시기심, 질투
- ☐ become: 어울리다
  ex) This green jacket becomes you well.: 이 녹색 잠바는 너에게 잘 어울린다.
- ☐ run through: 빗을 빗다
- ☐ take back: 도로 물리다[가져가다], 취소하다

Come with me to the sea of love.

: 나와 사랑의 바다로 갑시다.

Every body got ready for the fight.

: 모든 사람이 싸움을 위하여 준비되어있었다.

» **원문**

… "Come with me to my father's castle and you shall be my bride."
Snow-White was glad and went with him. And soon everything was
got ready for a splendid wedding. …

» **Note**

- ☐ come with me: 나와 함께 가자. (즉, 형태는 '명령문'이지만 내용상으로는 '청
  유형[...하자]'이다.)
- ☐ get ready for...: ...을 준비하다.

029

The Twelve Dancing Princesses(adapted)

- J & W Grimm

작품 소개: 공주님들은 조용하고 행실이 좋아야 하지만, 이 책에 나오는 12명의 공주들은 즐겁게 노는 것을 좋아한다. 공주들이 밤에 춤을 추러 몰래 빠져나간다는 사실을 알게 된 아버지가 더는 춤추는 것을 금지하게 하는데… 과연 그럴 수 있을까?

I was worn out after exercise.

: 나는 운동 후에 녹초가 되었다.

» **원문**

… Don't be so foolish," said the eldest sister, "you caught it on some nail or other, that is all." …

… Here they danced till three in the morning, when they were obliged to stop, because their shoes were worn out. …

» **Note**

□ catch on: (1)…에 걸리다 (2)인기를 얻다 (3)이해하다 (4)기회를 재빨리 포착하다 (5)취직하다

□ wear out: 달아 떨어지다, 오래가다, 녹초가 되게 하다

Hansel and Gretel(adapted)

- J & W Grimm

작품 소개: 커다란 숲 가장자리에 가난한 나무꾼이 그의 아내와 두 아이와 같이 살고 있었다. 소년의 이름은 헨델이고, 소녀의 이름은 그레텔이다.

I ordered some delicious food, so make a great feast of it.
: 맛있는 음식을 주문했습니다. 그러므로 그것을 실 컷 드십시오.

The sailer took me across the river to the dock.
: 뱃사공은 나를 강을 건너 잔교에 데려다 주었다.

» 원문

… And whenever she got them into her clutches, she cooked them and ate them and made a great feast of it. …
… "Nor is there any boat, either," said Gretel, but there swims a white swan. I will ask her to take us across. …

» Note
- □ clutch: 꽉 잡은 손, 마수
- □ make a great feast of it: 그것을 마음껏[실컷] 먹다
- □ take 목적어(A) across: (A)를 건네다 주다

172

The Adventures of Sindbad the Sailor(adapted)

- J & W Grimm

작품 소개: 「아라비안 나이트」에서 불가사의한 항해를 일곱 번 하는 뱃사람의 모험을 그린 이야기다.

The beauty <u>caught my eye</u>.
: 그 미인은 <u>나의 시선을 끌었다</u>.

I was embarrassed <u>more than ever</u>.
: 나는 <u>여느 때보다 더 많이</u> 당황했다.

She <u>wrung her hands and tore her hair</u>, and at last cried out.
: 그녀는 <u>그녀의 손을 비틀고 머리채를 쥐어뜯더니</u> 결국은 소리를 질렀다.

The natives welcomed us and <u>led us to their huts</u>.
: 원주민들은 우리 를 환영했고 <u>그들의 오두막집으로 우리를 안내했다.</u>

... The first thing that <u>caught my eye</u> was a huge white dome, that seemed to rise from the center of the island, unlike anything I had ever seen before. I climbed down the tree, and made way towards the white dome as quickly as I could, but when I reached it, <u>it puzzled me more than ever</u>. ...

... but when the captain looked earnestly at the island, <u>he wrung his hands, tore his hair</u>. "We are lost!" he cried, "for this is no other than the Mountain of Apes." ...

... We had <u>not</u> gone far <u>when</u> we were met by a crowd of black savages, who surrounded us, and <u>led us to their huts</u>. ...

» Note

- ☐ catch one's eye: 시선을 끌다
- ☐ more than ever: 여느 때보다
- ☐ wring one's hands: 손을 비틀다
- ☐ tear one's hair: 머리카락을 쥐어뜯다
- ☐ not...when...: ...하자마자...하다 즉, 시제에 주의할 것
- ☐ lead (A) to (B): (A)를 (B)로 이끌다[안내하다]

032

Little Red – Cap(adapted)

- J & W Grimm

작품 소개: 귀여운 소녀 빨간 모자는 할머니의 병문안을 가게 된다. 병문안을 가던 길에 만난 늑대가 이 사실을 알게 된다. 할머니와 여우가 사냥꾼에게 쫓기고 있다. 사냥꾼을 피해 도망가던 여우는 나무꾼을 만나게 된다. 여우는 나무꾼에게 부탁을 한다.

She was lying <u>with her cap pulled over her eyes</u> so that her mother could not recognized her as a daughter.

: 그녀는 <u>그녀의 모자를 그녀의 눈 위까지 푹 쓴 채로</u> 누워 있었다. 그래서 그녀의 어머니는 그녀의 딸을 알아채지 못했다.

» **원문**

… Then she remembered her mother's words and said in a loud voice, "Good morning," but got no answer. So she went to her grandmother's bed. She was lying <u>with her cap pulled over her eyes</u>, and looked strange …

» **Note**

  □ with her cap pulled over her eyes: 그녀의 모자를 그녀의 눈 위로 푹 쓰고 (분사구문)

033
Doctor Know –All(adapted)
- J & W Grimm

작품 소개: 가난에서 벗어나기 위해 무엇이든지 다 아는 의사 흉내를 내는데 우연한 기회로 어떤 부자의 돈을 찾아주게 된다.

If you are free this evening, please come and see the show and we'll give some freebies <u>into the bargain</u>.
: 오늘 저녁 만약에 시간이 있다면, 와서 쇼를 구경하세요 그러면 <u>덤으로</u> 경품을 주겠습니다.

<u>I'll take you to the wonderful restaurant</u>, if you don't mind.
: 괜찮으시다면 <u>멋진 식당으로 당신을 모시겠습니다</u>.

» **원문**

... They said, "We will return the money and give you much money <u>into the bargain</u>, if you don't betray us ; for if you do, we may lose our lives."
Then <u>they took him to the place</u> where the money was hidden. ...

» **Note**

□ into the bargain: 덤으로
□ take 사람(A) to 장소(B): (A)를 (B)로 데려가다

The Stars

- Alphonse Daudet

작품 소개: 풍부한 서정과 잔잔한 묘사로 애독되는 프로방스 지방 목동의 이야기는, 우연히 주인 집 딸과 하룻밤을 보내게 된 양치기 소년의 이야기로 많은 이들에게 감동을 주었던 소설이다.

작가 소개: 19세기 후반 프랑스의 소설가다. 고향 프로방스 지방에 대한 애착심을 주제로 하여 인상주의적인 매력 있는 작품을 썼다.

The problem was so easy that even a slow student such as I could solve it.

: 그 문제는 너무나 쉬워 가지고 나 같은 공부를 잘하지 못하는 학생도 그러한 문제를 해결할 수가 있었다.

I'll take pleasure in sending you a copy.

: 내가 복사한 한 부를 당신께 기꺼이 보내드리겠습니다.

» **원문**

… Some people asked me how a poor mountain shepherd such as I should be interested in those things, and I answered that I was twenty and that Mile Stephanette was the most beautiful thing that I had ever seen in my life. …
… but I was so confused that I could not find a single word. I believe that she noticed it, but the mischievous girl took pleasure in increasing my embarrassment. …

» **Note**

☐ such as… : …같은(like…)
☐ take pleasure in+…ing: …하는데 즐거움을 갖다, …하는 것을 즐기다

A Woman of Arles

- Alphonse Daudet

작품 소개: 수려한 외모를 가진 '쟝'이라는 총각은 아를르의 파티에서 한 아가씨를 만나 사랑에 빠지고 결혼을 결심한다. 그러나 어느 날 그녀를 알고 있는 한 사람으로부터, 그녀는 이미 정부가 있으며 그 누구도 사랑할 수 없는 여자라는 말을 듣게 된다. 그녀를 너무 사랑한 나머지, 쟝은 괴로워하다가 결국 자살을 하게 된다.

Even if they are not accustomed to foreigners, the natives did not cold-shoulder me.

: 비록 그들이 외국인에게 익숙해져 있지 않을 지라도, 그 원주민들은 나에게 냉랭하게 대하지 않았다.

Sometimes I remain reserved, at other times I remain outgoing.

: 때때로 나는 말수가 적다. 다른 때에는 나는 매우 외향적이다.

» **원문**

… but since your son wanted her to marry him, both she and her parents have cold-shouldered me. …

… Sometimes he passed days all alone in a corner, without moving; at other times he worked in the fields with enormous energy and did single-handed the work of ten labourers. …

… "Oh, well! Listen, Jan, if you want her after all, we'll manage somehow …" His father, flushed with shame, lowered his head …

» **Note**

☐ give the cold shoulder to…=cold-shoulder…: …에게 냉랭하게 대하다

036

To M. Pierre Gringoire, Lyric Poet in Paris

- Alphonse Daudet

작품 소개: 파리에 사는 서정시인 피에르 그랭그와르 씨에게 바치는 이야기다. 배고픈 시인인 친구에게 충고 차 쓴 편지 안에 담긴 내용이다.

What is it that you want?

: 당신이 원하는 것은 <u>무엇입니까?</u>

When we quarrel about something, our teacher always take the part of my friend.

: 우리가 무엇인가에 대해 다툴 때, 우리 선생님은 나의 <u>친구를 편든다.</u>

» 원문

… "No, I don't want it longer, M. Seguin." "Then, what do you need? <u>What is it that you want?</u>" … "I want to go to the mountain, M. Seguin. …

… You smile, Gringoire? Oh yes! <u>I believe you take the part of the goat</u> against this good M. Seguin. We'll see how long you can go on smiling …

» Note

☐ It is (A) that (B): (B)하는 것은 (A)이다(일종의 '강조구문'). 위의 문장을 분석하면, It is what that you want.(강조구문) → What is it that you want?(의문문)

☐ take part with…=take the part of…: …을 편들다
  cf) take A' part[role]: A의 역할[배역]을 하다

179

The Fall of the House of Usher — Edgar Allen Poe

작품 소개: 전통 있는 가문의 후에인 로데릭 이셔의 초대를 받은 '나'는 이느 흐긴 기을 헤 질녘, 호반의 낡은 저택을 찾아간다. 오랜만에 만난 로데릭은 심한 우울증에 빠져 있었고, 그의 쌍둥이 누이동생 매덜린의 갑작스러운 죽음으로 장례를 치르게 된다. 어느 폭풍우 몰아치던 밤, 가사 상태로 장례가 치러진 매덜린이 나타나 책을 읽고 있던 로데릭을 향해 쓰러지자 그도 죽고 만다. 이 끔찍한 사건을 목격한 '나'는 겁에 질려 뛰쳐나와 저택을 뒤돌아보니, 그 낡은 집은 두 동강 나 시커먼 늪 속으로 침몰해갔다. 현실과 환상이 교차하는 괴기소설의 백미다.

작가 소개: 미국의 시인이자 소설가, 비평가다. 추리소설의 시조로서도 유명한 포는 「황금벌레」(1843), 「도난당한 편지」(1845), 「모르그가의 살인사건」(1841) 등의 명작을 발표했다.

The pop singer was born of a royal family.
: 그 팝 가수는 왕족출신이다.

When the storm happened, the door was thrown open.
: 폭풍이 발생했을 때, 문이 활짝 열렸다.

» 원문

… I knew only that he was born of a family noted for the fine arts and generous deeds of charity. I knew also that his family lay in the direct line of descent without any branch. …

… The valet now threw open a door. and showed me into the presence of his master. The room in which I found myself was very large and high. The windows were long, narrow, and pointed, and were placed high up from the black oaken floor. …

… Many books and musical instruments lay scattered about, but failed to make the room cheerful. …

» **Note**

- be born of...: ... 출신이다
- direct line of descent: 직계 가계[혈통]
- throw open: 활짝 열다
- lay scattered about: 이리저리 흩어져 놓여있다

When he heard that his team was defeated in the championship, he <u>buried his face in his hands</u> and burst into tears.

: 그의 팀이 결승전에서 졌다는 것을 들었을 때, 그는 <u>그의 손을 얼굴에 묻고</u> 울음을 터뜨렸다.

I talked her about her appearance <u>in jest</u> rather than <u>in earnest</u>.

: 나는 <u>진지하게</u> 보다는 <u>농담조로</u> 그녀의 외모에 관하여 말했다.

She was as strong as a man <u>by nature</u>.

: 그녀는 <u>선천적으로</u> 사내만큼 힘이 세었다.

» **Note**

- □ bury one's face in one's hands: 얼굴을 손에 묻다
- □ in jest rather than in earnest: 진지하게 보다는 농담 삼아
- □ by nature: 천성적으로

She is a wise yet strange girl.
: 그녀는 현명하지만 이상한 소녀다.

» **원문**

... He rocked his body from side to side <u>with a gentle yet constant and uniform movement</u>. I <u>went on with</u> the story of Sir Launcelot ...

» **Note**

- □ rock: 흔들다
- □ yet: 그러나, 아직
- □ go on with...: ...을 계속 진행하다
  cf) go on with+명사[go on ...ing]: 계속...하다

038

A Descent into the Malestrome - Edgar Allen Poe

작품 소개: 포에 의해 쓰인 첫 번째 단편소설 중의 하나다. 이 작품은 현대 공상과학 소설의 효시라고 간주 된다. 또한 포우의 추론(ratiocination) 이야기 중의 하나로 간주 된다.

The picture is the most beautiful when it was seen <u>at an angle of</u> ninety degrees.

: 그 그림은 그것이 <u>90도의 각도에서</u> 보여질 때 가장 아름답다.

When I heard some bombs falling down near my house, I <u>threw myself upon my face</u>.

: 일부 폭탄이 나의 집 근처에서 떨어지는 것을 들었을 때, 나는 <u>나의 얼굴을 대고 납작 엎드렸다.</u>

» **원문**

… <u>At an angle of some forty-five degrees</u>, it was speeding round and round with a bewildering rapidity, shrieking and roaring with a terrible voice …

… The mountain trembled to its base, and the rock shook. <u>I threw myself upon my face</u> and <u>clung to</u> the grass. …

… "The usually fishing grounds are <u>a great way lower down to the southward</u>. There fish can be got <u>at all hours</u>, without much risk, and therefore these places are preferred. …

» **Note**

- at an angle of...: ...의 각도로
- throw oneself upon one's face: 얼굴을 대고 납작 엎드리다
- cling to : 에 집착하다, 달라붙다
- lower down to the southward: 남쪽으로 아래로 내려와
- at all hours: 때를 가리지 않고, 언제나

The state of things was getting worse when they gave up their works.

: 사태는 그들이 그들의 일들을 포기했을 때 악화되고 있었다.

For my part, I think she is in the wrong.

: 나로서는 그녀가 틀렸다고 생각한다.

» **원문**

... "This state of things, however, did not last long enough to give us time to think about it." ...

... For my part, I threw myself flat on deck, with my feet against the edge of the side of the schooner." ...

» **Note**

- the state of things: (일의) 사태
  cf) the state of affairs: (일의) 사정, 사태
- for one's part: ...로서는
  cf) in one's opinion: ...의 입장에서는
- throw oneself flat on...: ...에 납작 엎드리다

I sang a song on the stage <u>at the top of my voice</u> when I was excited.

: 흥분되었을 때 나는 <u>최고의 음부로[목청껏]</u> 무대에서 노래를 불렀다.

The air-plane <u>made a half turn to the right</u> when the strong wind hit its right wing.

: 그 비행기는 강한 바람이 그것의 오른쪽 날개를 쳤을 때 <u>오른쪽으로 반 회전 돌았다.</u>

» **원문**

... "I tried to speak to my brother; I screamed <u>at the top of my voice</u> in his ear, <u>but in vain</u>. ..." ...

... "<u>The boat made a sharp half turn to the left,</u> and then <u>shot off</u> in its new direction like a thunderbolt. ...

... "It turned out as I had guessed. ...

» **Note**

☐ at the top of...: ...의 최고로, 최고의 ...로
☐ but in vain: 그러나 헛되었다
☐ make a half turn to the left: 왼쪽으로 반 회전 돌다
☐ shoot off: 쏜 살같이 나아가다
☐ turn out: ...의 결과를 낳다, 결론이 ...이 되다

185

039
The Purloined Letter
- Edgar Allen Poe

작품 소개: 가악한 계략가이자 정치가인 D장관이 왕비의 비밀편지를 훔쳐 가면서 시작된다. 도둑맞은 편지로 인해 곤경에 빠진 왕비는 파리 경시청장에게 수사를 의뢰하지만, 결국 실패하고 사설탐정 뒤팽에게 의뢰한다.

I am in the habit of taking a walk in the morning.
: 나는 아침에 산보하는 것을 습관으로 삼는다.

The policeman searched every nook and corner in the room to find out some evidence.
: 경관은 어떤 증거를 발견하기 위해 방의 구석구석을 수색했다.

As a matter of fact, I have completed my job already.
: 사실상 나는 나의 일을 이미 끝냈지.

» 원문

… He was in the habit of calling everything "odd" that was beyond his understanding. "Very true," said Dupin, as he supplied his visitor with a pipe, and pushed toward him a comfortable chair. …
… I think I have searched every nook and corner where it is possible that the paper can be concealed. …
… "You might have spared yourself this trouble," said Dupin. "D-, I believe, is not altogether a fool, and, if not, must have expected these waylayings, as a matter of course." …
… Including the two neighboring houses." "You must have had a great deal of trouble," I exclaimed. "We had; but the reward offered is very large." …

» **Note**

☐ be in the habit of …ing: …하는 것을 습관으로 삼다

   cf) make a point of …ing: …으레히 …하다

☐ search every nook and corner: 구석구석 수색하다

☐ spare oneself this trouble: …자신이 이러한 수고를 하다

☐ as a matter of course: 하나의 (당연한) 과정으로써

☐ must have had a great deal of trouble: 많은 수고를 했음에 틀림이 없다

   cf) must have p.p…: …했음에 틀림이 없다

The Gold Bug

- Edgar Allen Poe

작품 소개: 황금색 벌레에게 물린 윌리엄 레그런드(William Legrand)라는 사람이 수인공이다. 레그런드의 흑인 하인 주피터(Jupiter)는 레그런드가 벌레에 물린 뒤로 미쳐간다고 두려워하고, 레그런드의 친구인 이름을 알 수 없는 서술자는 친구를 걱정해 레그런드를 방문한다. 레그런드는 주피터와 서술자를 끌고다니며 해적 윌리엄 키드 선장의 매장금을 찾기 위한 모험을 떠나게 된다.

People's mind is subject to the weather.

: 사람의 마음은 날씨에 영향을 받기 쉽다.

The mayor was usually accompanied by his pet dog taking a walk in the morning.

: 시장은 보통 아침에 산책을 할 때 그의 애완견을 동행했다.

» 원문

... I found him well educated, with unusual powers of mind, but infected with misanthropy, and subject to persevere moods of alternate enthusiasm and melancholy. He had with him many books, but rarely employed them. ...

... In these excursions he was usually accompanied by an negro, called Jupiter, who had been manumitted before the reverses of the family ...

» Note
- □ well educated: 잘 교육받은
- □ unusual powers of mind: 똑똑함
- □ subject to...: ...을 받기 쉬운, ...을 조건으로 하는
- □ be accompanied by...: ...의해 동반되다, ...와 함께 동행하다

Her cancer cell was <u>the size of a pea</u> when it was recognized at first.

: 처음 발견되었을 때 그녀의 암세포는 <u>강낭콩 크기</u> 만했다.

They <u>were about to leave</u> the camp, when he came back after a long absence.

: 그들이 캠프를 <u>막 떠나려고 했을</u> 때, 한 참 동안 소식 없던 그가 돌아왔다.

» 원문

... "Nonsense! No!-the bug. It is of a brilliant gold colour-<u>about the size of a large hickory-nut</u>-with two jet black spots near one extremity of the back, and another, somewhat longer, at the other. The antennas are ..." ...

... He received the paper very peevishly, and <u>was about to crumple it</u>, apparently to throw it in the fire, when a casual glance at the design seemed suddenly to rivet his attention. ...

... Presently he took from his pocket a wallet, placed the paper carefully in it, and deposited both in a writing-desk, which he locked. <u>He now grew more composed in his demeanour</u>; but his original air of enthusiasm had quite disappeared. Yet <u>he seemed not so much sulky as abstracted</u>. ...

- nonsense: 말도 안 되는 소리
- about the size of (A): 대략 (A)같은 크기
- be about to =be just going to…=be on the point of…ing¹ 막 …하려고 하다
- not so much (A) as (B): (A)라기 보다는 오히려 (B)

"It's all right, you'll be better." said my herb doctor feeling my pulse.

: "괜찮아요, 당신은 나으실 거예요." 나의 맥박을 짚어보며 한의사가 말했다.

To say the truth, I take second place, not first place.

: 솔직히 말해, 일등이 아니라 이등을 했다.

Let's be off right now, we have no time to lose.

: 지금 떠나자, 우리는 지체할 시간이 없다.

» **원문**

… "My dear Legrand," I cried, interrupting him, "you are certainly unwell, and had better use some little precautions, You shall go to bed, and I will remain with you a few days, until you get over this. You are feverish and …" …

"Feel my pulse," said he. I felt it, and, to say the truth, found not the slightest indication of fever. …

… "I am anxious to oblige you in any way," I replied; "but do you mean to say that this infernal beetle has any connection with your expedition into the hills? …

… "Yes; I promise; and now let us be off, for we have no time to lose." With a heavy heart I accompanied my friend. We started about four o'clock-Legrand, Jupiter, the dog, and myself. …

» Note

» Note

- □ had better+동.원(or 명사)…: …하는 편이 낫다
- □ feel one's purse: 맥박을 짚어보다
- □ to say the truth: 솔직히 말하면
- □ be anxious to+동.원: …간절히 바라다
- □ oblige…: …도움을 주다
- □ be off: 떠나다
- □ have no time to lose: 지체할 시간이 없다

Up with you. Now it's high time to have a great view.

: 올라와라. 경치를 즐길 최고의 시간이다.

The singer looks more beautiful in semblance than in reality.

: 그 가수는 실제보다 외형상으로 더 아름답게 보인다.

Never mind the weather, we can play the game any time.

: 날씨는 신경 쓰지 말라, 우리는 어느 때라도 경기를 할 수가 있다.

» 원문

… Then up with you as soon as possible, for it will soon be too dark to see what we are about." How far mus go up, massa?" inquired Jupiter. …

… "What de matter now, massa?" said Jup, evidently shamed into compliance; "always want for to raise fuss wid old nigger. Was only funnin anyhow. Me feered de bug! what I keer for de bug?" Here he took cautiously hold of the extreme end of the string, and, maintaining the insect as far from his person as circumstances would permit, prepared to ascend the tree. …

… Thus the difficulty of ascension, in the present case, lay more in semblance than in reality. …

… Never mind the sky, but attend to what I say. Look down the trunk and count the limbs below you on this side. How many limbs have you passed?" …

» **Note**

- □ Up with you=(You) go up: 올라오세요.
  cf) Away with you!=(You) Go away!: 꺼져라!
- □ shamed into compliance: 모욕당하여 승낙한 모습이 되어
- □ in semblance: 외형상으로
- □ in reality: 실제적으로
- □ never mind: 신경 쓰지 않다

He reached his hand <u>to the fullest extent</u> and struggled to grab the rope.

: 그는 <u>최대한도로</u> 그의 손을 뻗었다 그리고 그 밧줄을 잡고자 몸부림쳤다.

The knight <u>fell upon his knees</u> and begged the lady to marry him.

: 그 기사는 <u>무릎을 꿇었다</u> 그리고 그 숙녀에게 자기와 결혼해달라고 간청했다.

Our players fought against the opposite players <u>clenching their teeth</u>.

: 우리 선수들은 <u>이를 악물고</u> 상대방 선수들과 싸웠다.

Waterfalls falls from the top to the bottom <u>in the nature of things</u>.

: <u>사물의 본질상[천성적으로]</u> 폭포는 위로부터 아래로 떨어진다.

» **원문**

... Legrand strode up to Jupiter, and seized him by the collar. The astonished negro opened his eyes and mouth <u>to the fullest extent</u>, let fall the spades, and <u>fell upon his knees</u>.

"You scoundrel!" said Legrand, hissing out the syllables from <u>between his clenched teeth</u>-"you infernal black villain! speak, I tell you!-answer me this instantly without prevarication!-which is your left eye?" ...

... Legrand appeared exhausted with excitement, and spoke very few words. Jupiter's countenance wore, for some minutes, as greatly a pallor as it is possible, <u>in the nature of things</u>, for any negro's visage to assume. ...

» **Note**

- □ to the fullest extent: 최대한으[도]로
- □ fall upon one's knees: 무릎을 꿇다
- □ between one's clenched teeth: 꽉 다문 이 사이
- □ in the nature of things: 사물의 성질상[천성적으로]

I <u>called</u> the words that my fellow gave to me <u>to mind</u> and remembered the formula to solve the difficult problem with.

: 나는 나의 동료가 나에게 준 말을 <u>상기했다.</u> 그리고 난제를 풀기 위한 공식을 기억해냈다.

In front of the judge I said 'No' but I <u>admitted to myself</u> 'I am guilty.'

: 재판관 앞에선 나는 아니라고 했지만 <u>내심은</u> 죄가 있다고 <u>생각했다.</u>

… When you first made this assertion, I thought you were jesting; but afterwards I <u>called to mind</u> the peculiar spots on the back of the insect, and admitted to myself that your remark had some little foundation in fact. …

… In a few minutes, the pan having become throughly heated, I removed the slip, and, <u>to my inexpressibly joy</u>, found it spotted, in several places, with what appeared to be figures arranged <u>in lines</u>. Again I placed it in the pan, and <u>suffered it to remain another minute</u>. …

» **Note**

  □ call to mind: 상기하다
  □ admit to oneself: 스스로 인정하다[내심 맞는다고 생각하다]
  □ to my inexplicably joy: 말로 표현할 수 없는 정도로 기쁘게도
  □ in lines: 여러 줄로
  □ suffer: 잠자코 …하게 하다

This foot prints may <u>have some reference to</u> the missing bear.

: 이 족적들은 행방불명된 곰에 대한 참고사항이 될 수가 있다.

<u>After some demur</u>, the border guard consented to go through the border.

: <u>약간의 이의 (신청) 후에</u>, 그 보초인은 그 국경을 통과하라고 승락했다.

» **원문**

… that this "Bishop's hotel" might <u>have some reference to</u> an old family, of the name of Bessop, which, <u>time out of mind</u>, had held possession of an ancient manor-house, about four miles to the northward of the island. Accordingly I went over to the plantation, and re-instituted my inquiries among the older negroes of the place. …

… "I offered to pay her well for her trouble, and, <u>after some demur</u>, she consented to accompany me to the spot. We found it without much difficulty, when, dismissing her, I <u>proceeded to examine the place</u>. …

» **Note**

☐ have some reference to…: …에 대해 참조가 되다

☐ time out of mind: 옛날부터

☐ after some demur: 약간의 이의 후에

☐ proceed to+동원=계속 …하다

The Murders in the Rue Morgue

- Edgar Allan Poe

작품 소개: 추리소설의 효시로 인정되는 작품이다. 파리 모르그 가에서 잔혹한 모녀 살인 사건이 벌어지고 파리 경찰은 속수무책에 빠지는데 뒤팽은 뛰어난 추론과 분석을 통해 미궁의 사건을 해결한다. 1841년 발간된 작가의 최초의 추리소설이다.

His adventure story is beyond my comprehension, so I began to feel bored.

: 그의 모험소설은 나의 이해를 뛰어넘었다. 그러므로 나는 지루해지기 시작했다.

My boss is in the habit of drinking a cup of coffee on arriving at the office early in the morning.

: 나의 사장님은 이른 아침 사무실에 출근 하자마자 의례껏 커피한잔을 마신다.

He is a native of Seoul.

: 그는 서울태생이다.[토박이다.]

» **원문**

... 'Dupin,' said I gravely, 'this is beyond my comprehension. I do not hesitate to say that I am amazed, and can scarcely credit my senses. How was it possible you should know I was thinking of ...? Here I paused, to ascertain beyond a doubt whether he really knew of whom I thought. ...

... 'Pierre Moreau', tobacconist, deposed that he has been in the habit of selling small qualities of tobacco and snuff to madame L'Espanaye for nearly four years. Was born in the neighbourhood, and has always resided there. ...

... Odenheimer, restaurteur. This witness volunteered his testimony. Not speaking French, was examined through as interpreter. Is a native of Amsterdam. Was passing the house at the time of the shrieks. ...

» **Note**

☐ beyond comprehension: 이해를 뛰어넘는, 즉 이해할 수가 없는

☐ in the habit of...ing: ...하는 습관 하에 있다, 늘 ...하곤 한다

☐ a native of...: ...의 토박이, ...태생

The little kid always deposits his allowance in small sums.

: 그 작은 꼬마는 소액으로 항상 그의 용돈을 저축한다.

The king in person got out of the court to welcome his loyal courtier.

: 왕은 그의 충성스런 신하를 맞이하기 위해 몸소 궁궐로부터 나왔다.

There is no English equivalent for this korean word.

: 이 한국말에 대한 어떤 등가의 영어가 없다.

... Made frequent deposits in small sums. Had checked for nothing until the third day before deat.h, when she took out in person the sum of 4000 francs. This sum was paid in gold, and a clerk sent home with the money. ...

... 'Alberto Montani', confectioner, deposes that he was among the first to ascend the stairs. Heard the voices in question. The gruff voice was that of a Frenchman. Distinguished several words. The speaker appeared to be expostulating. ...

... I have said that the whims of my friend were manifold, and that Je les menageais-for this phrase there is no English equivalent. ...

» **Note**

□ in small sums: 소액으로

  cf) in large sums: 거액으로

□ in person: 몸소

□ in question: 문제의

□ equivalent for...: ...에 대한 등가물[상대물]

The thought that he got lost in such bad weather flitted over my mind.

: 그가 길을 잃었다는 생각이 나의 마음속에 스치고 지나갔다.

When I hear some wolves crying out in the cave, I felt a creeping of the flesh.

: 내가 동굴 속에서 늑대들이 우는 것을 들었을 때, 나는 소름이 끼쳤다.

I'll pledge the natives the honour of a Korean.

: 나는 한국인의 명예를 걸고 그 원주민에게 맹세를 할 것이다.

» **원문**

… <u>At these words</u> a vague and half-formed conception of the meaning of Dupin <u>flitted over</u> my mind. I seemed to be <u>upon the verge of</u> comprehension, without power to comprehend, as men at times find themselves <u>upon the brink of</u> remembrance, without being able in the end to remember. My friend <u>went on with</u> his discourse. …

… <u>I felt a creeping of the flesh</u> as Dupin asked me the question. 'A madame,' I said, 'has done this deed-some raving maniac escaped from a neighbouring Maison de Sante.' …

… You can get him in the morning. Of course you are prepared to identify the property?" 'To be sure I am, sir.' 'I shall be sorry to <u>part with</u> him,' said Dupin. 'I don't mean that you should be at all this trouble for nothing, sir,' said the man. …

… 'My friend,' said Dupin in a kind tone, 'you are <u>alarming yourself</u> unnecessarily-you are indeed. We mean you no harm <u>whatever</u>. <u>I pledge you the honour of a gentleman</u>, and of a Frenchman, that we intend you no injury. …

» **Note**

- ☐ at these words: 이 말에
- ☐ flit over…: …스쳐가다
- ☐ (up)on the verge of…: …막 하려고 할 즈음에
- ☐ go on with+명사…: …을 계속하다
    cf) go on …ing: …계속 ..하다
- ☐ feel a creeping of the flesh: 소름이 끼치다
- ☐ part with…: …와 헤어지다
- ☐ for nothing: 무료로, 헛되어
- ☐ alarm oneself: 염려하다
- ☐ whatever: 부정문과 결합하여 전혀 …않는(일종의 강조표현)
- ☐ pledge (A) the honour of (B): (A)에게 (B)의 명예를 걸고 맹세하다.

199

Up from Slavery

- Booker T. Washington

작품 소개: 「노예 신분으로부터의 상승(Up From Slavery)」(1901)은 출세를 위한 자신의 성공적인 노력에 관해 이야기하고 있다.

작가 소개: 교육자이자 당대 가장 두드러진 흑인 지도자였다. 해방된 미국 흑인들을 미국 사회의 주류에 포함하기 위하여 주장한 백인들과의 타협 정책은 유명한 애틀랜타 박람회 연설문(1895)에 드러나 있다.

Our festival is <u>drawing near</u>.

: 우리의 축제가 <u>다가오고 있다</u>.

The scandal of the respectable leader had more ring than expected.

: 그 존경할 만한 지도자의 스캔들은 기대되었던 것보다 <u>더 반향이 컸다</u>.

» 원문

… I am not very sure of the exact place or exact date of my birth, but <u>at any rate</u> I suspect <u>I must have been born somewhere and at sometime</u>. …

… As <u>the great day drew near</u>, there was more singing in the slave quarters than usual. It was bolder, <u>had more ring</u>, and <u>lasted later into the night</u>. …

… There was little, <u>if any</u>, sleep that night. All was excitement and expectancy. Early the next morning word was sent to all the slaves, <u>old and young</u>, to gather at the house. …

» Note

- □ had more ring: 반향이 더욱 커졌다
- □ draw near: 다가오다, 가까워지다
- □ if any: 있다 할지라도
- □ old and young: 나이를 먹었든 젊었던 간에

Please order two <u>portions</u> of chicken.
: 두 <u>몫</u>의 치킨을 주문해주세요.

She <u>sets her heart upon</u> her sweetheart while he is away for the army service.
: 그녀는 자기의 애인이 군에 복무하고 있는 동안 늘 <u>애인에 대해서만 생각하고 있다.</u>

» 원문

… My mother, who was standing by my side, leaned over and kissed her children, <u>while tears of joy ran down her cheeks.</u> …

… In some way, within a few weeks, <u>I mastered the greater portion of the alphabet.</u> In all my efforts to learn to read my mother shared fully my ambition, and sympathized with me and aided me in every way that she could. …

… But <u>my boyish heart was still set upon going to the day-school,</u> and I let no opportunity slip <u>to push my case.</u> …

» Note

- □ portion: 몫, 부분
- □ sympathize with…: …와 공감하다
- □ set one's heart upon: …에 대해서만 늘 생각하다
- □ push my case: 나의 경우를 관철시키다

I showed her to the gate.

: 나는 그녀를 대문 쪽으로 <u>안내했다</u>.

When my friend induced me to go on the gamble, I tried to <u>tear myself away</u> from it.

: 나의 친구가 도박을 하도록 나를 유인했을 때, 나는 그것으로부터 <u>나 자신을 뿌리치고자</u> 노력했다.

» **원문**

... After <u>all the other passengers had been shown into rooms</u> and were getting ready for supper, I shyly <u>presented myself</u> before the man at the desk. ...

... and yet he was but a type of that Christlike body of men and women who went into the Negro schools <u>at the close of the war</u> by the hundreds to assist in lifting up my race. ...

... She had so often expressed the wish that she might be permitted to live to see her children educated and <u>started out in the world</u>. ...

... but I had become so much observed in my work in West Virginia that I dreaded to give up. However, <u>I tore myself away from it</u>. I did not know how to refuse to perform any service that General Armstrong desired of me. ...

» **Note**

- ☐ show=guide=see: ...을 안내하다
- ☐ present oneself: 출석하다[나타나다]
- ☐ at the close of...: ...의 막바지에
- ☐ start out in the world: 사회에 첫 걸음을 내딛다
- ☐ tear one's self away: 뿌리치고 떠나다

He is far <u>above</u> me in skiing.

: 그는 스키 타는 데 있어 나<u>보다</u> 훨씬 <u>우위에</u> 있다.

They get paid <u>in proportion to[as]</u> their job ability.

: 그들은 그들의 업무 능력<u>에 비례하여</u> 보수를 지급 받는다.

» **원문**

… I knew that <u>the average Indian felt himself above the white man</u>, and, of course, <u>he felt himself far above the Negro</u>, largely on account of the fact of the Negro having submitted to slavery …

… How often I have wanted to say to white students that they <u>lift</u> themselves <u>up</u> <u>in proportion as</u> they help to lift others, and the more unfortunate the race …

… These gentlemen seemed to <u>take it for granted</u> that no coloured man suitable for the position could be secured, and they were expecting the General to recommend a white man for the place. …

» **Note**

☐ above…: …보다 우위에

☐ in proportion to[as]…: …에 비례하여

☐ take (A) for granted: (A)를 당연하게 여기다

In this country, immigrants <u>outnumbered</u> the natives by three to two.

: 이 나라에서 이민자들이 3대 2로 원주민보다 <u>수적으로 많다.</u>

<u>People above forty years of age</u> can take some medical check-up.

: <u>40세 이상의 사람들만이</u> 일부 건강진단을 받을 수가 있다.

» **원문**

… I found Tuskegee to be a town of about two thousand inhabitants, nearly one-half of whom were coloured. <u>It was in what was known as the Black Belt of the South.</u> In the county in which Tuskegee is situated the coloured people <u>outnumbered</u> the whites <u>by about three to one.</u> In some of <u>the adjoining and near-by</u> counties the proportion was not far from six coloured persons to one white. …

… A great many more students wanted to enter the school, but it had been decided to receive only <u>those who were above fifteen years of age</u>, and who had previously received some education. <u>The greater part of the thirty</u> were public-school teachers, and some of them were nearly forty years of age. …

» **Note**

- ☐ outnumber: 수적으로 앞서있다
- ☐ by about three to one: 약 3대 1로
- ☐ the adjoining and near-by: 부속하고 이웃하는
- ☐ those who were above fifteen years of age: 나이가 15세 이상인 사람들
- ☐ the great part of the thirty: 30명 중의 대부분

I am all the time in favor of you.

: 나는 늘 당신을 지지한다.

This is three dollars' worth of book.

: 이것은 3달러짜리[가치의] 책이다.

» **원문**

... Gradually, though, I noted with satisfaction that a sentiment in favour of work was gaining ground. ...

... Twenty years have now passed since I made the first humble effort at Tuskegee, in a broken-down shanty and an old hen-house, without owning a dollar's worth of property, and with but one teacher and thirty students. ...

» **Note**

□ gain ground: 우세하게 되다
□ a dollar's worth of property: 1달러 가치의 재산

Black Beauty

- Anna Sewell

작품 소개: 동물 애호 작가라는 애칭을 가진 애나 슈얼(Anna Sewell)의 작품으로, 주인공인 검은 말, 블랙 뷰티가 다양한 성격의 주인들과 만나며 겪게 되는 행복과 고난을 그린 감동적인 동화다.

작가 소개: 발이 불편하여 평생 말을 타고 다니면서 말을 좋아하게 되었다. 앞으로 18개월 밖에 못 산다는 선고를 받고 죽기 전에 말을 위한 글을 써야겠다고 결심, 침대 위에서 몇 줄씩 쓴 원고를 그녀의 어머니가 옮겨 써 「검은말 뷰티」를 출간했다.

They all the way treat me <u>with a good will</u>.

: 그들은 늘 좋은 마음을 가지고 나를 대한다.

I love Susan living <u>next door to</u> Helen.

: 나는 Helen 옆에 살고 있는 Susan을 사랑한다.

» **원문**

… I hope you will grow up gentle and good, and never learn bad ways; do your work <u>with a good will</u>, lift your feet up well when you trot, and never bite or kick <u>even in play</u>." …
… I had one white foot, and a pretty white star on my forehead. <u>After my master broke me in</u>, he sold me to Squire Gordon. …
… They think a great deal of me, and so does James. Are you going to live <u>next door to</u> me in the box?" …

» **Note**

- □ with a good will: 좋은 마음을 가지고
- □ in play: (1)농[장난]으로 (2)시합 중에
- □ break in: (1)길들이다(tame) (2)침입하다 (3)참견하다
- □ next door to…: … 옆[이웃]에

How does it go?

: 어떻게 지내니?

Her opinion has a point in its way.

: 그녀의 의견도 그 나름대로 일리가 있다.

» **원문**

… As we came back through the Park we met the Squire and his wife walking. 'Well, John, how does he go?' asked the Squire. …

… 'That's no wonder,' said John, 'didn't you know that farmer Grey's old Duchess was the mother of them both?' …

… John was very proud of me and talked to me a great deal. I grew very fond of him, he was so gentle and kind. James Howard, the stable boy, was just as gentle and pleasant in his way, so I thought myself well off. …

» **Note**

- □ How do 주어(A) go?: (A)는 어떻게 지내지[돼가니?]
- □ That's no wonder.: 좋은 일 없어.[그저 그래.]
- □ grow fond of…: …을 좋아하게 되다
- □ in one's way: …의 나름으로

I have been out all day so I am done up now.

: 나는 하루 종일 밖에 있었다. 그러므로 지금 녹초가 되어있는 상태다.

She stroked down her blond hair.

: 그녀는 그녀의 금발을 쓰다듬어 내렸다.

207

... 'The worst of it is,' he said, 'that my horse has been out all day and is quite done up ; my son has just been sent for, and he has taken the others. ...

... John stood by me and stroked my neck; I was very hot ...

... 'No! no! John,' said the Doctor, 'I hope not,' and in a minute we had left John far behind. When we came to the hill, the Doctor drew me up. ...

» Note

- □ be out: 밖에 나와 있다
- □ done up=exhausted=worn out: 녹초가 되어있는, 지쳐버린
- □ stroke: 쓰다듬다
- □ hot: 성적으로 흥분한
- □ in a minute: 잠시 후에
- □ leave (A) (far) behind: (A)를 (멀리) 뒤로 남겨 놓다
- □ draw up: (1)끌어 올리다 (2)(문서를)작성하다 (3)다가오다 (4)멈춰 세우다

They worked hard **night and day** so that they could succeed.

: 그들은 성공하기 위하여 밤낮으로 열심히 일했다.

The award for MVP **was too much for the player.**

: MVP라는 그 상은 그 선수에게는 너무나 과분했다.

... John nursed me night and day; he would get up two or three times in the night to come to me; my master, too, often came to see me. ...

... Master thanked John for his long and faithful service; but that was too much for John. 'Please don't, sir, I can't bear it; ...

... York came round to our heads and shortened the rein himself, one hole, I think; every little makes a difference, and that day we had a steep hill to go up. ...

» **Note**

□ night and day: 밤낮으로

□ That was too much for John.: 그것은 John에게는 과분한 일이야.

□ I can't bear It.: 나는 그것을 참을 수가 없다.

□ Every little makes a difference.: 모든 작은 것이 큰 것[중요한 일]을 만든다.

They attended the meeting <u>later than usual</u> but participated <u>more than ever.</u>.

: 그들은 여느 때보다 늦게 그 회의에 참여했다 그러나 여느 때보다 더 많이 참여했다.

» **원문**

… One day my lady came down later than usual, and the silk rustled more than ever. …

… 'Raise them at once, and let us have no more of this humouring and nonsense.' …

… When we came to the door, the gentleman seemed very uneasy. 'How is this? he said, are you tir.ed of your good Black Auster?' …

… There was no more to be said ; he placed her carefully on the saddle and then mounted me. …

» **Note**

□ later than usual: 여느 때보다 더 늦게

□ more than ever: 여느 때보다 더 많이

□ humoring: 비위를 맞춤

□ How it this?: 어찌된 일이요?(상대방에게 설명을 구할 때의 상투문구)

□ There was no more to be said.: 더 이상 한 말이 없었다.

He gathered himself together and succeeded in solving the tough problem.

: 그는 정신을 집중했다 그리고 그 어려운 문제를 해결하는 데 성공했다.

The hungry Eagle stooped down over the river and spotted a big swimming duck.

: 배고픈 독수리가 강 위를 굽어보았다 그리고 커다란 헤엄치고 있는 오리 한 마리를 목격했다.

The leaves were cut all to pieces by his sword.

: 잎들이 그의 칼에 의해 베어져 산산조각 났다.

» **원문**

... He gave me a steady rein, I gathered myself well together, and with one determined leap cleared both dike and bank. ...

... One of the men jumped out, and stooped down over it. 'It is Ruben!' he said, 'and he does not stir.' ...

... 'Hallo! he's bad in his foot as well as his knees; look here-his hoof is cut all to pieces; he might well come down, poor fellow! ...

» **Note**

☐ gather oneself up[together]: 전력을 집중하다, 기운을 내다, 정신을 차리다

☐ Look here.=Say.: 여보세요.(주위를 환기시킬 때 쓰는 표현)

☐ stoop down over...: ...위를 굽어보다

☐ stir: 동요하다, 움직이다

☐ be cut all to pieces: 잘려 (모두) 산산조각나다(이 표현은 '결과'적으로 해석 하는 것이 좋다.)

They <u>were hard on</u> the captives.

: 그들은 포로들에게 <u>가혹하게[심하게]</u> 대했다.

I prepared for a small gift <u>in answer to</u> his kindness.

: 나는 그의 친절함에 <u>답하기 위해</u> 조그만 선물을 준비했다.

<u>Look out for</u> the icy field to skate on.

: 스케이트를 탈 그 얼음판을 <u>찾아보아라.</u>

» **원문**

… I shall never forget my new master; he had black eyes and a hooked nose. <u>He was hard on the men, and the men were hard on the horses.</u> …

… He gave me a kind pat on the neck. <u>I put out my nose in answer to his kindness</u>; the boy stroked my face. …

… 'Oh! grandpapa, <u>how glad I am you bought him</u>!' 'So am I, my boy, but he has to thank you more than me; we must now be <u>looking out for</u> a quiet genteel place for him, where he will be valued.' …

… After this it was quite decided to keep me and <u>call me by old name of</u> 'Black Beauty.' …

» **Note**

- □ be hard on…: …에 가혹[엄]하게 대하다
- □ How glad I am you bought him!=I am very glad (that) you bought him!: 당신이 그를 구입하다니 나는 얼마나 기쁜가!
- □ in answer to…: …에 답하여
- □ look out: …을 찾다(…for), 주위를 딴 데로 돌리다, 경계하다(…for), 주의하다(…for)
    ex) Look out for the icy sidewalk.: 그 빙판 길을 주의하라.

The Golden Touch in a Wonder–Book for Boys and Girls - Nathaniel Hawthorne

작품 소개: 작가에 의해 다시 각색된 그리스 신화의 6개의 전설에 관한 것이다. 1850년 4월과 7월 사이에 작가는 이「원더 북」을 썼다.

작가 소개: 대표작「주홍 글씨」(1850)는 청교도 엄격함의 교묘한 묘사, 죄인의 심리 추구, 긴밀한 세부구성, 정교한 상징주의로 19세기의 대표적 미국소설이 되었다.

A great idea <u>occurred to me</u>.

: 한 좋은 생각이 <u>나에게 떠올랐다</u>.

<u>The moment</u> she saw me she ran away as soon as possible.

: 그녀는 나를 보자마자 그녀는 가능한 빨리 줄행랑을 쳤다.

I don't have a mind to do that. It is just <u>a passing thought</u>.

: 나는 그것을 할 마음이 없다. 그것은 단지 <u>스쳐 가는 생각</u>뿐이다.

» **원문**

… So he thought, and thought, and thought. At last, <u>a bright idea occurred to him</u>. Raising his head, he looked the shinning stranger in the face. …

… He <u>lifted a spoonful of coffee to his lips</u>, and, tasting it, was surprised to find that, <u>the moment his lips touched it</u>, it became molten gold, and, the next moment, hardened into a lump! …

… These reflections so troubled wise King Midas, that he began to doubt whether, after all, riches are the one desirable thing in the world, or even the most desirable. <u>But this was only a passing thought</u>. …

» Note

- □ occur to...=happen to...: ...에게 발생하다
- □ a spoonful of (A): 한 숟가락[가득]의 (A)
  ex) a bucketful of water: 한 양동이 가득의 물
- □ the moment...=the instant...: ...하자마자
- □ a passing thought: 스처 가는 생각

She **started from her chair** when she heard a good news.

: 그녀는 좋은 소식을 들었을 때 <u>의자로부터 벌떡 일어섰다.</u>

The policeman <u>forced his way through</u> the crowd.

: 그 경찰은 군중을 <u>통하여 헤집고 지나갔다.</u>

» **원문**

... Then, with a sweet and sorrowful wish to comfort him, <u>she started from her chair</u>, and running to Midas, <u>threw her arms affectionately about his knees.</u> ...

... As he scampered along, and <u>forced his way through the bushes</u>, they turned yellow behind him, as if the autumn had been there, and nowhere else. On reaching the rivers's bank, he jumped headlong in, without waiting so much as to pull off his shoes. ...

» **Note**

- □ start: 뛰어 오르다, 벌떡 일어나다
  ex) start from one's chair: ...의자로부터 벌떡 일어서다
- □ throw: 던지다, 갑자기 움직이다
  ex) throw about...: ...둘레로[주위로] 던지다
- □ force one's way through...: ...향하여 길을 뚫고 지나가다

The Three Golden Apples
in a Wonder–book for Boys and Girls

- Nathaniel Hawthorne

작품 소개: 작가에 의해 다시 각색된 그리스 신화의 6개의 전설에 관한 것이다. 1850년 4월과 7월 사이에 작가는 이 「원더 북」을 썼다.

She took pleasure in helping the poor people.
: 그녀는 가난한 사람을 돕는 것을 낙으로 삼는다.

Keep fast hold of this rope lest you should fall into the river.
: 강 속으로 떨어지지 않도록 이 밧줄을 꽉 잡아라.

» 원문

... They took pleasure in helping him to this simple food ; and, now and then, one of them would put a sweet grape between her rosy lips, lest it should make him bashful to eat alone. ...

... Besides all this, he took to himself great credit for having cleaned out a stable. ...

... "Keep fast hold of the Old one, when you catch him!" ... Only hold him fast, and he will tell you what you wish to know." ...

... Sometimes he swung his club in the air, and broke in pieces a mighty oak with a single blow. ...

... What they have already done seems less than nothing. ...

» Note

☐ take pleasure in +...ing: ...하는 데 즐거움을 찾다
☐ lest ...should...: ...하지 않도록

214

- ☐ keep fast hold of...: ...을 꽉 잡다
- ☐ swing his club in the air: 허공 속으로 그의 곤봉을 빙빙 돌리다
- ☐ break in pieces: 산산조각나다
- ☐ with a single blow: 단 일격으로
- ☐ less than nothing: 전혀 무의미한
- ☐ take[get, have] (the) credit for...: ...을 자기의 공적으로 삼다
- ☐ take credit to oneself in...=take credit to oneself for...: ...을 자기의 공적으로 돌리다

As the fall is coming around, some leaves of trees begin to take on some colours.

: 가을이 다가옴에 따라, 일부 나뭇잎들이 어떤 색깔을 띠기 시작한다.

His ability was on a level with mine in solving the problem.

: 그 문제를 푸는 데 있어 그의 능력은 나의 능력과 같은 수준이다.

» **원문**

... You must understand that the Old Man of the Sea could take on any shape he pleased. ...

... Thanking the Old Man of the Sea, and begging his pardon for having handled him so roughly, the hero resumed his journey. ...

... Most wonderful of all, the giant held up his great hands and appeared to support the sky upon his head! This does really seem almost too much to believe. ...

... "But, if you were to take your stand on the summit of that nearest one, your head would be pretty nearly on a level with mine. You seem to be a fellow of some strength. What if you should take my burden on your shoulder, while I do your business for you?" ...

» **Note**

- ☐ take on...: ...을 띠다
- ☐ most wonderful of all: 모든 것 중 가장 놀라운 것은
- ☐ on a level with...: ...와 동일 수준에, ...에 동격으로
- ☐ what if...?: ...만약 ...한다면 어떤 일이 일어날까?

The Scarlet Letter

- Nathaniel Hawthorne

작품 소개: 17세기 미국의 어둡고 준엄한 청교도 사회를 배경으로, 죄지은 자의 고독한 심리를 묘사하였다. 치밀한 구성과 심오한 주제 등으로 19세기 미국문학의 걸작으로 꼽힌다.

The respectable professor <u>went so far out of the right way</u> and took the bribery from the students and gave a good grade to them.

: 그 명망 있는 교수는 <u>정도에서 너무 어긋났다</u>, 그리고 그의 제자들로부터 뇌물을 받았고 그들에게 좋은 학점을 주었다.

The uniform of the soccer player came <u>in harmonious combination of</u> the blue jacket and white trunk.

: 그 축구 선수의 유니폼은 푸른색 상의와 흰색의 반바지<u>의 조화로운 조합을</u> 이루었다.

The old woman <u>looked hard at her family</u>.

: 그 노파는 <u>그녀의 가족을 빤히 쳐다보았다</u>.

» 원문

… "People say," another said, "the Reverend Mr. Dimmesdale is greatly grieve.d that a woman under his care should have <u>gone so far out of the right way</u>." …

… At that moment the wearer of the scarlet letter discerned, on the outskirts of the crowd, an Indian in his native dress and a white man <u>in a strange combination of civilized and savage clothing</u>. …

… During this conversation, <u>Hester Prynne was looking hard at the stranger</u>-so hard that there were moments when all other objects in the visible world seemed to vanish, leaving only him and her, which would be terrible. …

» Note

- □ go so far out of the right way.: 정도로부터 너무 멀리 일탈하다
- □ in a combination of…: …와의 조합 속에서
- □ look hard at…: …를 빤히 쳐다보다

Her cheerful and husky voice <u>called his attention</u> in the midnight.

: 그녀의 명랑하고 쉰듯한 목소리는 한 밤중에 <u>그의 주목을 끌었다</u>.

We <u>are</u> all <u>responsible for</u> our future lives.

: 우리는 우리의 미래의 삶에 <u>대하여 책임을 저야 한다</u>.

» 원문

… The voice that <u>called her attention</u> was that of the Reverend John Wilson, the eldest clergyman of Boston. …

… But he opposes me, saying that it would be wrong to force you to lay open your heart's secrets in such broad daylight and in the presence of so many people. …

… "Mr. Dimmesdale," he said, <u>you are responsible for this woman's soul</u>. "It is your duty, therefore, to exhort her to repentance and confession." …

What good does it do to harm this poor beggar?

: 이와 같은 불쌍한 거지에게 해를 가하는 것은 무슨 소용이 있나요?

I feel sorry I would wrong all of you without my intention.

: 본의 아니게 당신 모두에게 모욕을 준 것을 죄송하게 생각합니다.

What had I to do with those faults?

: 내가 그 잘못들과 무슨 관계가 있나요?

» 원문

... "Foolish woman!" responded the physician. "What good does it do to harm this unhappy child? ...

... "I have greatly wronged you," Hester murmured. "We have wronged each other," he answered. "What had I, such a misshapen bookworm as I am, to do with youth and beauty like your own? ...

» Note

☐ What good...?: 무슨 이익 ...?
  rf) do good: 이익이 되다, 도움을 주다

☐ wrong: 모욕을 주다, 오해하다

☐ (A) have (B) to do with (C): (A)는 (C)와 (B)한 관계에 있다
  ex) I had what to do with her.: 나는 그녀와 무슨 관계가 있었다. (즉, 이것을 의문문으로 고치면, What had I to do with her?: 내가 그녀와 무슨 관계가 있었는가?)

I threw open the door and rushed into the room to announce the good news.

: 좋은 소식을 알리기 위해 나는 <u>문을 활짝 열고</u> 방안으로 들어갔다.

You don't look well. It shows itself in your face.

: 당신은 건강이 좋지 않은 것처럼 보이는군요. 그것은 당신의 얼굴에 <u>나타나 있어요.</u>

» **원문**

… Hester Prynne's <u>term</u> of <u>confinement</u> came to an end. <u>Her prison door was thrown open</u>, and she <u>came forth</u> into the sunshine, which seemed to her sick heart to reveal the scarlet letter on her breast. …

… "<u>A bodily sickness</u>," the physician said one day, "<u>is but a sign of some spiritual disease. A sickness in your spirit immediately shows itself in your body</u>. …

… "You have such a friend in me!" Again she hesitated but brought out the words with an effort. "And you have long had such an enemy and lived with him under the same roof!" …

» **Note**

☐ term: 형기
☐ throw open: 문 따위가 홱하고 열다[열리다]
☐ come forth…: …로 나오다
☐ a sigh of…: …의 신호
☐ show itself: 스스로 보여주다[나타나다]

A young man <u>thrust himself through</u> the crowd and announced the news of breaking out a war.

: 한 젊은 남자가 군중 속으로 뚫고 지나갔다. 그리고 전쟁이 발발했다는 소식을 알렸다.

They <u>support me up that stage</u> and let me give a congratulatory speech.

: 그들은 나를 무대 위로 부축해 올렸다 그리고 나로 하여금 축하 연설을 하도록 허락했다.

» **원문**

... At this instant old Roger Chillingworth <u>thrust himself through the crowd and rushed forward</u>. "Madman! What are you going to do?" he whispered. "<u>Wave back that woman!</u> ...

... To do what I could not do seven years ago, come here now and support me. <u>Support me up that scaffold!</u>" ...

» **Note**

- □ thrust oneself through...: ...을 통하여 헤치고[뚫고] 나가다
- □ wave back: 답례로 손을 흔들다
    cf) wave: 손을 흔들다.
- □ support: 지지[지탱]하다
- □ up: ...위로

David Swan

- Nathaniel Hawthorne

작품 소개: 단편 소설인 「David Swan」은 David라는 인물이 한 시간 동안 잠을 자는 동안 일어난 이야기를 다루고 있다.

I am a native of Seoul.

: 나는 서울 토박이다.

» **원문**

… David Swan was a native of New Hampshire, born of respectable parents, and had received an ordinary school education, with a classic finish by a year at Gilmanton Academy. …

… How sweet a picture! This good deed accomplished, with quickened breath, and a deeper blush, she stole a glance at the youthful stranger for whom she had been battling with a dragon in the air. …

» **Note**

- □ a native: 토박이, 원주민
- □ born of…: …로부터 태어난
- □ classic finish: 고전과정 수료
- □ steal a glance at…: …을 힐끗 보다

048

The Great Stone Face
- Nathaniel Hawthorne

작품 소개: 나다니엘 호손의 대표적인 단편 「큰 바위 얼굴」은 성말 뛰어난 것은 논이나 냉예, 권력과 같은 것이 아니라 끊임없는 자기 성찰을 거쳐 얻어진 말과 사상과 삶의 일치라는 평범한 진리를 말해준다. 이 작품은 조그만 골짜기 마을에서 태어나고 일생을 살았던 어니스트와 그 조그만 마을을 떠나 더 큰 세상으로 나갔던 4명을 대비 시켜 이야기를 풀어나가고 있다.

I did see little or no likeness about the twines.
: 나는 그 쌍둥이에 관해 거의 또는 어떤 유사성도 못 보았다.

The old gentleman bent forward to see it closely.
: 그 노인은 그것을 자세히 보기 위해 몸을 앞으로 굽혔다.

» **원문**

... "No!" said Ernest, bluntly, "I see little or no likeness." ...
... As Ernest listened to the poet, he imagined that the Great Stone Face was bending forward to listen too. He gazed earnestly into the poet's glowing eyes. ...

» **Note**

- □ little or no likeness about...: ...관해 거의 또는 어떤 유사성이 없는
- □ bend forward to+동원: ...하기 위해 앞으로 몸을 구부리다

049

Sir Isaac Newton

- Nathaniel Hawthorne

작품 소개: 아이작 뉴턴(1642~1727)과 관련된 전기물이다. (아이작 뉴턴은 물리학자이자 천문학자이며 수학자로 역학 체계를 세우고 만유인력의 원리를 도입했다. 또한 미적분 창시와 빛의 스펙트럼 분석 등의 공적을 남겼다. 1687년 프린키피아(자연철학의 수학적 원리)를 저술했다. 근대과학 성립의 최대 공로자다. 후에 지폐국 장관 및 영국왕립협회장을 역임했다.)

The war orphan was left <u>to the care of</u> the famous social worker.

: 그 전쟁고아는 유명한 사회사업가<u>의 보호 하</u>에 맡겨졌다.

<u>With the aid of</u> some rich men, the homeless can manage to live.

: 몇몇의 부자들<u>의 도움으로</u> 그 집 없는 사람들은 그럭저럭 살아가게 되었다.

» 원문

… Isaac's father being dea.d, Mrs. Newton was married again to a clergyman, and went to reside at North Witham. Her son was left <u>to the care of</u> his good old grandmother, who was very kind to him and sent him to school. In his early years Isaac did not appear to be a very bright scholar, but was chiefly remarkable for his ingenuity in all mechanical occupations. He had a set of little tools and saws of various sizes manufactured by himself. <u>With the aid of these</u> Isaac contrived to make many curious articles, at which he worked <u>with so much skill</u> that he seemed to have been born with a saw or chisel in hand. …

» **Note**

  □ to the care of...: ...의 보호아래
  □ with the aid of...: ...의 도움으로
  □ with skill: 기술로 기술을 가지고

When I was a young boy, I had a taste for a fine art.
: 내가 어린 소년이었을 때 나는 미술에 취미가 있었다.

In due time, come and see me.
: 적절한 때에 나를 보러 오세요.

I was suspected of stealing some books.
: 나는 약간의 책을 훔쳤다고 혐의를 받았다.

» **원문**

... Others probably thought that little Isaac was destinate.d to be an architect, and would build splendid mansions for the nobility and gentry, and churches too, with the tallest steeples that had ever been seen in England. ...

... The boy seemed to have a taste for mathematics, which would be very useful to him in that profession. And then, in due time, Isaac would set up for himself, and would manufacture curious clocks ...

... To be sure, he had not a very good character for honesty, and was suspected of sometimes stealing a portion of the grain which was given him to grind. ...

» **Note**

  □ be destinate.d to 동원: ...하도록 운명지워지다
  □ have a taste for...: ...에 취미[취향]를 가지고 있다
  □ in due time: 적절[당]한 때에
  □ set up oneself: 자립하다, 스스로 개업하다
  □ be suspected of...: ...에 대해 의심[혐의]을 받다

When I was left to myself, I was usually absorbed in reading.

: 홀로 남겨져 있을 때 나는 보통 책을 읽는데 몰입했다.

In her free time, she turns her attention to knitting

: 자유로운 시간에 그녀는 그녀의 주의력을 뜨개질하는 데 돌린다.

» **원문**

… All day long, if left to himself, he was either absorbed in thought or engaged in some book of mathematics or natural philosophy. …

… For a year or two, therefore, he tried to turn his attention to farming. But his mind was so bent becoming a scholar that his mother sent him back to school, and afterwards to the University of Cambridge. …

» **Note**

☐ left to…: …에 남겨져 있는

☐ be absorbed in…=be engaged in…: …에 몰입[열중]에 있다

☐ turn one's attention to…: …의 주의력을 …로 돌리다

Newton lived to be a ninety year old man.

: Newton은 살아 90세의 노인이 되었다.

I care little for gambling.

: 나는 도박에는 거의 관심이 없다.

... Newton lived to be a very old man, and acquired great renown, and was made a member of Parliament, and received the honour of knighthood from the king. But he cared little for earthly fame and honors, and felt no pride in the vastness of his knowledge. All that he had learned only made him feel how little he knew in comparison to what remained to be known. ...

... But this sort of ingenuity is but a mere trifle in comparison with the other talents of such men." ...

... But what would Newton have done had he been blind? or if his eyes had been no better than mine?" ...

» Note

- □ grow to 동원=자라서...이 되다
- □ care little for...에 대해 거의 관심이 없다
- □ in comparison to[with]...: ...에 비교해 보아
- □ What would Newton have done had he been blind?: 만약에 Newton이 장님이었다면 무슨 일을 했을까?('가정법 과거완료'로 주절의 If가 생략되었기 때문에 if he had been blind가 Had it been blind로 도치가 됨.)

050

Biographical Stories

- Nathaniel Hawthorne

작품 소개: Benjamin Franklin(미국의 정치가이면서 과학자(1706~90))의 전기 이야기다.

We <u>are</u> all <u>expected to be punished</u> because of cheating.

: 우리들 모두는 부정행위 때문에 <u>벌 받기로 되어있다.</u>

In his manhood, Schweizer <u>contributed to treating</u> the sick Africans.

: 청년시절에 Schweizer는 병든 아프리카인들을 <u>치료하는데 이바지했다.</u>

» 원문

… But on those days boys <u>were expected to be silent</u> in the presence of their elders. However, Ben Franklin was looked upon as a very promising lad, who would talk and act wisely by and by. …

… Thus, you see, <u>in his early days, as well as in his manhood</u>, his labors <u>contributed to</u> throwing light upon dark matters. …

… "How can that be, father?" asked Ben. "Because," answered his father, "in building your wharf with stolen materials, <u>you have committed a moral wrong</u>. There is no more terrible mistake than to violate what is eternally right <u>for the sake of</u> a seeming expediency. <u>Those who act upon such a principle</u> do utmost in their power to destroy all that is good in the world." …

    □ be expected to...: ...하기로 기대[예상]되다
    □ in one's early day: ...의 유년시절에
    □ in one's manhood: ...의 청년시절에
    □ contribute to (동)명사: ...하는 데 공헌[이바지]하다
    □ for the sake of...: ...을 위하여
    □ act on...: ...에 따라 행동하다

I bought three thousand won worth of notebooks yesterday.

: 나는 3천원 가격의 공책을 어제 샀다.

After playing three games straight, I was worn out and fell fast asleep.

: 세 게임을 계속한 후에 나는 거의 탈진에 되어 곧 잠에 푹 빠졌다.

The deal was suited to our condition.

: 그 협상[거래]은 우리의 조건에 잘 맞는다.

» 원문

... In this way our friend Benjamin spent his boyhood and youth, until, on account of some disagreement with his brother, he left his native town and went to Philadelphia. He landed in the latter city, a homeless and hungry young man, and bought threepence worth of bread to satisfy his appetite. Not knowing where else to go, he entered a Quaker meeting-house, sat down, and fell fast asleep. ...
... "I have read some of those proverbs," remarked Edward; "but I do not like them. They are all about getting money or saving it." "Well," said his father, "they were suited to the condition of the country; and their effect, upon the whole, has doubtless been good, although they teach men but a very small portion of their duties." ...

» Note

    □ on account of...: ... 때문에
    □ three pence of bread: 3펜스 가격의 빵
    □ be suited to...: ...에 어울리다[잘 맞다]
    □ a small portion of (A): 매우 작은 부분[몫]의 (A)

051

The Bible Story

- Nathaniel Hawthorne

작품 소개: 성경에 관한 이야기를 집약해 알기 쉽게 스토리 형식으로 쓴 이야기다.

They shall be praised for some good conducts.
: 그들은 선행 때문에 칭찬 받을 것이다.[우리가 그들을 칭찬해줄 것이다.]

I never tell a lie in the sight of my teacher.
: 나는 담임선생님 앞에서 전혀 거짓말하지 않는다.

By degrees, the rain cloud began to clear.
: 점진적으로, 비구름이 걷히기 시작했다.

» 원문

… And God said to Cain, "If any one harms Cain, he shall be punished for it." And the Lord God placed a mark on Cain, so that whoever met him should know him, and should know also that God had forbidden any man to harm him. …

… But even in those bad times God saw one good man. His name was Noah. Noah tried to do right in the sight of God, and talked with him. and Noah had three sons; their names were Sem, and Ham, and Japheth. …

… Then God sent a wind to blow over the waters, and to dry them up ; so by degrees the waters grew less and less. First mountains rose above the waters, then the hills rose up, and finally the ark ceased to float and lay on a mountain which is called Mount Ararat. …

□ he shall be punished for it: 그는 그것 때문에 벌을 받게 될 것이다

□ in the sight of...: ...이 보는 가운데, ...의 앞에

□ by degrees: 점진적으로

□ grew less and less: 점점 더 덜해졌다[적어졌다]

Every time the boss <u>looked down on</u> his men.

: 매번 사장은 그의 직원들을 멸시했다.

» **원문**

... The little girl-who was Miriam, the baby's sister ran quickly as she could and brought the baby's own mother to the princess. Miriam showed in this act that she was a wise and thoughtful little girl. ...

... She named him "Moses," a word that means "drawn out," because he was drawn out of the water. So Moses, the Hebrew boy, lived in the place among the nobles of the land, as the son of the princess. ...

... So Samuel chose as their king a tall young man named Saul, who was a farmer's son of the tribe of Benjamin. ...

... And all the people shout, "<u>God save the king! Long live the king!</u>" ...

... They showed no respect to the king, and in their hearts <u>looked down on</u> him. But Saul said nothing, and showed his wisdom by appearing not to notice them. But in another thing he was not so wise. ...

» **Note**

□ God save the king!: 주여 왕을 구해주소서!

□ Long live the king!: 왕이여 장수하시길 기원합니다!

□ look down on...: ...을 멸시하다

The pop star is plain <u>in his look</u>, but agreeable <u>in talking</u>, so he is very popular with his fans.

: 그 팝 스타는 <u>외모는</u> 평범하지만 <u>말하는 방법은</u> 부드럽다. 그러므로 그의 팬들에게 인기가 높다.

The two sides <u>were set against</u> each other to fight against each other.

: 양측은 상대방과 싸우기 위해 <u>대치하고 있었다.</u>

They <u>fell down on their faces</u> to avoid the flying shots.

: 그들은 날아가는 탄환들을 피하기 위하여 <u>그들의 얼굴을 대고 엎드렸다.</u>

» **원문**

… One of the young man said: "I have seen a young man, a son of Jesse in Bethlehem, who can play well. <u>He is handsome in his looks, and agreeable in talking.</u> …

… At one time, when David was still with his sheep, the camps of the Philistines and the Israelites <u>were set against</u> each other on opposite sides of the valley of Elah. …

… They knew at once that this was the king; and they <u>fell down on</u> their faces and worshipped him as the Lord. Then they brought out gifts of gold and precious perfumes, frankincense, and myrrh, which were used in offering sacrifices; and they gave them as presents to the royal child. …

» **Note**

☐ in one's looks: …의 외모는
☐ in talking: 말하는 태도는
☐ be set against…: …에 대치상태에 있다
☐ fall down on one's faces: 얼굴을 대고 엎드리다

231

052

Little Woman

- Louisa May Alcott

작품 소개: 어려운 가정환경에도 아름답고 당당하게 성장하는 네 자매 이야기다. 네 자매는 서로를 오해하고 다투기도 하지만 결국 가족의 소중함을 깨달으며 조금씩 더 성장하게 된다.

작가 소개: 1832년 미국 펜실베이니아에서 태어났다. 어렸을 때부터 집안 살림을 위해 가정교사, 가사 도우미 등 다양한 일을 해 왔다. 자신의 경험을 바탕으로 한 「병원 스케치」, 「작은 아씨들」 등의 작품으로 독자들의 사랑을 받았다.

She is very <u>particular and prim</u> about her food.

: 그녀는 음식에 특히 <u>까다롭고 꼼꼼해.</u>

The meeting ended in <u>a burst of laughter.</u>

: 그 회의는 <u>한 바탕의 웃음</u>과 함께 끝났다.

» **원문**

... I know I do, ... , when I'm longing to enjoy myself at home," began Meg, in the complaining tone again. "You don't have half such a hard time as I do," said Jo. ...

... It didn't matter so much when you were a little girl; but now you are so tall, and <u>turn up your hair</u>, you should remember that you are a young lady." ...

... As for you, Amy," continued Meg, "<u>you are altogether too particular and prim. Your airs are funny</u> now, but you'll grow up an affected little goose if you don't take care. ...

... "No, it's the toasting-fork, with mother's shoes on it instead of the bread. Beth's stage-struck!" cried Meg, and <u>the rehearsal ended in a general burst of laughter.</u> ...

» **Note**

- □ half such a hard time as...: ...만큼의 그렇게 어려운 시간의 반
- □ turn one's hair: ...의 머리를 틀어 올리다
- □ particular and prim: 까다롭고 꼼꼼한
- □ airs: 뽐내는 태도
- □ a burst of laughter: 한 바탕의 웃음

They enjoyed their welcoming party to their heart's content.

: 그들은 <u>마음껏</u> 그들의 환영 파티를 즐겼다.

The enemy took their breath away by making surprise attack.

: 적은 불시의 기습공격을 함으로써 <u>그들을 놀라게 했다.</u>

» **원문**

... Hannah, who had carried wood, made a fire, and stopped up the broken panes with old hats and her own cloak. ...

... No gentlemen were admitted; so Jo played male parts to her heart's content, and took immense satisfaction in a pair of russet-leather boots given her by a friend, who knew a lady who knew an actor. ...

... It very took their breath away; and they stared first at the table and then at their mother, who looked as if she enjoyed it immensely. ...

... What in the world put such a thing into his head? We don't know him!" exclaimed Meg. ...

... but says he's very proud, and doesn't like to mix with his neighbours. He keeps grandson shut up when he isn't riding or walking with his tutor, and makes him study very hard. ...

233

» **Note**

- stop (up) A with B: A를 B로 채우다
- admit: 입장시키다, 입회시키다
- play a part: 역할을 하다
- to one's heart content: ... 마음껏
- take one's breath away: ... 깜짝 놀라게 하다
- mix with...: ...와 교제하다, 어울리다
- shut up: 격리시키다

    ex) keep (A) shut up: (A)를 격리된 상태로 유지시키다

053

After Twenty Years

- O. Henry

작품 소개: 「20년 후」는 어릴 적 약속을 지키기 위해 20년 만에 만난 두 친구의 이야기다. 20년이란 긴 세월 동안 각자의 삶을 살다 약속의 날 약속의 장소에서 만나게 된 Bob과 Jimmy, 그들은 사뭇 다른 삶을 살고 있다. 마지막 장면에서 Bob이 Jimmy의 편지를 읽는 순간, Bob은 Jimmy가 누구인지 알게 되는데…

작가 소개: 서민의 삶을 다채롭게 그려낸 300여 편의 그의 작품은 유머와 인간애가 넘치며 특히 '오 헨리식 결말'이라는 이름이 붙을 정도로 반전 있는 결말로 잘 알려져 있다. 그의 이야기의 주제를 이루는 휴머니티는 여전히 우리에게 독특한 따뜻함을 느끼게 해 준다.

The old building was <u>torn down</u> by strong wind yesterday.

: 그 낡은 건물은 어제 강풍에 의해 <u>허물어졌다.</u>

There <u>used to be</u> a mill house right here long ago.

: 오래전에 방앗간이 바로 <u>여기에 있었다.</u>

Where are you going, Max? I am <u>on the way</u> home.

: 어디에 가고 있니? 집에 가는 중이야.

» **원문**

… About that <u>long ago there used to be a restaurant</u> where this store stands-'Big Joe' Brady's restaurant." "Until five years ago," said the policeman. "it <u>was torn down then</u>." …

… "Did pretty well out West, didn't you?" asked the policeman. "<u>You bet!</u> I hope Jimmy has done half as well. …

… The policeman twirled his club and took a step or two. "<u>I'll be on my way</u>. Hope your friend comes around all right. …

» **Note**

- □ used to+동사의 원형: ...이었다(즉, 지금은 아니다)
- □ tear down: 허물다
- □ You bet!: 정말이야!
  - *cf*) You bet?: 정말이야?
- □ I'll on the way: 나는 계속 할 것이다.
  - *cf*) on the way: 계속 하는[진행]중에 있는

He hung about at the park <u>with coat turned high</u>.

: 그는 <u>코트 깃을 올린 채로</u> 공원을 어슬렁거렸다.

Is that you, Tom?

: <u>그게 바로 너냐</u>, Tom?

» **원문**

... The few foot passengers astir in that quarter hurried dismally and silently along <u>with coat turned high</u> and pocketed hands. ...

... About twenty minutes he waited, and then a tall man in a overcoat, <u>with collar turned up to his ears</u>, hurried across, from the opposite side of the street. ...

... He went directly to the waiting man. "<u>Is that you, Bob?</u>" he asked, doubtfully. "Is that you, Jimmy Wells?" cried the man in the door. ...

» **Note**

- □ with 목적어(A) 목적보어(B): (A)가 (B)한 채로('부대상황'의 뜻)
  - *ex*) with collar turned up to his ears: 칼라를 목까지 올린 채로
- □ Is that you, (A)?: 그것이 당신이냐 (A)?(상대방을 뜻밖으로 만났을 때 놀라며 묻는 말)

054

A Retrieved Reformation

- O. Henry

작품 소개: 주인공 Jimmy Valentine(지미 발렌타인)은 주로 은행의 금고를 따서 먹고사는 일을 한다. 스프링필드(Spring field)라는 곳에서 잡히는 바람에 감옥 생활을 하던 중에 자기 친구의 도움으로 특별사면을 받게 된다. 그러나 지미 발렌타인이 출소한 지 2일 후 또다시 금고가 깨끗이 털리는 사건이 발생하는데…

Brace up, you can win the game.
: 힘을 내, 너는 그 경기를 이길 수가 있다.

As he grew up, Bill made a man of himself.
: 계속 자라며, Bill은 사람다운 사람이 되었다.

I didn't help a friend of mine (to) succeed in his job. So my friend had it in for me.
: 나는 나의 친구가 성공하는 것을 도와주지 않았다. 그러므로 그는 나에게 원한을 품었다.

» 원문

… Now, Valentine," said the warden, "you'll go out in the morning. Brace up, and make a man of yourself. You're not a bad fellow at heart. Stop cracking safe, and live straight." …
… Or was it simply a case of a mean old jury that had it in for you? It's always one or the other with you innocent victims." …
… "Got any thing on? asked Mike Dolan, genially. "Me?" said Jimmy, in a puzzled tone. "I don't understand I'm representing the New York Amalgamated Short Snap Biscuit Cracker and Frazzled Wheat Company. …

» Note

- brace up: 힘을 내다
- Make a man of yourself.: 사람다운 사람이 되시오.
- at heart: 마음은
- jury: 배심원, 심사위원회
- had it in for…: …에 대하여 원한을 품다
- (Have you) got anything on?: 무얼 할 작정인가?

237

055

The Cop and the Anthem

- O. Henry

작품 소개 부랑자인 소피는 겨울이 다가오자 하루 세끼를 무료로 먹으며 겨울을 날 수 있는 교도소에 가기로 결심한다. 그래서 돈 없이 식당에 들어가서 식사를 하고, 가게의 진열창을 깨는 등 나쁜 행동을 하지만, 교도소에 가는 것은 매번 실패하고 만다. 그러다 우연히 교회에서 흘러나오는 아름다운 찬송가를 듣고 꿈과 희망을 되찾겠다고 결심하지만, 그 순간 교회 앞에서 서성거렸다는 이유로 교도소에 가게 된다.

What has this job to do with me?

: 이 일이 나와 무슨 관계가 있습니까?

She all the time has an excuse to go home early.

: 그녀는 늘 집에 일찍 가기 위한 변명을 일삼는다.

» **원문**

... An old, old ivy vine, gnarled and decayed at the roots, climbed half way up the brick wall. ...

... "What have old ivy leaves to do with your getting well? And you used to love that vine so, you naughty girl. ...

... I want to turn loose my hold on everything, and go sailing down, down, just like one of those poor, exhausted leaves. ...

... No, I will not pose as a model for your fool hermit-dunderhead. ...

... The doctor came in the afternoon, and Sue had an excuse to go into hallway as he left. ...

» **Note**

- □ half way up: 반쯤 위로
- □ have what to do with...: ...와 무슨 관련이 있다
- □ turn loose: 풀어주다
- □ go sailing down: 날려 떨어지다, 아래로 침몰하다[미끄러지다]
- □ pose as a model: 모델로써 자세[포즈]를 취하다
- □ have an excuse to...: ...하기 위한 변명을 만들어내다

056

The Sketch Book

- Washington Irving

작품 소개: 영국을 방문한 미국인으로서의 견문기를 중심으로 영국의 전통과 미국의 전설을 은연중에 대비시키며 묘사하고 있다. 수록된 작품의 일반적 경향은 작가가 현실 세계에서 느끼고 있던 위화감과 과거의 세계에서 품고 있던 향수를 나타내고 있다.

작가 소개: 워싱턴 어빙(Washington Irving)(1783~1859)은 미국 최초의 소설가로 꼽히는 인물이다. 그는 주로 미국의 독립을 전후한 사회상을 작품으로 그려냈다.

His words added fuel to my rage.
: 그의 말은 <u>나의 격정을 더욱 키웠다</u>.

When his wife nags at him, he usually beats a hasty retreat and gets out of his room.
: 그의 아내가 그에게 바가지를 긁을 때, 그는 보통 <u>한 발 뒤로 물러선다</u>. 그리고 방으로부터 빠져나간다.

» **원문**

> … <u>The greatest defect in Rip</u> was his unsurmountable dislike for all kinds of useful labor. <u>This disposition</u> could not be from the want of industry or patience. …
>
> … This, however, always <u>added fuel to her rage</u> and made her abuse him afresh; so that he had usually to <u>beat a hasty retreat</u> and go to the outside of the house …

» **Note**

 □ beat a retreat: (1)북을 쳐서 황급히 후퇴를 알리다 (2)도망가다, 후퇴하다 (3) 사업에서 손을 떼다

 □ add fuel to rage(or, the fire, the flame): 불에 기름을 붓다, 격정을 더욱 키우다

At these words, I was very encouraged and got to try my best.

: 이 말을 듣고, 나는 고무되었고 결국은 최선을 다하게 되었다.

When I was left alone at home, I felt a vague uneasiness rising within me.

: 나 홀로 집에 남게 되었을 때, 나는 막연한 불안감이 내부로부터 일어나는 것을 느꼈다.

» **원문**

... At these words Wolf would wag his tail, look his master in the face attentively, and if dogs have feelings, I firmly believe he shared the sentiment with all his heart. ...

... Rip now felt a vague uneasiness rising within him; he looked anxiously in the same direction, and noticed a strange man slowly coming up the valley ...

» **Note**

☐ at these words: 바로 이 말에, 이 말을 듣고

☐ look 목적어(A) in the face: (A)의 얼굴을 들여다보다

   ex» look his master in the face: 그의 주인의 얼굴을 들여다보다

☐ feel a vague uneasiness rising within him: 막연한 불안감이 내부에서 일어나는 것을 느끼다

When he saw the big boy as a fighting partner, <u>his heart turned within him.</u>

: 그가 그 덩치 큰 소년을 보았을 때, <u>그는 기가 꺾였다.</u>

I <u>am tempted to eat</u> it easily whenever I see any kind of food.

: 어느 종류의 음식을 볼 때마다 나는 그것을 <u>먹도록</u> 쉽게 <u>유혹 받는다.</u>

» **원문**

... As Rip and his companion approached them they suddenly stopped playing, and stared at him with such fixed gaze, and with strange, clumsy, spiritless countenances, that <u>his heart turned within him</u> and his knees knocked each other. ...

... He was <u>by nature</u> fond of alcoholic drinks, and was <u>tempted to</u> drink much more freely. ...

» **Note**

☐ his heart turned within him: 그의 기가 꺾였다
☐ by nature: 천성적으로
☐ be tempted to+동사의 원형: ...하도록 유혹 받다

He was walking up to his house in a hurry and <u>tripped up</u> on a rock.

: 그는 그의 집으로 황급히 가고 있었다. 그리고 돌덩이에 <u>걸려 넘어졌다.</u>

He came back to his home <u>with a heavy heart</u> when he heard his house was burnt down.

: 그는 그의 집이 불에 탔다는 것을 들었을 때 <u>무거운 마음으로</u> 그의 집으로 돌아왔다.

» 원문

... He whistled after him and called his name, but all was in vain; the echoes repeated his whistle and call, but no dog put up its appearance. ...

... and being sometimes <u>tripped up</u> or entangled by the wild grapevines that twisted their coils or tendrils from tree to tree, and spread a kind of network in his path. ...

... As he rose to walk, <u>he found himself stiff in the knee-joints</u> and wanting in his usual activity. ...

... with a <u>heavy heart full of and anxiety</u>, turned his steps toward home. ...

» **Note**

- □ trip up: 넘어지다
- □ entangle: 엉키다
- □ with a heavy heart: 무거운 마음으로

My teacher always <u>calls</u> us <u>by name</u>.

: 나의 선생님은 항상 <u>이름으로</u> 우리를 <u>부르신다.</u>

I <u>was given a cold shoulder</u> from my room mate who, I believed, loved me very much. That was <u>the most unkind cut of all.</u>

: 나는 나를 대단히 사랑한다고 믿었던 방 동료부터 냉대를 받았다. 그것은 모든 것 중 가장 불친절한 처사였다.

» 원문

... <u>Rip called him by name</u>, but the dog barked, showed his teeth, and went away. <u>This was the most unkindest cut of all.</u> ...

... In place of these, a lean gloomy-looking fellow, with his pockets full of handbills, <u>was making a loud harangue</u> about rights of citizens ...

» Note

□ call ...by name: 이름으로 ... 을 부르다
□ the most unkindest cut of all: 가장 불친절한 처사
□ make a harangue: 장황한 연설을 하다

With a knowing air, he is explaining something in front of the classmates.

: 아는 척하는 태도를 가지고 그는 항상 급우들 앞에 나와 무언가를 설명하고 있다.

He stands up with one arm akimbo.

: 그는 한쪽 팔을 허리에 대고 서 있다.

» 원문

... At this moment, a self-important gentleman, with a knowing air, who wore a sharp cocked hat, made his way through the crowd and pushed them to the right and left with his elbows as he passed. Then he planted himself before Van Winkle, with one arm akimbo and the other resting on his cane, his keen eyes and sharp hat penetrating, as it were, into his very soul. ...

» Note

□ plant oneself: 자리 잡다, 서다, 지위를 확보하다
□ akimbo: 손을 허리에 대고 팔꿈치를 굽혀서
　　ex) stand with arms akimbo: 양손을 허리에 대고 팔꿈치를 굽히고 서다
□ as we were: 즉, 말하자면

The Necklace(adapted)

- **Maupassant**

‖ **작품 소개:** 주인공 루와젤은 친구 프레스티에 부인의 목걸이를 빌려 무도회에 나간다. 그러나 무도회에서 돌아오다가 루와젤은 목걸이를 잃어버리고, 빚을 내어 다른 다이아몬드 목걸이를 사서 되돌려준다. 루와젤은 10년 동안에 걸쳐 빚과 이자를 갚은 후 그것이 가짜였다는 것을 알게 된다.

‖ **작가 소개:** 「비곗덩어리(Boule De Suif)」로 문단에 데뷔한 모파상은 이후 장편소설 「여자의 일생(A Woman's Life, 1883)」 등을 발표하며 프랑스를 대표하는 작가가 되었다. 인간의 한계와 전쟁의 비인간성을 날카롭게 그려낸 그의 작가정신은 오늘날까지 높이 평가되고 있다.

What's that to me?

: 그것을 내가 알아 무얼 해요?

It occurred to me that he left for the England without notice.

: 예고 없이 그가 영국으로 떠났다는 생각이 나에게 번뜩 떠올랐다.

» **원문**

… She did not seem delighted. On the contrary she flung the invitation card on the table, and said spitefully: "What's that to me?" …

… "What do you expect me to wear at a party like that?" It occurred to him that she had no pretty dresses nor jewels. He replied hesitatingly: "Why, the dress you wear when you go to the theater looks very nice to me?" …

… She burst into tears. Why did she marry such dull, stupid fellow? Only because she was born into a poor family. Oh, cruel trick of destiny! …

» Note

□ What's that to me?=What is that related to me?: 내가 그까짓 것 알아서 무얼 해요?

□ It occurred to them that...: ...하는 것이 그들에게 번뜩 떠오르다

□ burst into tears: 갑자기 울음을 터뜨리다

□ cruel trick of destiny: 잔인한 운명의 장난

<u>Mind</u> you're their teacher when you behave before them.

: 당신이 그들 앞에서 행동할 때 그들의 선생님이라는 것을 명심하시오.

You're <u>out of sort</u> today. How come?

: 당신은 오늘 기분이 언짢은 것처럼 보입니다. 왜 그러시죠?

» 원문

... "I'm not sure, but I think <u>I could manage with four hundred francs.</u>" ...

... "All right. You shall have four hundred francs. <u>Mind you get a really nice dress.</u>" ...

... "What is the matter?" her husband asked. "<u>You look out of sorts these days.</u>" ...

... "The diamond necklace is gone!" "<u>What? How? Impossible!</u>" They searched the folds of her skirt and cloak, her pockets, everywhere ; but <u>the necklace was nowhere to be seen.</u> "<u>You had it on when you left the ball?</u>" ...

» Note

□ manage: 그럭저럭 해내다, 관리[경영]하다

□ out of sort: 짜증이 나는, 시무룩한

□ nowhere to be seen: 어느 곳에서도 보이지 않는

□ had (A) on: (A)를 입고 있었다

She flung oneself from the room.

: 그녀는 방으로부터 날듯이 나왔다.

She wore the very picture of despair when she was omitted from the visit application form.

: 그녀는 그녀가 방문 신청서에 누락되었다는 것을 알았을 때 실망의 표정을 지었다.

At last she reported to the police the fact that she had been stalked from somebody.

: 그녀는 마침내 그녀가 누군가에 의해 미행되어왔다는 사실을 경찰에 신고했다.

» **원문**

... He hurried out. She flung herself down in a chair, and remained there blankly, the very picture of despair. About seven o'clock he returned empty-handed, then he reported to the police and made inquires among the horse-riding company ...

... They bought nothing except daily necessaries, which they tried to do without often enough ...

» **Note**

☐ fling oneself down: 몸을 날려 앉다
☐ blankly: 멍하니
☐ the very picture of despair: 바로 그 실망의 상[모습]
☐ report to...: ...에 보고[신고]하다
☐ daily necessaries: 일상생활 용품

They worked so hard, and then they went to the sea <u>to divert their mind from</u> the stressful work.

: 그들은 열심히 일했다 그리고 스트레스 쌓이는 일로부터 기분을 전환시키고자 바다로 갔다.

She <u>uttered a cry of disappointment</u> when she heard she failed in the mid-term exam.

: 중간시험에 낙제했다는 소식을 듣고 그녀는 실망의 비명을 질렀다.

What made you come here?

: <u>무엇이 당신을 여기에 오게 했습니까?</u> [즉, 왜 여기에 오셨습니까?]

> *ex)* What brought you here?=Why did you come here?=What did you come here for?=How come you came here?

» **원문**

… One Sunday she went for a stroll in the Champs-Elysees <u>to divert her mind from the labours of the week</u>, when she caught sight of a lady with a child. It was madame Forestier! …

… <u>Madame Forestier uttered a cry of surprise</u>. Oh, my poor Mathilde! What's happened to you? You're very a stranger!" …

… <u>What makes you say so?</u> You returned it to me." …

» **Note**

☐ divert (A) from (B): (A)를 (B)로부터 전환시키다

　　ex) divert her mind from the labours of the week: 주중의 노동으로부터 그녀의 마음[기분]을 전환시키다

☐ utter a cry of surprise: 놀람의 비명을 지르다

☐ What makes you say so?: 무엇이 당신을 그렇게 말하도록 만드시오? (즉, 왜 그렇게 말하시오? Why do you say so?의 뜻)

Boule de Suif(adapted)

- Maupassant

작품 소개: 프로이센군에 점령된 루앙으로부터 디에프로 가는 역마차 안에서 생긴 일은 그린 작품이다. 뚱뚱해서 '비곗덩어리'라는 별명이 붙은 창녀가 합승객의 희생이 되어 프로이센 장교에게 몸을 맡기는데, 일이 끝나자 합승객은 절박한 고비에서 구조를 받은 은혜도 잊고서 그녀를 경멸하고 멀리한다는 이야기다.

When they saw the beautiful sight before them, the looking-good couple talking about something <u>broke off</u> and then enjoyed the scenery.

: 그들 앞에 펼쳐진 아름다운 광경을 보았을 때 무엇인가에 대해 이야기를 하고 있던 그 멋있는 커플은 <u>중단하고</u> 그 광경을 즐겼다.

We're in the same boat.

: 우리는 공동 운명체다.

The politician <u>accepted the offer</u> when given a lot of money by some lobbyists

: 그 정치가는 일부 로비스트들에 의해 거액의 돈을 제공 받았을 때 <u>그 제의를 받아들였다.</u>

» 원문

… <u>It so happened that</u> all the woman were seated on the same table. Next to the Countess sat two nuns. …

… She raised her head and looked at them so defiantly that they became silent, with their eyes cast down; Loiseau, sensitive to feminine charms, <u>cast stealthy glances of curiosity at her.</u> …

… She broke off, for fear of being rebuffed. Loiseau <u>took the cue.</u> "<u>We are in the same boat</u>, as the saying is," he said. "We should help one another. Come, ladiess and gentlemen, <u>accept her offer.</u>" …

» **Note**

- ☐ It so happened that…: …하는 것은 우연히 발생한 일이다, 즉 우연히… 했다
- ☐ break off: 관계를 끊다, 말을 끊다
- ☐ for fear of …ing: …하는 것이 무서워
- ☐ take the cue: 암시[언질]을 하다
- ☐ We are in the same boat.: 우리는 같은 운명체다.
- ☐ as the saying is: 속담이 말하듯이
- ☐ accept one's offer: …의 제의를 받아들이다

There was no choice for them but to laugh when they saw the funny sight.

: 그들이 그 우스운 광경을 보았을 때 그들에게 단지 웃는 것 외에는 다른 대안이 없었다.

We resumed the conference after taking a ten minute break.

: 10분 동안의 휴식을 취한 후에 우리는 그 회의를 재개했다.

» **원문**

… Will you get out, ladies and gentlemen?" There was no choice for them but to obey. They followed the offer into the great kitchen of the inn …

… When Boule de suif was gone, they tried to guess why she had been summoned. They wondered what they would say if they were called in their turn. …

… He was the very picture of the insolence of a victor. At last he said; "What do you want?" The count acted the part of spokesman. "Sir, we wish to resume our journey." "you can't." "Might I ask why we can't?" …

- □ There was no choice for (A) but to obey.: 복종하는 것 외에는 (A)에게 대안이 없었다. 즉, (A)는 따르지 않을 수가 없었다.
- □ in one's turn: 그들은 교대로
  cf) in turn: 교내로
- □ the very picture of the insolence of a victor: 승리자의 오만함 바로 그 자태
  cf) the very: 바로 그
- □ resume: ...을 다시 시작하다

Don't get on her nerves when she concentrates on something.

: 그녀가 무엇인가에 집중하고 있을 때 그녀의 신경을 건들지 말라.

She all the time puts on airs whenever she stands in front of her boy-friend.

: 그녀는 그녀의 남자 친구 앞에 있을 때마다 늘 점잔을 뺀다.

I had a hard time in talking her around.

: 나는 그녀를 설득하는데 어려움을 겪었다.

We put our heads together over our future plan and made up a good idea

: 우리는 미래의 계획에 대해 얼굴을 맞대고 생각했다. 그리고 좋은 생각을 생각해냈다.

» **원문**

... By lunch time the situation was getting on their nerve. Naturally their thoughts underwent a subtle change. ...

... I know her policy at Rouen was 'Let anyone come, and I am his mistress.' And now, when we are in trouble, she puts on airs. ... "We must talk her round," he said. Then they put their heads together over the plan, every one giving an opinion with cruel enthusiasm. ...

» Note

- □ get on one's nerves: 남의 신경에 거슬리다, 성가시게 하다, 애태우다
- □ assume[put on] airs 또는 give oneself airs: 점잔을 빼다
- □ talk (A) around=persuade(A): (A)를 설득시키다
- □ put one's heads together over...: ...에 대해 머리를 맞대고 의논하다

What she beat him so harshly without notice was too much.

: 그녀가 예고 없이 그렇게 심하게 그를 때린 것은 너무나 가혹했다.

When we heard our team lost the game we were struck dumb for a moment.

: 우리 팀이 졌다는 것을 들었을 때 우리는 잠시동안 어안이 벙벙했다.

The day was so hot and humid, and we are so worn out, but when we were given some food and iced water we pulled ourselves together and began to walk on.

: 날씨는 너무 덥고 후덥지근했다 그러므로 우리는 녹초가 되었다. 그러나 약간의 음식과 시원한 물을 제공받았을 때 정신을 가다듬고 다시 계속 걷기 시작했다.

… At last he said: "What makes you grudge him a favour which has been a matter of course to you at Rouen?" Boule de Suif made no reply. …

… About midnight, Cornudet, who had remained silent through the dinner, suddenly stood up. Glaring at the company, he said, "This is too much," and strode out of the room. Everyone was struck dumb for a moment. Loiseau, however, soon pulled himself together, laughed heartily. …

» **Note**

☐ grudge(or envy)+목적어(A)+목적어(B): (소유물, 성공 따위로) (A)에게서 (B) 를 시기하다, 질투하다

☐ This is too much.: 이것은 너무 가혹하다[지나치다].

☐ Everyone was struck dumb for a moment.: 모든 사람들은 어안이 벙벙해 졌다.
  cf strike+사람(A)+dumb: 남을 놀라게 하여 말이 안 나오게 하다. (즉, 앞의 표현은 이 숙어형태의 수동형이다.)

☐ pull oneself together: 정신을 가다듬다, 기운을 되찾다

A I failed in the Math exam.: 나는 수학시험을 낙제했어.

B You don't say so! I know you are good at math.: 설마 그 럴라구! 너는 수학을 잘한다고 알고 있는데.

Jack served his right! He disgraced himself by deceiving his faithful girl friend.

: Jack은 그래 싸다! 그는 그의 정숙한 여자 친구를 속임으로써 스스로 치욕 을 초래했다.

» **원문**

... Every one, mystified, wanted an explanation, which he furnished with the air of one letting out a most important secret. "What! You don't say so!" "Yes. I saw it with my own eyes." "And he was rejected?" "Yes; perhaps because of the Prussian officer in the next room." "Fancy that!" ...

... The count shrugged his shoulders, while Madame Loiseau laughed silently and murmured. "Serve her right! She disgraced herself." ...

» **Note**

☐ You don't say so!: 설마 그럴라구!(Are you sure?)

☐ I saw it my own eyes.: 나는 나 자신의 눈을 가지고 그것을 보았소. (즉, 'own(...자신의, ...고유의)'은 소유격을 강조한다.)

☐ Prussian: 프러시아의(즉, 옛 독일 연방의 왕국의)

☐ (Just) fancy that!: 정말 놀랐는걸!(즉, 놀람을 나타내거나 주의를 촉구하는 감탄사로 쓰인다)

☐ Serve one's right!: ...는 그래 싸다!

☐ She disgraced oneself!: 그녀는 스스로 불명예[치욕]를 초래했어!

God Sees the Truth, but Waits(adapted)
- Leo Nikolaevich Tolstoy

작품 소개: 상인 악쇼노프는 장사를 하기 위해 길을 떠났다가 여관에 들게 되고, 다른 상인과 함께 차를 마신 뒤 옆방에서 잠을 자게 된다. 이튿날 새벽 혼자서 부지런히 길을 나선 악쇼노프는 경찰에 의해 제지를 받는데, 그 과정에서 악쇼노프의 봇짐 속에서는 뜻밖에도 피 묻은 칼이 나온다. 꼼짝없이 살인죄의 누명을 뒤집어쓴 악쇼노프는 이후 세미요니치의 자백으로 법원으로부터 석방 명령을 받게 되지만, 악쇼노프는 이미 죽고 난 뒤였다.

작가 소개: 러시아의 작가, 개혁가, 도덕 사상가다. 세계적인 소설가 중의 한 사람으로 꼽히며, 대표작으로는 불후의 명성을 안겨준 '전쟁과 평화', '안나 카레니나'가 있다.

How is it that he suddenly canceled his project? He said that he would never change his mind.
: 그가 갑자기 그이 계획을 취소한 것은 어찌된 된 일이냐? 그는 결코 그의 마음을 바꾸지 않겠다고 말했어.

What more do you want of me?
: 도대체 당신은 나로부터 무엇을 더 많이 원해?

This door was locked from within[inside].
: 이 문은 내부로부터 잠긴다.

» **원문**

… Aksyonof, astonished, only stammered, "It's not mine, sir. <u>How is it, in the name of God, that's it is in my bag?</u>" …

… <u>The house was locked from inside</u>. You were the only person who was there. …

… "<u>What more do you want of me?</u>" Aksyonof asked. "<u>What have you come here for?</u>" Semyonitch <u>bent close over him</u> and whispered. "Oh, Aksyonof, forgive me!" …

» **Note**

- □ How is it?: 그것은 어째서냐? 그것은 왜냐?
- □ in the name of God: 신의 이름으로, 맹세코, 〈의문문 강조〉도대체
- □ lock from inside: 내부로부터 잠그다
- □ What more…?: 무엇을 더 (많이)…?
    rf) (A) more: (A)를 더 (많이)
- □ What… for?=Why?
- □ bend over…: …위로 몸을 구부리다.

255

What Man Lives(adapted) - Leo Nikolaevich Tolstoy

// **작품 소개**: 미카엘 대천사가 신의 명령을 어기고 인간 세상에서 하느님이 진름 세 가지에 대한 답을 얻어올 것을 명받고 인간이 되어 그것을 깨달아가는 과정의 이야기다.

[A] **Excuse me but could you tell me the way to the city hall?**: 실례합니다만 시청으로 가는 길을 알려 주시겠습니까?

[B] **I'm sorry I am a stranger here, too.** : 죄송합니다만 저도 이곳을 잘 몰라요.

My teacher is always hard with some bad students.
: 나의 선생님은 항상 불량한 학생들에게 가혹하다.[심히 다룬다.]

Was it cold outside? Come on in to the stove and warm yourself.
: 밖이 추었는가? 난로가에 와서 몸을 녹여라.[불을 쬐어라.]

» 원문

… When he reached the shrine at the bend of the road on his way home, he saw something white behind the shrine. In the twilight he could not make out what it was at first. …

… The man began to walk-but so nimbly that Simon wondered at his steps. "Where do you come from?" Simon asked. "I am a stranger here." "How is it that you came by the shrine?" "I can not tell." "Was someone hard with you?" "No, no one was hard with me. I was punished by God." …

… Simon was surprised at this answer, but said, "You are freezing. Come home with me warm yourself."…

» **Note**

- at the bend of...: ...의 모퉁이에
- on one's way (to) 장소(A): (A)로 가는 도중에 I am a stranger here.: 이곳을 잘 몰라요. (즉, 'I am new to here'의 뜻)
- How is it that...?: ...한 것은 어째서냐[왜냐]?
- be hard with...: ... 번거로움[말썽, 고통]이 되다
  cf) go hard with...: ...에게 번거로움[말썽, 고통]을 주다
- You are freezing.: 당신은 얼어붙고 있습니다. (매우 한기를 느낀다는 뜻)
- Come with me.: 나와 함께 갑시다.
- warm oneself: 불을 쬐다

Don't raise your eyes any time when your teacher punishes you.

: 선생님이 벌 줄 때 너의 눈을 치켜 올리지 말라.

She went to office with her new blouse on.

: 그녀의 새로 산 블라우스를 입은 채로 그녀는 출근했다.

The beggar lay down on the bare ground, naked, half frozen, and motionless.

: 그 거지는 발가벗고, 반쯤 언 채로, 움직이지 않고 맨땅에 누워 있었다.

... Raising her eyes, she saw her husband, seemingly ashamed, with only a shirt on, standing with a stranger fellow, hatless, with her husband's coat on and wearing felt boots. "he has been drinking," she thought, "and brought a good-for-nothing fellow home." ...

... And this man was sitting by the shrine, naked and half frozen. ...

... Matryona saw the stranger sitting on the edge of the bench, motionless, his eyes closed, as if in pain. her heart softened towards him. ...

» **Note**

- □ raise one's eyes: 〈놀람, 경멸 따위로〉눈을 치켜 올리다
- □ with only a shirt on: 단지 셔츠만 입은 채로
  (즉, 여기의 표현들을 보면, 'with+목적어(A)+목적보어(B)=(A)가 (B)한 채로'처럼 정식적인 문법 형식에 따라 '부대상황'의 뜻을 표현하는가 하면, 단지 '형용사'나, '분사(과거분사나 현재분사)', 또는 '접속사+절 형태(주어+be동사의 생략)
  ex) while (we are) reading을 써서 '부대상황'을 나타내는 경우가 구어체 표현에서는 허다하다.
- □ a good-for-nothing: 쓸데없는
- □ naked and half frozen: 발가벗고 반쯤 얼은 채로
- □ motionless: 움직임 없이
- □ with his eyes closed: 그의 눈을 내린 채로
- □ as if in pain: 마치 고통상태에 있는 것처럼

See to it that your house is locked safely when you get out.
: 외출할 때 너의 집이 안전한지 조치를 취하라.

I am remotely related to the celebrity.
: 나는 그 명사와 먼 친척이다.

» **원문**

… "What are you smiling at foolishly?" the gentleman roared. "See to it that my boots are ready in time." …

… "Then you are not their mother?" she asked. "No, I am not their mother, nor am I related to them in any way. I adopted them." …

… Matryona said with a sigh, "As the saying goes, even without parents children grow up, but without God we can not live." …

» **Note**

☐ see to it that...: ...하도록 조치를 취하다.

☐ be related to...: ...와 관련[친분]이 있다.

☐ 부정어 ... in any way: 어떤 면에서든지 ...아닌

☐ as the saying goes: 속담이 말하는 것처럼

The Story of Ivan the Fool(adapted)

- Leo Nikolaevich Tolstoy

작품 소개: 러시아의 민속동화 「바보 이반」을 재구성한 작품이다. 표면적으로는 러시아 우화의 재구성으로 보이지만, 내포된 작가의 뜻은 작가스스로의 정치적 성향인 기독교 아나키즘 성향이 표출된 작품이다. 러시아 귀족들의 무위도식과 탐욕을 비판하고, 땀을 흘려가며 정직하게 일하는 러시아 농민들의 성실함을 찬양하는 사회비판소설이다.

He went bankrupt because of the bad condition of his company, so he ran into debts.

: 그는 회사의 상태가 안 좋기 때문에 부도를 냈다. 그러므로 빚더미에 쌓였다.

You can turn your time into good account.

: 당신은 당신의 시간을 잘 활용할 수가 있다.

A Can you come to the party in time, tonight?

: 오늘 밤 늦지 않게 파티에 올 수가 있겠니?

B No problem. I can make it.

: 문제 없고 말고. 제시간에 델 수가 있지.

I was seated astride the fence and looked out into the gymnasium.

: 나는 담장 위에 걸터앉았다. 그리고 체육관 안을 들여다보았다.

» **원문**

... He spent all his money and <u>ran into debts,</u> from which he will never be free. ...

... But of what use are soldiers?" "<u>You can turn them into good account</u>. They will do anything for you." they will do anything for you." ...

... "At last," the spirit thought. "<u>I've made it</u>. He can no longer work. Well, <u>I'll take a rest</u>." He <u>was seated asride</u> a branch and chuckled to himself. ...

» **Note**

- □ run into debts: 빚더미에 쌓이다
- □ turn (A) into good account: (A)를 잘 활용하다
- □ I've made it.: 나는 그것을 해냈어.
  - *rf*) make it: 제시간에 대다(or 해내다)
  - *ex*) I can make it.: 나는 제 시간에 댈 수가 있어.
- □ be seated astride: 걸터앉다
  - *ex*) ride a horse astride: 말에 걸터앉다

Mind your own job. It's no business of yours.

: 너의 일에나 신경 써. <u>그것은 너의 일이 아니야.[네가 알 바가 아니야.]</u>

I don't love her. On the contrary, she loves me very much.

: 나는 그녀를 좋아하지 않는다. <u>오히려 그와는커녕,</u> 그녀가 나를 매우 사랑한다.

... "Where did you get those soldiers and where did you take them?"
"It's is no business of yours." "On the contrary, it is my business. ...
... The soldiers took corn and cattle, but no villagers resisted. The
same state of things awaited the soldiers when they went on to
another village. ...

☐ It's no business of yours.=It's none of your business.: 네가 알 바가 아냐.
☐ on the contrary: 그와는커녕, 그와는 반대로
☐ the state of things=the thing of affairs: 일의 사태[상황]

I make it a rule to take a walk every morning.
: 나는 매일 아침 산보 하는 것을 규칙으로 삼는다.

Never be offend. Every thing is going well.
: 화내지 말세요. 모든 일이 잘 될 것이요.

... "All right," Ivan said, "But," he continued. "we make it a rule not
to give any food to those who do not work with their hands except
the scraps that were left over. ... Don't be offended, sir," Ivan's wife
said. "I'm sorry, but your hands show no sign of labour. ...
... The Devil talked at length how to work with the head instead of
the hands, but the people only stared at him in blank surprise. They
were unable to make head or tail of his speech. ...

☐ make it a rule to+동사의 원형(또는 that +절): ...하는 것을 규칙으로 삼다,
　의례히 ...하다
☐ Don't be offended.: 화 내지 말아요.
☐ in blank surprise: 멍한 놀라움 속에
☐ make a head or tail of one's speech: 말의 앞뒤를 이해하다

Darling(adapted)

- Anton Chekhov

\# **작품 소개:** 등장인물 올렌카는 사람마다 보는 시각이 다를 수 있지만, 아마 저자는 여성스러움의 본질을 순수하게 잘 간직하고 있으면서도, 주체성을 상실한 온순한 노예같은 인물로 평가되고 있는 올렌카의 모습을 묘사했다고 볼 수 있다.

\# **작가 소개:** 러시아의 소설가 겸 극작가다. 객관주의 문학론을 주장하였고 시대의 변화와 요구에 대한 올바른 목소리를 전달하기 위해 저술 활동을 벌였다.

What's the use of regretting your test result after you didn't prepare your exam?

: 시험 준비를 하지 않은 후에 너의 시험 결과를 후회하는 것은 무슨 소용이 있느냐?

I saw the drunken man to his house.

: 나는 그 술 취한 사람을 그의 집까지 바래다주었다.

Stop fighting! Make up with your wife.

: 싸우는 것을 멈춰라! 너의 아내와 화해하라.

» **원문**

… She sat in his office and looked after things in the theater, keeping the account and paying out wages. …

… Olenka, my dear, what's the matter? Make the sign of the Cross!" …

… What's the use of going to the theater?" …

… "Well, may God keep you," she would say to him at parting, as she saw him to the door by candlelight. "Thank you for coming to see me. …

… "Make up the quarrel with your wife, my friend." …

□ keep account: 기장하다, 치부하다

□ make the sign of the cross: 성호를 긋다.

□ what's use of ...?: ...하는 것은 무슨 소용이 있는가? (즉, 'use'는 '소용', '이익'의 뜻)

□ see (A) to (B): (A)를 (B)까지 바래다주다

□ make up...: ...화해하다

The fact is that we fall short of air. Come on, hurry up.

: <u>사실은</u> 우리가 지금 공기가 부족하다는 것이다. 자, 빨리 움직여라.

Don't put in your word when we are talking about our business.

: 우리가 우리의 용무를 이야기 할 때 <u>참견하지 말라.</u>

» **원문**

... She began to find her new happiness in his company. <u>The fact was</u>, Olenka could not live a single year without loving somebody, and she did not try to keep it secret. ...

... "Why do you talk about what you don't understand? I've asked you not to. When I'm talking with my friends, <u>please don't put in your word</u>. <u>It's really annoying.</u>" ...

... Besides, it is time for my boy to go to school. <u>I have made up with my wife</u>, you know." ...

» **Note**

□ The fact[The thing] is...: 사실은...(것)이다

□ put in one's word: 참견하다

□ annoying: 괴로운, 성가신

□ make up with...: ...와 화해하다

I saw my foreign friend off to the harbor.

: 나는 나의 외국인 친구를 항구까지 배웅했다.

As compared with her classmate, Helen is taller than her.

: 그녀의 반 친구와 비교해볼 때 Helen은 그녀보다 더 키가 크다.

» 원문

… "What a troublesome boy you are! she would say, seeing him off to school. "You must work hard and do as you are told by your teachers." …

… Her former attachments were nothing as compared with the maternal love Sashenka aroused in her. …

» Note

☐ troublesome: 귀찮은, 성가신, 다루기 힘든
☐ see (A) off: (A)를 배웅하다
☐ as compared with…: …와 비교해 볼 때

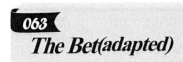

The Bet(adapted)

- Anton Chekhov

작품 소개: 부유한 은행가와 젊은 은행가가 사형제도에 대한 말다툼(사형과 무기형 중에 무엇이 더 인간적인 처벌인가) 끝에 젊은 변호사가 15년의 홀로 사는 생활을 견디면 은행가가 2만 달러를 주기로 하는 내기로 시작된다.

He hasn't eaten any food and drink for three days so his cheek is hollow and sunken.

: 그는 어떤 음식물도 3일 동안 먹지 않았다. 그러므로 <u>그의 볼은 움푹 패이고 쑥 들어갔다.</u>

I <u>don't like mixing with</u> any other people in character.

: 나는 성격상으로 어떤 다른 사람들과 <u>어울리는 것을 좋아하지 않는다.</u>

» 원문

... The colour of his face was that of the earth; <u>the cheeks were hollow and sunken</u>; and the hand on which he leaned his head was so thin and skinny as to reveal the bones. ...

... For fifteen years <u>I have been kept from mixing with people</u>, but this earthly life I have diligently studied ...

» Note

☐ hollow: 움푹 패인
☐ sunken: 푹 꺼진, 내려앉은
☐ mix with...: ...와 섞다, ...와 교제하다

064

Once a Year(adapted)

- Anton Chekhov

작품 소개: 백작부인은 일 년에 한 번 자기의 세례명인 성인의 생일을 축하하는 날 아무도 축하하지 않는 것이 못마땅하다. 많은 보살핌으로 키워준 부인의 조카 Jean은 부인이 재산이 많았을 때는 아는 체하다가 재산이 없어지자 아는 체 하지도 않고 불규칙한 생활을 하고 있고… 부인의 하인 Mark가 찾아가 설득 끝에 결국 축하하기 위하여 부인을 방문하고 만나는 대가로 약간의 루블을 받기로 한다.

They are due to come here at seven o'clock.

: 그들은 7시까지 여기에 오기로 되어있다.[올 예정이다.]

His face was swollen.

: 그의 눈은 부어올랐다.

Have your heart in the right place.

: 마음을 곱게 잡수세요.

» 원문

… "Baron Trumb, Prince Khalakhadze, General Bitkov, and others-they are due to come here already. I must say, Mark, that they've deserted me! …

… He found the count sprawling on his bed, with his eyes dimmed still with last night's drinking. His face was purple and swollen. …

…"You want to sleep?" "How do you dare to say that sort of thing to me?" "Shut up, you old fool!" …

… "Go and see her, your Lordship. She's terribly hurt by your-what shall I say?-lack of feeling." …

… "Please, sir, do have your heart in the right place. She is old. Do have pity on her, your Lordship." …

267

- due...: ...할 예정인
- with his eyes dimmed: 그의 눈이 희미한 채로
- swollen: 부풀어 오른
  rf) swell-swelled-swollen
- How do you dare to say that sort of thing to me?: 당신은 감히 그런 말을 나에게 하느냐?
- What shall I say?: 무엇이라고나 할까?(혼잣말로 판단)
- do have your heart in the right place: 마음을 곱게 잡수세요

065

Gusev(adapted)

- Anton Chekhov

작품 소개: 평범한 인생에서 길어낸 비극적 유머 "사랑에 관하여". 이 책은 삶과 죽음의 경계, 진정한 사랑과 부조리한 현실의 기로, 욕망과 윤리의 갈등, 젊음과 회한의 대립에 이르기까지, 다양한 색채와 화법으로 삶과 인생을 투영한 폭넓은 체호프의 작품 세계를 일목요연하게 보여 주는 대표 선집이다. 구세프는 이 작품 속에 나오는 부속 이야기 중의 하나다.

My brother was discharged from the service three days ago.

: 나의 형님은 3일 전에 제대하셨다.

The water is still tepid

: 그물은 여전히 미지근하다.

It was nice and warm in the morning so I walked farther as ever.

: 아침에 날씨가 너무 좋고 기분도 좋았다 그러므로 나는 여느 때처럼 더 멀리 걸었다.

» **원문**

… Darkness was coming on the ship. Gusev, a soldier discharged from service, sat up in his hammock and said in a low voice. …
… He gulped down a glass of water. The water was tepid, disgusting. The ship was rising and falling as ever. …

» **Note**

☐ discharge from service: 병역으로부터 제대
☐ tepid: 미지근한
☐ as ever: 여느 때처럼

269

066

The Call of the Wild
- Jack London

작품 소개: 알래스카의 대자연을 배경으로 야성의 삶과 모험을 그리고 있다. 작가인 런던에게 소설가로서의 명성을 안겨 준 작품으로, 환경이 생물에 미치는 불가항력이나 야생과 폭력의 세계를 뛰어난 문체로 표현하고 있다. 모험과 영웅주의가 독자들을 사로잡는다. 문명에 길들여진 개가 알래스카로 팔려 가면서 겪는 모험을 다룬 소설이다.

작가 소개: 미국의 소설가 잭 런던(Jack London)(1876~1916)의 본명은 존 그리피스 체이니(John Griffith Chaney)로 체험을 통해 해양 문학의 걸작품을 많이 그려냈다.

I added one to the rest and then the balls made a total of nines.
: 나는 하나를 그 나머지에다 더했다. 그러자 그 공들은 전체 아홉 개를 만들었다.[총 아홉 개가 되었다.]

The temperature was twenty degrees below zero Celsius.
: 온도는 섭씨 영하 20도였다.

» 원문

… Three more huskies were added to the team, making a total of nines. …

… Dave was pulling just in front of the sled; then came Buck and sol-leks. The leader was Spitz. Before the end of the day Buck mastered his work. …

… Then something unexpected happened. The camps was suddenly alive with hungry huskies, 80 or 100 in all. …

… Many times Perrault fell through the ice and was saved by the long pole he carried. The temperature was fifty below zero. …

» Note

  □ husky: 에스키모 개
  □ then came+주어(A): (A)가 오다 (즉, 부사(구) 때문에 도치가 된 구문)
  □ in all=all told: 모두 합하여
  □ below zero: 영하

When somebody was stalking me, I turned off into a small bright corner.

: 누군가가 나를 미행했을 때, 나는 조그마한 밝은 모퉁이로 돌아 들어갔다.

A school of minnows went up round bend after bend along the creek.

: 한 떼의 피라미들이 굽이치며 샛강을 따라 올라갔다.

I cut across the path to save my time.

: 나는 시간을 절약하기 위하여 지름길을 택하였다.

» 원문

  … The rabbit sped down the river, turned off into a small creek, and ran lightly on the surface of its frozen bed. …
  … Buck led the pack, round bend after bend, his splendid body flashing forward in the white moonlight. …
  … Spitz, cold and calculating, left the pack and cut across a narrow neck of lands where the creek made a long bend. …

» Note

  □ turn off: 돌다
  □ pack: 한패
  □ round bend after bend: 굽이를 따라 이리저리 돌며
  □ bend: 굴곡진 부분, 즉 굽이
  □ cut across: 가로질러 달리다, 가까운 길을 택하다
  □ neck: 애로, 해협, 지협
  □ The creek made a long bend.: 강이 길게 굽이쳐있었다.

Let's meet another man. We can not set our heart on him.

: 또 다른 사람을 만나자. 우리는 그에게 희망을 걸 수가 없다.

We exchanged our extra clothes for food for survival.

: 우리는 생존을 위해 우리의 여분의 옷들을 식량과 교환했다.

» **원문**

… At night Buck lay down near the fire, hind legs crouched under him, forelegs stretched out in front, head raised, and eyes blinking dreamily at the flames. …

… He could not set his heart on the work. …

… When they stopped at John Thornton's camp at the mouth of White River, the dogs dropped down as if they had all been …

… Hal exchanged the whip for the club. Buck did not move under the rain of heavier blows. …

» **Note**

- □ crouch: 웅크리다
- □ stretch out: 앞으로 쭉 뻗다
- □ set one's heart on…: … 에 희망을 걸다, 탐내다, 열중하다
- □ at the mouth of…: … 어귀에
- □ exchange (A) for (B): (A)를 (B)와 교환하다

The drunken man <u>staggered to his feet</u>, took a few steps and then he fell down again on the ground.

: 그 술취한 사람은 <u>비틀거리며 일어났다</u> 그리고 몇 발짝 내디뎠다. 그리고 난 후 다시 땅에 넘어졌다.

It was getting colder and colder, and the drunken man began to <u>come to himself</u>.

: 날씨가 점점 더 추워지기 시작했다. 그리고 그 술취한 사람은 <u>제정신이 들기</u> 시작했다.

I'll <u>bet you this money on</u> the result of the game.

: 나는 그 경기 <u>결과에 대해 당신과 이 돈을 걸겠다.</u>

» **원문**

… He <u>staggered to his feet</u> and fell down. But when the faint sound of Thornton's voice came to him, it <u>acted on</u> him like an electric shock. He <u>sprang to his feet</u> and ran up the bank ahead of the men where he had set out before. …

… When Thornton <u>came to himself</u>, he saw that Buck was <u>as limp as a rag</u> and apparently lifeless. …

… "I've got a thousand dollars. Here it is. <u>I'll bet you this money that he can't</u>" Thornton flushed. …

» **Note**

☐ stagger to one's feet: 비틀거리며 일러서다
☐ act on...: ...작용하다, ...따라 행동하다
☐ spring to one's feet: 벌떡 일어서다
☐ come to oneself: 제정신 나다
☐ as limp as a rage: 넝마처럼 절름거리는
☐ bet 사람(A) (B): (A)에게 (B)를 걸다

We have only to help the poor regardless of money.

: 우리는 돈과 상관없이 단지 그 가난한 사람들을 돕기만 하면 된다.

The newly-born calf began to rise on his hind legs.

: 그 갓 태어난 송아지는 그의 뒷다리를 대고 일어나기 시작했다.

» **원문**

... Buck now swung to the left. The crackling turned into a snapping, the runners slipping several inches to the side. The sled began to move. ...

...The dogs had only to pull in the animals that Thornton shot. Buck spent long hours dreaming by the fire. As he was lying in the camp, falling asleep lazily now and then in the heat of the day, he felt as if someone were calling him. ...

... The wolf turned, rose on his hind legs, snarling and bristling, snapping his teeth together. ...

» **Note**

- ☐ swing-swung-swung: 방향을 바꾸다
- ☐ have only to+동사의 원형=단지...하기만 하면 되다
- ☐ rise on one's hind legs: ...의 뒷다리를 지지하고 일어서다(이 경우 'on'은 '부착, 지지'를 표현)

067

Daisy Miller

- Henry James

\# **작품 소개:** 주인공 윈터본은 유럽 사회에 대해 벗어날 수 없는 콤플렉스를 가진 미국인의 한 사람으로 그려져 있고, 그 콤플렉스 때문에 자유분방하게 사는 데이지의 순진함을 있는 그대로 이해할 수가 없다. 헨리 제임스가 작품의 테마로 자주 사용하는 '겉모습과 마음속의 진실'을 그려낸 작품으로, 리얼하고 섬세한 윈터본의 의식에 대한 묘사를 통해 이야기의 비극성이 부각되고 있다.

\# **작가 소개:** 미국의 소설가 헨리 제임스는 조이스와 프루스트에게 결정적인 영향을 주었고, 콘래드를 거쳐 사르트르까지도 그를 중요한 작가라고 평했다. 1940년 이후에는 그에 관해 '유럽과 미국에서 20세기의 소설에 관해 이야기할 때 빼놓을 수 없는 존재'라는 평가가 내려지고 있다.

Take care that you are not caught in the shower.

: 당신이 소나기를 맞지 않도록 조심하라.

I am sorry that I went too far, but it's not my intention.

: 제가 너무 지나치게 굴어 죄송합니다. 하지만 그것은 나의 의도가 아니었습니다.

I don't mean to say I hate her.

: 내가 그녀를 싫어한다고 말할 의향은 아니었습니다.

» **원문**

… He poke his alpenstock into Winterbourne's bench, and tried to crack the lump of sugar with his teeth. …
… "Take care you don't hurt your teeth," he said. …
… He wondered whether he had gone too far, when she turned to the boy and said, "I would like to know where you got that pole." "I bought it," said Randolph. "You don't mean to say you're going to take it to Italy?" …
… She did not stop teasing him till he promised her to come down to Rome in the winter. …

275

» **Note**

☐ poke: 찌르다

   ex) poke (A) into (B): (A)를 (B)속으로 찌르다

☐ Take care...: ...하는 것을 주의하라

☐ You don't mean to 동사의 원형: ...하는 것을 의미[의도]하지 않다

☐ stop ...ing: ...하는 것을 멈추다

068

Wuthering Height

- Emily Bronte

작품 소개: 주인공인 주워온 아이 히스클리프가 집안 후계를 이어가는 과정에서 히스클리프와 캐서린 언쇼가 서로에게 끊임없이 집착하고 사랑을 열망하면서 거칠고 격정적인 인간의 애증 심리를 잘 보여주고 있는 작품이다.

작가 소개: 영국 여류 소설가 겸 시인이다. 유일한 소설 「폭풍의 언덕」은 오늘날에는 셰익스피어의 「리어왕(King Lear)」, H.멜빌의 「백경」에 필적하는 명작이라고까지 평가되고 있다.

I happened to see my old teacher in the United States when I was on business trip.

: 사업상 여행하고 있을 때 나는 미국에 살고 있는 나의 오래된 은사님을 우연히 만났다.

When she met her long-forgotten daughter after long absence, she flung her daughter's neck.

: 오랫동안 만나지 못한 후에 그녀가 딸을 만났을 때, 그녀의 어머니는 딸의 목을 와락 껴안았다.

» 원문

... I sat still, but, when I happened to make faces at them, she got angry and leaped on my knees. I flung her back and put the table between us. ...

... She was slender, almost a girl; had small, fair features and golden ringlets hanging loose on her delicate neck, and pretty eyes, in which, however, there was something between scorn and desperation. ...

☐ make(or pull) faces(or a face) at...: ...에게 인상을 찌푸리다
☐ happen to 동사의 원형=chance to 동사의 원형=우연히 ...하다
☐ fling: 던지다, 껴안다
　　ex) fling-flung-flung
☐ hang loose: 느슨하게 걸다

Strange to say, the twins are so different in their appearance. One is on their mother's side, the other is on their father's side.

: 이상하게 들릴지 모르지만, 그 쌍둥이는 외모 상으로 매우 다르다. 한 쪽은 어머니 쪽을 닮았고, 다른 똑은 아버지를 닮았다.

They were not so familiar with each other. So I tried to dispel the awkward atmosphere prevailing between them.

: 그들은 상호간에 너무나 잘 알지 못하고 있었다. 그러므로 나는 그들 사이에 만연해 있는 어색한 분위기를 쫓아내고자 노력했다.

... I began to doubt whether he was a servant or not
: his hands were brown like those of a common labourer, and his bearing was so free and haughty. Five minutes afterwards Heathcliff entered, to my relief. ...
... I thought I must dispel the awkward silence prevailing there. "I say, Mr. Heathcliff, you must be very happy, with your lovely lady, and surrounded by your family." ...
... "Yes; and her husband was her cousin also: one on the mother's, the other on the father's side: Heathcliff married Mr. Linton's sister." ...

» **Note**

  □ bearings: 뽐내는 태도(airs), 관련성
  □ haughty: 거만한
  □ prevailing: 만연하고 하고 있는, 충만하고 있는
  □ one...the other...: 한 쪽은... 다른 쪽은 ..., 즉, 둘 사이에 쓰인다

I had a peep at the fighting sight. It was really very pleasant thing.

: 나는 그 싸우는 장면을 몰래 보았다. 그것은 정말로 즐거운 일이었다.

A short time after we met each other, I began to become thick with her.

: 우리가 함께 만나고 얼마 안 있어, 나는 그녀와 친해지기 시작했다.

As soon as I met her, I took to her without any special reason.

: 내가 그녀를 만나자 마자, 나는 어떤 특별한 이유 없이 그녀를 좋아하기 시작했다.

» **원문**

... We crowded round, and over Miss Cathy's head, I had a peep at a dirty, ragged, black-haired child. ...
... Hindly, who was a boy of fourteen, hated him; but Miss Cathy, who was hardly six years old, became very thick with him. ...
... He took to Heathcliff strangely, believing all he said and petting up far above Cathy, who was too mischievous and wayward for a favorite. ...

279

- crowd round: 떼를 지어 모이다
- take to...: ...이 좋아지다, 의지하다, 돌보다, 전념하다
- mischievous: 장난 끼가 심한, 해로운
- wayward: 외고집의
- favorite: 가장 좋아하는 것

The old fashioned furniture is good for nothing for the newly-moved house.

: 그 낡은 가구는 새로 이사한 집을 위해 아무 쓸모가 없다.

It degraded me to marry such a unfaithful woman.

: 내가 그와 같은 정숙치 못한 여인과 결혼한 것은 나의 명예를 훼손시켰다.

» **원문**

... Mr. Earnshaw agreed, though with a heavy spirit, saying, "Hindly is good for nothing." ...

... Strange to say, she was very fond of Heathcliff. ...

... But it would degrade me to marry Heathcliff now; so he shall never know how I love him; and that, not because he's handsome, Nelly, but because he's more myself than I am. ...

... He was indulgent, not from affection, but from pride. He wished earnestly to see her bring honour to the family by an alliance with the Lintons. ...

» **Note**

- be goof for...: ...에 좋다
- Strange to say: 이상하게 들리지만
- not from (A) but from(B): (A)로부터가 아니라 (B)로부터
  rf) not (A) but (B): (A)가 아니라 (B)

069

The King of the Golden River - John Ruskin

작품 소개: 석양의 빛을 받아 금이 쏟아지는 것처럼 보인다고 하여 황금 강이라고 불리는 폭포가 있었다. 이 계곡의 주인 슈바르츠, 한스, 글룩이라는 삼 형제는 황금강의 왕을 만나고 그는 황금 강이 황금으로 변하게 되는 방법을 알려준다. 황금을 찾아 떠나는 슈바르츠, 한스, 글룩. 과연 황금을 찾는 사람은 누구일까?

작가 소개: 영국의 비평가이자 사회사상가(1819~1900)다. 예술미의 순수감상을 주장하고 "예술의 기초는 민족 및 개인의 성실성과 도의에 있다."라고 하는 자신의 미술 원리를 구축해 나갔다.

The landlord <u>turned</u> the poor beggar <u>out</u> of the gate without saying a word.

: 그 집주인은 불쌍한 거지를 일언반구 없이 대문 <u>밖으로</u> 내 쫓았다.

The brothers are so different from each other in appearance and in character.

: 그 형제들을 <u>외모와 성격면에선</u> 상호간에 너무 다르다.

》 **원문**

… They worked their servants without any wages, till they would not work any more, and then quarrelled with them and <u>turned them out of doors without paying them</u>. …

… The youngest brother, Gluck, was very different from his brother <u>in appearance and character</u>. …

… He did not get on very well with his brothers, or rather, they did not treat him well. …

281

His moustaches <u>curled</u> twice on each side of his mouth, and his hair <u>fell over</u> his shoulder.

: 그의 구렛나루는 그의 양 입가에서 두 번 말렸다, 그리고 그의 머릿결은 그의 어깨 <u>위로 떨어졌다.</u>

Could you <u>spare</u> some moments?

: 짬을 내주실 수가 있습니까?

» **원문**

… He had a very large nose, slightly brass-coloured skin; his cheeks were round, and very red; his eyes twinkled merrily through long silky eyelashes, <u>his moustaches curled twice round like a corkscrew on each side of his mouth, and his hair, curiously black and white, fell over his shoulder.</u> …

… I'm very, very hungry, sir. <u>Couldn't you spare me a bit of bread before I go?</u>" …

» **Note**

□ curl: 소용돌이치다, 말아 올리다, 곱슬거리게 하다

□ on each side of his mouth: 그의 양 입가에

□ fall over…: …위로 떨어지다

□ spare: 절약하다, 남겨두다, 할애하다

282

I gave place to an old woman when I took a subway.
: 나는 지하철을 탔을 때 한 노파에게 자리를 양보했다.

I drew myself up to my full height and began to take some exercise.
: 나는 완전히 온 몸을 폈다, 그리고 운동하기 시작했다.

Under pretence of bowing at him I slipped into the room.
: 그에게 인사를 하는 것을 핑계삼아[한다는 미명 아래], 나는 교실로 살짝 들어갔다.

» 원문

… Then his amazement gradually gave place to his curiosity, and he asked a very delicate question. …

… The little man turned sharply round, walked straight up to Gluck, and drew himself up to his full height. "I am," the little man said, "the King of the Golden River." …

… Therefore, Hans went to the evening service for the first time in his life, and, under pretence of crossing himself, stole a cupful and returned home, very glad of his success. …

… The bottle was two-thirds empty. But Gluck went on again bravely. The path became easier to walk on, and two or three blades of grass appeared upon it …

» Note

☐ give place to…: …에게 양보하다
☐ draw oneself up to one's full height: 허리를 펴고 꼿꼿이 서다
☐ under the pretence of…: …하는 구실로
☐ two-third empty: 3분의 2가 빈

283

When I was in sight of the wonderful castle, I cried out with exclamation.

: 멋있는 성이 나의 눈 안에[시야에] 들어왔을 때, 나는 감탄과 함께 소리 질렀다.

I worked my way under the dark tunnel.

: 나는 깜깜한 터널아래에서 나의 길을 헤쳐 나갔다.

» 원문

... When he came in sight of the Treasure valley, a river, like the Golden River, was springingly from a new opening of the rocks above it and was flowing in many streams among the dry heaps of red sand. ...

... And, even to this day, the inhabitants of the valley are glad to trace the Golden River working its way under the ground till it comes out in the Treasure Valley. ...

» Note

☐ in sight of...: ...의 시야에 있는
  ex» come in sight of...: ...의 시야에 들어오다
☐ work one's way: (애써)나아가다.

Abraham Lincoln(adapted)

- Autobiography

\# **작품 소개:** "링컨 자서전 명연설문"은 소통과 통합의 정치를 꿈꿨던 에이브러햄 링컨의 사상, 그리고 민주주의의 정수가 담긴 연설, 교서, 편지를 모아 엮은 책이다.

\# **작가 소개:** 미국의 16대 대통령이다.

How much of the water shall I drink?
: 어느 정도의 물을 내가 마실까요?

Daejeon is a few miles south of our city.
: 대전은 우리 시로부터 몇 마일 남쪽으로 떨어져 있다.

» 원문

… "How much of it shall I cut?" "All of it," Mr. Crawford answered. …

… He did not hesitate to go all over the country to borrow books. …

… The new home was located on the north bank of the Sangamon River, a few miles west of Decatur. Abraham was hired out to split fence rails for neighbors. …

… New Salem gave him 277 votes in a poll of 284-all but seven. He was not elected, however, only because he was not known throughout the county. …

» Note

☐ How much of it shall I cut?: 그것의 어느 정도를 베어들일까요?
☐ a few miles west of Decatur: Decatur로부터 몇 마일 서쪽에 있는
☐ poll: 투표수
  cf) exit poll: 출구 조사
☐ all but…: …을 제외하고 모두

285

When you punishes your students, be sure to <u>turn to</u> the use of reason instead of the use of emotion.

: 당신이 당신의 학생들을 벌 줄 때, 감정의 사용보다는 이성의 사용에 <u>의존할 것</u>을 분명히 하라.

Smith is <u>setting me against</u> my friend.

: Smith는 <u>나를 나의 친구와</u> 이간질 시키고 있다.

The colony people living in this country can <u>exercise their rights</u> to vote for their favorite president.

: 이 나라에 살고 있는 식민지 국민들은 그들이 좋아하는 대통령을 지지하는 투표를 하기 위한 <u>그들의 권한을 행사할</u> 수가 있다.

» **원문**

... "He is working on the passions of men, so that they may <u>turn to the use of force instead of law</u>. He is setting brother against brother!
...

... "<u>I am not stirring up the people to rebel</u>. I don't have to. This country belongs to the people who live in it. ...

... "When they are not satisfied with their government, <u>they can exercise their right to change it</u>. ...

» **Note**

□ work on: (1)효력이 있다 (2)설득하다 (3)연구하다
  ex) work on the passions of them: 그들을 부추기고 있다.
□ set (A) against (B): (A)가 (B)에 대하여 반감을 품게 하다, 대항하게 하다
□ turn to...: (1)...의지하다 (2)...좋아하다
□ stir up: ...선동하다
□ exercise: 운동하다, 연습하다, 행사하다, 실행하다
  ex) exercise one's right: ...의 권력을 행사하다

The game <u>was close</u>.

: 게임은 <u>팽팽했다</u>.

<u>The things having come to this pass</u>, we can not but fight against the enemy.

: <u>사태가 이러한 형편에 이른 이상</u>, 우리는 적과 싸우지 않을 수가 없다.

Our government <u>expressed its concerns about the war between the two countries</u>.

: 우리 정부는 그 두 나라사이에 있는 <u>전쟁에 대하여 깊은 우려를 표시했다</u>.

» 원문

... <u>The election on November 2 was close</u>. The republican polled 125,430 votes for their state ticket against 121,609 for the Douglas Democrats. ...

... <u>Things having come to this pass, there is no choice but to fight</u>," Douglas said. "I think so, too, but ..." ...

... The government of France, Italy, Prussia, Belgium, Turkey, Austria and Swizerland <u>expressed deep regret</u>. ...

» Note

□ close: 막상막하의, 대접전인

□ Things have come to this pass.: 사태가 이 지경[형편]에 이르다.

□ there is no choice but to+동사의 원형: ...하지 않을 수가 없다

□ express deep regret: 깊은 유감을 표명하다

287

071

Tom Sawyer Detective

- Mark Twain

\# **작품 소개:** "탐정 톰 소여(Tom Sawyer, Detective)"는 마크 트웨인이 톰 소여의 모험 시리즈의 속편이다. 19세기 미국 남부 미주리주에 있는 가공의 마을인 세인트 피터즈버그(St. Petersburg)를 배경으로 하고 있으며, 귀여운 말썽꾸러기 톰 소여의 익살맞은 모습을 통해 기성세대를 조롱하는 것이 특징이다.

\# **작가 소개:** 미국 현대문학의 아버지로 불리는 문학적 업적을 이루었을 뿐 아니라, 물질문명과 종교와 전쟁의 부조리를 날카롭게 파헤치고 불의와 제국주의에 맞서 신랄한 비판을 가했다.

I'll take back what I said, if you say, 'I'm sorry.'

: 만약에 죄송하다고 말한다면, 나는 내가 한 말을 철회하겠다.

A What is she like?

: 그녀는 어떠한가?

B She is very kind and considerate.

: 그녀는 매우 친절하고 사려 깊다.

It beats anything I ever heard of.

: 그것은 내가 일찍이 들어왔던 어느 것보다 낫소.

» **원문**

… and imagine a lot of sickness and dangers and objections, and she'll take back what she said. Let me alone. I know how to work her." …

… And he's a twin." "What's the other twin like?" "Just exactly like

Jupiter-so they say, but he hasn't been seen for seven years. He got to robbing when he was nineteen or twenty, and they jailed him; but he broke and got away. …

… Tom was astonished, and so was I. He said: "Aunt Polly, it beats anything I ever heard of. Why, Uncle silas was as gentle as a lamb." …

» **Note**

- ☐ take back...: ...을 취소하다
- ☐ What is (A) like?: (A)는 어떠한가? (즉, (A)의 '성격'이나 '속성'을 물을 때 쓰인다.)
  cf) What does (A) look like?: (A)는 어떻게 보이는가? (즉, '외모'를 물을 때 쓰인다.)
- ☐ got to+동사의 원형/(동)명사: ...하기에 이르다
- ☐ break and get away: 부수고 도망가다 즉, 탈옥하다
- ☐ beat...: ...능가하다

The pop star is not so popular as he used to be.
: 그 가수는 과거만 큼 그렇게 인기가 있지 못하다.

You are the image of your mother.
: 당신은 당신의 어머니상이다.[어머니와 인상이 똑같다.]

Don't worry, Buddy. I'll never tell on your father.
: 걱정하지 마세요, 친구. 나는 결코 너의 아빠에게 고자질하지 않을 것이다.

» **원문**

… Your aunt Sally says he hates to go into the pulpit. He isn't so popular as he used to be." …

… Because if you aren't Jupiter Dunlap you're the other twin, Jake. You're the image of your brother." "Well, I am Jake. but look here, how did you come to know as Dunlap's?" …

… "Then I'm saved. I'm saved, sure! I'll go home. They'll hide me and save my life. But you must never tell on me. Swear you'll keep silent. I'm burned day and night." …

» **Note**

- □ 주어(A) used to be: (A)가 …였던 것, 즉 (A)의 과거

  ex) I'm not what I used to be.: 나는 과거의 내가 아니다.
- □ You're the image of your brother.: 당신은 당신 형제의 상[모습, 외모]다. 즉, 당신은 당신의 형제와 똑같다.
- □ tell on: 고자질하다
- □ I'm burned day and night.: 나는 매일 낮과 밤 녹초가 된다.

What do you think it was (that) he bought?

: 당신은 그가 구입한 것이 무엇이라고 생각하니?

Something flashed on me and took my breath away.

: 무엇인가가 나에게 번뜩 생각났다, 그리고 나를 깜짝 놀라게 했다.

» **원문**

… It was Bud Dixon. I watched him in secret. Now what do you think it was he bought?" "What was it he bought, Jake?" "You'd never guess in the world. It was a screwdriver." "A screwdriver! What did he want with it?" …

…"Where did he hide the diamond? I thought and thought. Then something flashed on me and took my breath away. …

» **Note**

☐ 원래 표현은 다음과 같다: Now do you think?+What was it (that) he bought? 다시 말해, 'do you think'는 '삽입절'이 되고, 의문사 what이 의문문이 되기 위해 문장 앞에 오고, 관계대명사 'that'이 생략된 구문이다. 이때의 'it'는 선행사라고 볼 수가 있다.

    cf) 다음의 문장 'It was what (that) he bought.'는 2가지로 해석 가능하다. (1)what이 강조된 '강조구문(그가 구입한 것은 무엇이다.)'으로 해석할 수가 있다. (2)what이 '선행사이고, 목적격 관계대명사 that이 생략된 구문(그것은 그가 구입한 무엇이다.)'처럼 해석할 수 있다.

☐ (A) flash on (B): (A)가 (B)에 번뜩 생각나다

☐ take one's breath away: …를 깜짝 놀라게 하다.

I'm sorry to have kept you waiting.

: 당신을 기다리게 해서 죄송합니다.

While talking about something, they stole a look towards their father.

: 무엇인가 말하면서, 그들은 그들의 아빠의 표정을 훔쳐봤다.

» **원문**

… You must be hungry, poor thing! Sit down, sit down." "I'm sorry to have kept you waiting. Tom and I came on foot; we wanted to take a smell at the woods," I said. …

… Whenever she lift her head a little and stole a look towards her father, you could see there were tears in her eyes. …

… It oughtn't to be going around in the day-time." "That's so, Tom. I've never heard the like of it before." …

□ I'm sorry to have kept you waiting.: 기다리게 만들어 죄송합니다.

□ steal: 살짝 훔치다, 살그머니 다가가다

    ex)) steal a look: 표정을 살짝 훔쳐보다

□ the like: 닮은 것

The players of our opposite team played it on us.

: 상대방 팀은 비열한 방법으로 우리를 앞질렀다.

As our parents were away, we have their house to ourselves.

: 양친들이 멀리 출타 중이었을 때, 우리는 그들의 집을 전유했다.

Listen up. Now it's high time to make a name for yourselves.

: 잘 들어라. 지금이 너희들이 이름을 떨칠 좋은 기회다.

She broke in the room and threw cold water on the good atmosphere.

: 그녀는 방으로 불쑥 들어왔다 그리고 좋은 분위기에 찬물을 껴 없었다.

» **원문**

... "Goo-goo-goo-goo," the way a deaf and dumb person does. "You do it well, and your disguise is excellent. You're right. Play it on us. Play it on us the same as on the others," Tom said. ...

... Everybody praised Brace Dunlap for being so good to that stranger. He let him have a little log cabin all to himself, and had his negros take care of it, and fetch him all the food he wanted. ...

... Here we've got a good opportunity to make a name for ourselves." However, old Jeff Hooker threw cold water on the whole business when we got to the blacksmith's shop and told him what we came for. ...

» **Note**

☐ play it on: 비열한 방법[수단]으로 (남)을 앞지르다.

☐ have(or keep) (A) to oneself: (A)를 혼자 전유하다

☐ make a name for oneself: 이름을 떨치다

☐ throw cold water on...: ...에 찬물을 끼얹다.

Stop it! I don't want to get her into trouble any more.

: 그만해! 나는 그녀를 더 이상 곤경 속으로 빠뜨리고 싶지 않아.

I got down on my knees and begged for my forgiveness.

: 나는 무릎을 꿇었다 그리고 용서를 구했다.

You bet! I had no hand in it!

: 정말이야! 나는 그것에 관여하지 않았어!

» **원문**

... With Tom it was awful. He seemed at a loss what to think, because he had got his uncle into a thousand times more trouble than ever. But pretty soon he said: "Uncle Silas, don't say another word like that. It's dangerous, and there isn't a shadow of truth in it." ... Then Uncle Silas was scared and sorry, got down on his knees and lift his head up. Before long Jupiter came to himself. ...

... "Sit down! A murder was done, but you had no hand in it!" A pin could have been heard to drop. The old man sank down, at a loss, in his seat, and Aunt Sally and Benny, astonished, were staring at Tom with their mouth open. ...

- □ get+사람(A)+into trouble: (A)를 곤경 속으로 몰아넣다
- □ a shadow of truth: 진리의 그림자
- □ get down on one's knees: 무릎을 꿇다
- □ come to oneself: 제정신이 들다
- □ have hand in...: ...에 관여하다
- □ A pin could have been heard to drop.: (가벼운) 핀 하나라도 떨어지면 소리가 들렸을 것이다.('가정법 과거완료'의 '주절'과 '종속절'이 혼합된 상태)
- □ sink down: 풀썩 주저앉다

072

The Prince and the Pauper
- Mark Twain

\# **작품 소개:** "왕자와 거지"는 에드워드와 톰의 각자 다른 삶의 체험을 통해 이상과 현실의 차이, 삶의 겉모습과 실제의 차이를 잘 보여준다. 어린아이들의 순수한 눈에 비친 왕궁의 사치와 허례 허식, 부당한 권력에 희생되는 백성들의 모습을 그려내 그 시대의 불합리한 현실을 풍자한다.

<u>At a distance</u>, I saw somebody running towards me.
: 멀리서 나는 누군가가 나에게 달려오는 것을 보았다.

He was <u>none other than</u> my long-forgotten close friend.
: 그는 다름 아닌 나의 오랫동안 잊혀졌던 친구였다.

What is it (that) you would like to say?
: 당신이 말하기를 원하는 것이 무엇입니까?

» **원문**

> … When the king left the inn with a man who told him that Hendon was lying wounded in the wood over there, there was a man following them <u>at a distance</u>. He showed his face when they came to the wood. <u>He was none other than John Canty!</u> …
> … Hendon <u>laid his hand upon</u> the arm of the constable and said in a low voice, ""I would like to say a word to you, sir." "<u>What is it (that) you would like to say?</u>" …

» **Note**
□ at a distance: 멀리서
□ none other than…: 다름 아닌…
□ lay one's hand upon…: …의 손을 …위에 얹다
□ What is it (that) you would like to say?: 당신이 말하고 싶은 그것은 무엇이 냐? (이 문장은 선행사가 it이고 목적격 관계대명사 that이 생략된 구문이라고 볼 수 있다.)

Our players looked down as our team didn't win the game, and so I tried to cheer them up with forced lightness.

: 우리의 팀이 이기지 못했기 때문에 선수들은 우울해 보였다. 그러므로 나는 억지의 밝은 표정을 가지고 그들을 격려하고자 노력했다.

What more do you mean to say, after finishing the hot debate between us?

: 우리 사이의 열띤 논쟁이 끝난 후에 당신은 무엇을 더 말하기를 원하니?

» **원문**

... "Shall I tell the judge? Well, it may cost you your neck." The constable was dumb with fear for a moment, then said with forced lightness, "I did it only for a joke." "Oh, do you mean to say that you kept the woman's pig for a joke?" ...

... "No, it is not strange. He has been wicked from his birth." "Oh, I didn't speak of him, Sir Miles." "Not of him? Then of what? What is it (that) is strange?" ...

... Even the mob was impressed by his heroic attitude, and the insulting clamour gave place to an admiring silence. ...

» **Note**

- □ with forced lightness: 억지로 만든 밝은 표정을 가지고
  ex) a forced smile: 억지 미소
- □ you mean to say...: ...라고 말할 작정이다
- □ from one's birth: 태어날 때부터

073

The Adventures of Huckleberry Finn

- Mark Twain

작품 소개: 「톰 소여의 모험」(1876)의 속편이다. 미국 서부의 자유인으로서의 의식을 가진 허크라는 인물의 창조, 성인들의 사회적 인습과 위선에 대한 통렬한 풍자, 웅대한 자연을 배경으로 구가하는 자유에의 찬가, 또한 방언의 구사와 문체의 예술성 등에 의하여 미국문학의 굴지의 걸작으로 평가된다. 헤밍웨이, 샐린저 등에게 영향을 주었다.

The nails sell <u>by the pound</u>.

: 그 못들은 <u>파운드 단위로</u> 팔린다.

<u>I am making a bad job of it</u>, so I want to stop the job and take a short break for a few days.

: 나는 이 일이 잘 안 풀리고 있다, 그러므로 나는 이 일을 중단하고 싶다 그리고 잠시 동안 며칠 휴식을 취하고 싶다.

» **원문**

…They sell such a fish as that <u>by the pound</u> in the market and everybody buys some of it. Its meat is s white as snow and makes a good fry. …

… I practiced wearing those clothes all day and soon I found I could do pretty well in them. Jim said I didn't walk like a girl. He said I should not pull up my gown to touch my trouser-pocket. …

… My hands shook, and <u>I was making a bad job of it</u>. When the woman stopped talking, I looked up. …

» **Note**

- □ by the pound: 파운드 단위로
- □ pull up: (위로)… 을 올리다
- □ make a bad job of it: 일이 잘 안 풀리다

What did you say your name was?

: 당신의 이름이 무엇이라고 했죠?

This is a seven hundred thousand dollars worth of stamp.

: 이것은 70만 달러 가치의 우표다.

It was still so dark, so I had to feel my way with my hands

: 여전히 캄캄했다. 그러므로 나는 나의 손을 가지고 더듬으며 나아갔다.

» **원문**

... The woman kept looking at me curiously, and I didn't feel comfortable at all. Soon she said: "What did you say your name was?" "M-Mary Williams." ...

... Every nights now I went up the shore about ten o'clock at some little village, and bought ten or fifteen cents' worth of meal, bacon or other things to eat. ...

... The deck side was so high out there. We went down the slope of it to the left side of the board, in the dark, feeling our way slowly with our feet, and spreading our hands to protect ourselves. ...

» **Note**

□ What did you say your name was?: 너의 이름이 무엇이라고 했지? (이 문장 은, Did you say?+What was your name?이다. 즉 이 두 문장이 하나로 결합 된 '간접의문문' 형태다.)

□ ten or fifteen cents' worth of meal: 10 내지 15센트 가치의 식사
  rf) 금액(A) worth of (A): (A)가치[가격]의 (B)

□ feel one's way: ...의 길을 더듬어 나가다

Put the robot toy out of sight, or they'll struggle to get it each other.

: 그 로봇 장난감을 눈에 보이지 않게 하라, 그렇지 않으면 그들은 그것을 쟁 취하기 위하여 분투할 것이다.

Don't do that, or you get into trouble.

: 그것을 하지 말라, 그렇지 않 으면 당신은 곤경에 처할 것이다.

Thank you for having taken any trouble to help me.

: 나를 도와주기 위해 어떤 수고를 하신 것에 대해 고맙게 여깁니다.

» **원문**

… One of the men put his head out just a few feet from me, and jerked it in again, and said: "Put the lantern out of sight, Bill!" …

… Then Bill came out and got in. …

… "Oh, what are they doing there? There is no chance for them if they don't get off very quickly. Why did they get into such a trouble?" …

… When he turned the corner, I went back and got into my boat. I felt comfortable because I took all the trouble for that gang on the wreck. …

» **Note**

- □ put (A) out: (A)를 내밀다
- □ jerk: 갑자기[홱] 움직이다
- □ put (A) out of sight: (A)를 안보이게 하다
- □ get into trouble: 곤경에 빠지다, 꾸지람을 듣다
    - *cf)* give (A) a trouble=get (A) into trouble: (A)에 폐를 끼치다
- □ take trouble: 수고하다, 노고를 아끼지 않다
- □ make a trouble: 말썽을 일으키다

299

The Adventures of Tom Sawyer - Mark Twain

작품 소개: 수무나 개구쟁이 톰 수여는 잖나에 관하 하 누구도 따라우지 무할 기발하 재치를 지닌 소년으로, 하루가 멀다 하고 온갖 말썽을 일으킨다. 그러던 어느 날 톰은 마을의 방랑객 인 친구 허크에게 해적이 숨겨놓은 보물을 찾아보자고 제안한다. 그러나 보물은 그들이 우연 히 목격한 살인 사건의 진범인 인디언 조의 수중에 들어가고, 톰과 허크는 두려움과 싸우며 보 물을 손에 넣기 위한 모험에 뛰어든다.

Once in a while Tom plays hooky.

: Tom은 이따금 수업을 빼먹는다.

The sports star is a object of admiration.

: 그 운동선수는 숭배의 대상이다.

That is the way she succeeded in her working area.

: 그것이 그녀가 그녀의 직업분야에 성공했던 방식이다.

» 원문

… Tom did play hooky, and he had a very good time. He got back home just in time to help Jim, the small colored boy, to saw and split the next day's fire-wood before supper …

… A stranger of any age, male or female, was an object of curiosity in the poor little village of St. Petersburg. …

… "I can't, Master Tom. The Mistress told me not to stay fooling around with anyone." "Oh, never mind what she said, Jim. That's the way she always talks. Give me the bucket. I won't be gone only a minute. She won't know." …

» **Note**

☐ play hooky=play truant: 농땡이 부리다

☐ any...어떤...라도(즉 긍정문의 'any'는 양보의 뜻이 있다.)

☐ object: 대상

☐ fool around with...: ...와 빈둥빈둥 거리며 놀다

☐ That's the way she always talks.: 그것이 그녀가 늘 말하는 방식이다.(직역)

　　rf) 그런 식으로 그녀는 늘 말한다.(의역)

<u>Jim is only human, too.</u> He can make a mistake.

: <u>Jim 역시 인간에 불과하다.</u> 그도 실수를 범할 수가 있다.

His opinion of the war <u>put the thing in a new light</u>.

: 전쟁에 관한 그의 견해는 <u>사태를 새로운 견지로 바라보게끔 했다</u>.

» **원문**

... "<u>Jim was only human.</u> <u>This temptation was too much for him</u>. He put down his pail and took the marble, and bent over the toe with great interest while the bandage was being unwounded. ...

... Well, I don't see why I shouldn't like it. Does a boy get a chance to whitewash a fence every day?" <u>That put the thing in a new light</u>. Ben stopped nibbling his apple. ...

» **Note**

☐ human: 인간

　　ex) human nature: 인간의 천성

☐ too 부사[형용사](A) for (B): (B)에 비해 너무나 (A)한[하게]

☐ That put the thing in a new light.: 그 말이 사태를 새로운 견지로부터 바라 보게끔 했다.

Tom expressed his opinion <u>with smile in his face but anger in his heart</u>.

: Tom은 얼굴에는 미소를 가지고 그러나 마음속으로는 노여움을 가지고 그의 의견을 피력했다.

<u>Now that</u> you arrived here, it's time to start for our trip.

: 이제 당신이 도착<u>했으므로</u> 여행을 위해 출발할 시간이다.

She tries to <u>show off</u> her newly bought dress in front of her friends.

: 그녀는 그의 친구들 앞에서 그녀의 새로 산 옷을 <u>과시하려고</u> 한다.

» **원문**

... Tom gave up the brush <u>with reluctance in his face but alacrity in his heart</u>. ...

... His soul was at peace, <u>now that</u> he had settled with Sid for <u>calling attention to</u> the black thread and <u>getting him into trouble</u>. ...

... Then he pretended that he did not know she was present, and <u>began to show off in all sorts of silly boyish ways</u> in order to win her admiration. ...

» **Note**

  □ with reluctance: 마지못해
  □ now that: (1)because: ...때문에 (2)since: ...이후로
  □ get 목적어(A) into trouble: ...에게 고통을 주다, 괴롭히다

There is nothing so good as our own house in the world

: 이 세상에는 우리 자신의 집만큼 그렇게 좋은 것은 아무 것도 없다.

Hold on. I'll connect you to your friend.

: 잠깐만 기다려라. 너의 친구를 연결해 줄게.

She hurried upstairs with Sid and Mary at her heel.

: 그녀는 그녀의 뒷자락에 Sid와 Mary를 데리고 이층으로 급히 올라갔다.

» **원문**

… Tom came up to the fence and leaned on it, hoping that she would tarry a little longer. She halted a moment on the steps and then moved toward the door. …

… Then he would tell, and there would be nothing so good in the world as to see that pet model "get it." …

… "Hold on, now, what're you belting me for? Sid broke it!" …

… But she hurried upstairs, nevertheless, with Sid and Mary at her heels, and her face grew white, too, and her lips trembled. …

» **Note**

☐ tarry: 머무적거리다, 늑장부리다
☐ so …. as to…: …하는 것만큼 그렇게 …한[…하게]
☐ get it: 벌 받다
☐ hold on: 잠깐 기다리다
☐ What…for?=Why…?: 무엇 때문에?, 왜?
☐ at one's heels: 남의 뒤를 바로 따라

303

What's that (that) you've got?
: 네가 가지고 있는 것이 무엇이냐?

The late boy student began to steal furtive glances at the beautiful girl student next door to his friend.
: 늦게 온 남학생은 자기의 친구 옆에 있는 그 아름다운 여학생에게 은밀한 시선을 보냈다.

» **원문**

... "Hello, Huckleberry! What's that you've got?" asked Tom. ...

... Thomas Sawyer, this is the most astounding confession I have ever listened to. You deserve a severe punishment. Take off your jacket." ...

... Presently the boy began to steal furtive glances at the girl. ...

» **Note**

□ What's that (that) you've got? 즉, 이 문장은 목적격관계대명사 that이 생략된 것이라고 볼 수가 있다.

cf) I realized (that) that is my money.(이 문장은 that이 원래 두 번 와야 되지만 오해를 방지하기 위해 지시 대명사 that만 살리는 경우가 많다. :

□ deserve...: ...받을[할]만한 가치가 있다

□ steal glance at...: ...을 몰래 훔쳐보다

A cute little girl dangled her legs against the bench in excess of joy.
: 한 귀엽고 작은 소녀가 기쁨에 겨운 나머지 의자에 기대어 그녀의 다리가 댕글댕글 매달리어 흔들거리고 있었다.

He kept that money under lock and key.
: 그는 그 돈을 안전하게 잠궈 보관했다.

… and when you get to the corner give the rest of them the slip and turn down through the lane, and come back." In a little while the two met at the bottom of the lane and when they reached the school they had it all to themselves. …

… That was agreeable. They sat happily, and dangled their legs against the bench in excess of contentment. …

… Then his pride was up, and he strode away and went outside. …

… Every day he took a mysterious book out of his desk and absorbed himself in it at times. He kept that book under lock and key. …

» **Note**

☐ slip: 쪽지
  ex) a pink slip: 해고 통지

☐ have(or keep) (A) to oneself: (A)를 독차지하다

☐ dangle …(A) against (B): (B)에 대항하여[기대어] (A)가 대롱대롱 매달리게 하다

☐ up: 위로 올라가는, 기분이 좋은, 새로운, 시간이 다 된
  ex) Time is up.: 시간이 다 됐다.

☐ under lock and key: 자물쇠로 채워 안전하게 보관하여

Don Quixote

- Miguel De Cervantes

작품 소개: 기사 소설에 탐닉하다가 정신을 잃어 기사가 되겠다고 나선 한 엉뚱한 미치광이의 이야기를 그린 작품이다. 성서 다음으로 지구상에서 가장 다양한 언어로 번역된 책이기도 하다.

작가 소개: 스페인의 소설가이자 극작가이며 시인(1547~1616)이다.

My mind is fully made up. Let's go for a walk.

: 마음이 완전히 결정되었어. 산보합시다.

I armed myself with some new weapons.

: 나는 신예 무기를 가지고 나 자신을 무장했다.

He hit on a good name to please all of us.

: 우리 전체를 기쁘게 해줄 좋은 이름이 그에게 떠올랐다.[그는 좋은 이름을 떠올렸다.]

» 원문

… "Yes, I will be a knight," he said to himself. "My mind is fully made up. I will arm myself in a coat of mail, I'll mount my noble steed, I will ride out into the world to seek adventures. …

… He studied over this for many days and at last hit upon a name which pleased him much. "It shall be Dulcina," he cried. "It shall be Dulcina del Toboso. No other name is so sweet, so harmonious, do like the lady herself." …

I am not a match for him.

: 나는 그에게 적수가 안 된다.

She left me without so much as saying good-bye.

: 그녀는 안녕이라는 말 한마디도 없이 나를 떠났다.

Let it be ever so difficult, I can solve the problem.

: 아무리 어렵다 할지라도, 나는 그 문제를 해결할 수가 있다.

» **원문**

... "Where are you wounded, uncle?" asked the niece. "Wounded! I'm not wounded. I'm only bruised. I had a bad fall from Rozinante while I was fighting ten giants. ...

... They were the wickedest fellows that ever roamed the earth; but I was a match for them." ...

... When he had eaten a hearty supper, he crept off to bed without so much as saying good-night. ...

... At length Sancho Panza spoke: "I beseech you, Sir Knight-errant, be sure to remember the island you promised me. I dare say I shall make out to govern it, let it be ever so big." ...

- wounded: 다친
- bruised: 타박상을 입은
- match=rival: 호적수

    ex) I am a match for you.: 나는 낭신의 호석수나.
- without so much as=not even: ...조차도 하지 않고
- Knight-errant: 편력 기사, 수습 기사, 의협가
- I dare say: (1)아마도 (2)분명코
- make out: (1)이해하다 (2)작성하다 (3)발견하다 (4)입증하다 (5)암시하다 (6) 잘 해내다(manage) (7)애무하다
- let it be ever so+(A): 아무리 (A) 할지라도

I will get even with my enemy.

: 나는 나의 적에게 복수할 것이다.

A good idea struck her and then she keeps it to herself.

: 좋은 생각이 그녀에게 떠올랐다. 그리고 그것을 혼자 간직하고 있다.

» **원문**

... but he changed them into windmills so that I should not have the honor of victory. But mind you, Sancho, I will get even with him in the end." "So be it, say I!" cried Sancho, as he dismounted from the donkey. ...

... Still, with the saddle on his shoulders, he trudged silently at the heels of Rozinante, and kept his thoughts to himself. ...

» **Note**

- mind you: 알겠나, 잘 들어 둬
- get even with...: ...와 복수하다
- So be it.: 그렇다면 좋다. 그렇게 하도록 해.
- keep (A) to oneself: (A)를 독차지하다

    ex) keep his thought to himself: 그의 생각을 혼자 독차지하다, 즉 혼자만 알고 있다

308

Pray have done with your preach.

: 제발 설교는 그만두게.

You need not go to any trouble about the matter.

: 당신은 그 문제에 관하여 어떤 걱정을 가질 필요가 없어.[고생할 필요가 없어.]

The hungry men watered at the thought of a well-done beef steak.

: 그 배고픈 사람들은 잘 익힌 스테이크 생각에 군침이 돌았다.

» 원문

... Every man for himself, and God for us all, say I. Little said is soonest mended. There is no padlocking of men's mouths; for a closed mouth catches no flies." "Pray have done with your proverbs," said Don Quixote, sternly. ...

... "Oh, you need not go to any trouble about it," said Sancho; "for I will tell the lady just the same. ...

... It was dinner time, and the odors of the kitchen filled the air. Sancho's mouth watered at the thought of a bit of hot roast beef; for he had tasted nothing but cold food for many days. ...

» Note

□ have done with...=have finished with...=get through with...: ...을 끝내다

□ Pray=Please: 제발, 부디

□ go to trouble: 수고하다, 고생하다

□ A mouth waters.: 군침이 돈다.

　　ex) My mouth waters.=I have a watering mouth.: 나는 군침이 돈다.

□ at the thought of...: ...의 생각에

309

It <u>deserves</u> attention.
: 그것은 주목할 <u>만한 가치가 있다.</u>

A I gave up getting first place.: 나는 일등 상 받는 것을 포기했다.

B How so?: 어떤 이유로?

» 원문

… They spoke to Sancho, and he was not a little surprised to meet them <u>in that out-of-the-way place.</u> …

… "Matter enough," he answered. "<u>I deserved the worst beating in the world,</u> for I have lost three donkeys which were as good as three castles." "<u>How so?</u>" asked the barber. "Were the donkeys in your pocket?" …

» **Note**

☐ in that out-of-the-way place: 낯선 장소로부터

☐ deserve+(동)명사: …받을[할] 가치가 있다.

    ex) He deserves helping.: 그는 도움을 받을 가치가 있다.

☐ How so?: 어떤 이유로 그런가?

I knew what you said by heart.

: 나는 네가 말한 것을 다 외웠다.

The rumor was passed down to all the people in town by word of mouth.

: 그 소문은 구전에 의해 마을에 살고 있는 모든 사람들에게 전달되었다.

His mother bade his son Godspeed on his way to the battle place.

: 그의 어머니는 전장으로 가는 중에 있는 그의 아들에게 행운을 빌었다.

» 원문

... As for Dulcinea's letter, I don't care a straw about that. I know it all by heart, and will carry it to her by word of mouth. ...

... He stroked the donkey with his hands; he kissed it again and again ; he called it by every endearing name. ...

... Samson Garrasco walked with them to the edge of the village, and there bade them Godspeed on their journey. ...

» **Note**

- □ learn[know] (A) by heart=memorize (A): (A)를 암기하다
- □ by word of mouth: 구전으로
  cf) in writing: 글로
- □ stroke: 쓰다듬다
- □ call (A) by (B): (B)에 의해 (A)를 부르다
- □ bid ... Godspeed on...: ...에게 ...대해 행운을 빌다

The mischievous student likes to play a trick on his classmates.

: 그 장난끼 많은 학생은 자기의 급우들을 놀리기를 좋아한다.

I am not particular about any food when I am on trip.

: 여행 중일 때 나는 음식에는 특별히 신경 쓰지 않습니다.

Pluck up your heart and just do it.

: 너의 기력을 불러 모으십시오 그리고 단지 그것을 하십시오.

» **원문**

... Sancho replied at leaving. "I'll be back here in a moment. The hare leaps out of the bush where we least expect hero. Faint heart never won fair lady." ...

... Why should I wish to play a trick on you? Come, ride out with me quickly, and you will see the princess coming. ...

... "I shall be very glad to the colts, master, and I thank you," said Sancho; "but as for spoils, they are so small that I'm not particular." ...

..."My master," he said, Pluck up your heart and cheer up if you can. Let us go home and quit seeking adventures in lands and places we do not know. ...

» **Note**

☐ play a trick on...: ...를 놀리다, 속이다
☐ particular: 신경을 쓰는, 까다로운, 특별한
   ex) I'm so particular about my dress.: 나는 나의 옷에 특히 까다롭다.
☐ pluck up: (담력, 기력 등을)불러 일으키다
   ex) pluck up one's spirit: ...힘을 내다

076

The Story of My Life

- Benjamin Franklin

작품 소개: 1장 My Childhood로부터 시작하여 14장 I Publish Poor Richand's Almanac까지 작가의 인생 과정을 기술한 작품이다.

작가 소개: 벤저민 프랭클린(1706~1790)은 18세기의 미국인 가운데 조지 워싱턴 다음으로 저명한 인물로 작가, 과학자, 정치인이다.

When I discuss something with my friends I don't usually put forward my opinion bluntly.

: 내가 친구들과 무언가를 의논할 때, 나는 보통 나의 의견을 버릇없이 내세우지 않는다.

When I grew up, I moved to the big city and established myself there.

: 내가 성장했을 때, 나는 그 대도시로 이사를 했고 그곳에 기반을 잡았다.

» **원문**

… I ceased to say so hastily to the opinions of others. Nor did I put forward my opinion positively or bluntly. I adopted a humble and inquiring attitude of scepticism. …

… At the time I established myself in Pennsylvania, there was not a good bookstore in any of the colonies to the south of Boston. …

- put forward: (1)앞으로 돌리다 (2)...을 제언하다 (3)남의 눈에 띠게 하다
  ex) put oneself forward: 주제넘게 나서다
- positively: 긍정적으로, 단호히
- bluntly: 무뚝뚝하게, 버릇없이
- establish oneself: (1)기반을 잡다 (2)개업하다

Jane Eyre

- Charlotte Bronte

\# **작품 소개:** 최초의 여성 성장 소설로 19세기 영국의 보수적이고 가부장적인 사회 분위기 속에서 이를 거부하고 당당한 여성으로서 독립적이고 주체적인 삶을 살고자 한 주인공 제인 에어의 시련과 극복, 사랑의 성취 과정이 1인칭 주인공 시점으로 그려져 있다.

\# **작가 소개:** 19세기 영국의 유명한 여류작가다.

I am just talking with them on terms of friendship.

: 나는 그저 우정 이라는 조건에서 그들과 이야기하고 있다.

By diligence, she could succeed in her working area without any connection.

: 근면성에 의해, 그녀는 어느 친분 없이도 그의 직업 분야에 성공할 수가 있었다.

» **원문**

… Leah is a nice girl, and John and his wife are decent people; but I can't talk with them on terms of equality. …

… "What a fool I was to think that I was a favorite with Mr. Rochester! Have you forgotten that you are a poor and plain governess without any connection?" …

» **Note**

☐ on terms of...: ...의 조건에서

　　rf) on good terms with...: ...와 좋은 사이에 있는

　　cf) in terms of...: (1)...의 말로, ...의 형[식]으로 (2)...에 의하여, (3)...으로 환산하여, (4)...의 견지에서 (5)면에서[...에 관하여]

☐ connection: 친척관계, 친분(relation)

I don't want to disturb you but let me know what the news is about?

: 당신을 방해하고 싶지는 않습니다만 그 소식이 무엇에 관한 것인지 말씀해 주시겠습니까?

[A] **What happened to the army?:** 무슨 일이 군에 발생했는가?

[B] **Nothing particular as usual.:** 여느 때처럼 특이한 사항은 없습니다.

They **became acquainted with** each other so soon since they met.

: 그들은 서로 만난 이후로 곧 바로 서로에게 친숙해졌다.

» **원문**

… "Why didn't you come and speak to me in the drawing room?" "I didn't want to disturb you; you seemed engaged, sir." "What have you been doing during my absence?" "Nothing particular. Teaching Adele as usual." …

… That night I had forgotten to draw the curtain and pull down my window blinds and that he had first become acquainted with Mr. Rochester there. …

» **Note**

☐ disturb: 방해하다, 교란시키다
☐ engaged: 바쁜, 약혼중인, 교전중인, 종사하고 있는, 예약된
☐ Nothing particular.: 특별한 일없음., 이상 무.
☐ as usual: 여느 때처럼
☐ draw a curtain: 커튼을 치다
☐ be acquainted with…: …와 친숙해지다

It was dated three years back. Then I happened to meet my wife in the bookstore.

: 그것은 3년 전으로 거슬러 올라갑니다. 그때 나는 우연히 책방에 당신을 만났습니다.

After a long spell of rainy season, the sky began to clear up partly.

: 장기간의 우기 후에, 하늘이 부분적으로 개이기 시작했다.

I swear an oath before my citizens that I'll keep our promise.

: 나는 내가 나의 약속을 지킬 것을 시민 앞에 맹세합니다.

» **원문**

… It was dated three years back. "Why didn't you tell me?" I asked.
…

… Summer came, and with it a long spell of fine weather. The fields around Thornfield were green …

… If an oath is necessary to satisfy you, I'll swear an oath. …

» **Note**

☐ date: 날짜가 적혀있다[날짜를 적다]
  ex) date back: 날짜가 거슬러 올라가다

☐ date from: …로부터 비롯되다
  ex) a friendship dating from(or back to) their college days: 대학 시절로부터 맺어온 우정

☐ a long spell of…: 장기간의 …
  rf) spell: 기간

The model student came a step forward from his row and was awarded a good conduct prize.

: 그 모범 학생은 <u>그의 줄로부터 앞으로</u> 한발 나왔다, 그리고 선행상을 받았다.

For a joke, they shut me out and closed the door.

: 농담으로, <u>그들은</u> <u>나를 밖으로 떼어놓았다.</u> 그리고 문을 닫았다.

» 원문

   … The service began. <u>The clergyman came a step forward</u> and said …

   … And <u>my heart ached to think how he would feel to find me gone</u>; but I could not stay here any longer. …

   … The door was closed gently and civilly, <u>but it shut me out</u>. …

   … The door <u>was clapped to and bolted from within</u>. …

» **Note**

   ☐ come a step forward: 한 발 짝 앞으로 나오다

   ☐ my heart ached: 나의 마음은 아팠다

   ☐ shut+목적어(A)+out: (A)를 못 들어오게 하다, 가로막다

078

Silas Marner

- George Eliot

\# **작품 소개:** 인과응보의 도덕성을 강조한 작품이다. 구성도 짜임새가 있고, 시골의 소박한 인정과 주인공의 심리변환 과정이 잘 묘사되어 있다. 엘리엇의 대표작으로 평가된다.

\# **작가 소개:** 영국의 소설가다. 주요 저서에는 대작 「미들마치」, 「다니엘 데론다」 등이 있다. 멋진 심리묘사와 도덕·예술에 대한 뛰어난 지적 관심에 의해 20세기 작가의 선구적 역할을 수행한 것으로 평가된다.

At that time I was seriously taken ill, so I could not join the event.

: 그 당시 나는 심각하게 병을 앓았다, 그러므로 그 행사에 참여 할 수가 없었다.

The two guards take their turns in the night-watching in the working place.

: 그 두 경비원은 그 작업장의 야간 경계근무를 교대로 한다.

His work is so much in demand but he was well paid.

: 그의 일은 너무나 힘들지만 보수는 좋다.

I work for the top rate company in Korea.

: 나는 한국에 있는 최고 수준의 회사에 일한다.

... At that time one of the ministers was taken dangerously ill. Young members of the church looked after him by turns, night and day. Silas frequently took his turn in the night watching with William. The one relieve the other at two in the morning. ...

... His work was much in demand, and he was well paid. His earnings in his native town, where he worked for a wholesale dealer, had been very low. ...

- ☐ take one's turn in ...ing: ...하는 데 교대로 하다
- ☐ relieve: 구제하다, 교대하다
- ☐ in demand: 〈많은 노동, 어려움〉을 요구하는, 필요로 하는
- ☐ well paid: 보수를 잘 받는
- ☐ work for...: ...에 근무하다

Seeing his father, her face took on expression of relief.

: 그녀의 아빠를 보자마자, 그녀의 얼굴은 안도의 표정을 띠었다.

Suddenly he rose to his feet and walked off of the office.

: 갑자기 그는 자리로부터 벌떡 일어섰다. 그리고 사무실로부터 빠져져나 갔다.

A wonderful idea came to his mind and then he smiled.

: 어떤 좋은 생각이 떠올랐다. 그러자 그는 미소를 지었다.

… The door opened. It was his brother Dunstan who entered. <u>Seeing him Godfrey's face took on expression of hatred.</u> …

… <u>He rose to his feet with the bags in his hand,</u> and closed the door behind him immediately. <u>The rain and darkness had got thicker,</u> and he was glad of it. He stepped forward into the dark night. …

… Now that all the hopes had vanished, <u>the idea of a thief came to his mind.</u> The thought gave him some new strength. …

» **Note**

- ☐ (on) seeing (A): (A)를 보았을 때, 보자마자
- ☐ take on...: ...을 띠다
- ☐ rise to one's feet: 벌떡 일어서다
- ☐ get thicker: 더욱 짙어지다
- ☐ an idea comes to one's mind: 한 생각이 ...에게 떠오르다

We had heavy rain all day long. <u>I'm as wet as a drowned rat.</u>

: 하루 종일 폭우가 왔다. <u>나는 물에 빠진 생쥐처럼 흠뻑 젖었다.</u>

I happened to meet my village friend whom <u>I have lost sight of</u> since I was young.

: 어렸을 때 <u>소식이 끊겼던</u> 나의 마을 친구를 우연히 만났다.

... "Master Marner, said the landlord, taking Marner by the shoulder, "come here and warm yourself at first. <u>You're as wet as a drowned rat</u>." ...

... He was sure Dunstan had ridden away with Wildfire. <u>It was a mistake that he had trusted his horse to Dunstan</u> ...

... It's Dunstan-my brother Dunstan that <u>we lost sight of sixteen years ago</u>. We've found him-found his body. The stone-pit has gone dry suddenly. ...

... Silas was hurt and uneasy. "I don't understand you, sir," he answered. "<u>Well, my meaning is this</u>, Marner," said Godfrey. ...

- ☐ as wet as a drowned rat: 익사한 쥐새끼처럼 온전히 젖은
- ☐ trust (A) to (B): (A)를 (B)에 맡기다
- ☐ lose sight of...: ...시야로부터 멀어지다, 연락이 끊기다
- ☐ meaning: 의미, 의도
    - *ex)* My meaning is...: 내 의도는 ...입니다
    - *rf)* My understanding is...: 나의 이해는 ...입니다

079

The Fir Tree(adapted)

- Hans Christian Andersen

작품 소개: 항상 만족하지 못하고 불평하는 전나무의 이야기다. 조금만 더 자랐으면, 좀 더 높은 자리에 앉았으면, 좀 더 행복해졌으면, 좀 더 돈이 많았으면 하면서 우린 항상 우리의 상황에 만족하지 못한다. 높은 자리에 가면 또 더 높은 곳을 바라보게 된다. 행복이란 뭘까? 그 자리에서 만족함과 감사함을 가진다면 그게 더없는 행복이지 않을까?

작가 소개: 덴마크의 유명한 동화작가다.

They are twins and I can not <u>tell</u> one <u>from</u> the other by appearance.

: 그들은 쌍둥이다. 그리고 외모에 의해서 나는 <u>하나를 다른 하나와 구별할</u> <u>수가 없다.</u>

Give my best wishes to your students.

: 너의 학생들에게 <u>안부를 전해주어라.</u>

» **원문**

… The next year the tree grew much taller, and the year after that its trunk became even bigger. <u>You can always tell the age of a fir tree by the number of rings it has</u>, but this dear little tree was not happy because it did not have many rings. …

… They had lovely masts that smell of fir-I am sure it was your friends, and they asked that <u>I give you their best wishes.</u> …

» **Note**

☐ tell: …을 분간하다, 구별하다
☐ give 목적어(A) best wishes: (A)에게 안부를 전해주다

Tom Thumb

- Hans Christian Andersen

작품 소개: 옛날 어느 마을에 작고 예쁜 아이를 가지고 싶어 하는 한 부인이 있었다. 부인의 간절한 소원을 들은 요정은 그녀에게 꽃 한 송이를 건넸고, 얼마 후 꽃 속에서 아주 작은 아이가 태어났다. 부인은 그 아이에게 엄지처럼 작다고 하여 '엄지공주'라는 이름을 붙여 주었다.

Even if the bug is <u>no bigger than</u> my thumb but it can jump high.

: 비록 그 벌레가 나의 엄지손가락보다 더 크지는 않을 지라도 그것은 높이 뛰어오를 수가 있다.

First of all, <u>get your mouth clear of dirty things</u> and take a deep breath.

: 우선, <u>너의 입을 더러운 오물로부터 깨끗이 청소하라</u> 그리고 심호흡을 하라.

This room is so stuffy that I can not bear it. <u>Let me out</u>.

: 이 방은 너무 후덥지근하여 도저히 참을 수가 없다. <u>나가게 해주세요.</u>

» 원문

… Even if he were no bigger than my husband's thumb, I would be satisfied." Merlin was much amused with the idea of a boy no bigger than a man's thumb, and he determined to grant the poor woman's wish. …

… But Tom, having by this time got his mouth clear of the batter, began to cry aloud: "Let me out! Let me out!" …

But Tom begged again and again and so earnestly that his father at last gave in. Then Tom asked his father to put him in the horse's ear …

» **Note**

☐ even if...: ...비록 ...일지라도

☐ no bigger than...: ...보다 더 크지 않은

☐ get (A) clear of...: (A)를 ...로부터 깨끗이 치우다

☐ Let (A) out: (A)를 나가게 하다 ↔ Let (A) in: (A)를 들어가게 하다

☐ at last: 마침내

☐ give in: 양보하다, 손들다

The Little Match Girl — Hans Christian Andersen

 # 작품 소개· 한 아이의 간절한 소망을 이야기하고 있는 이 동화는 작가가 빈곤하게 시절 시절을 보낸 어머니를 생각하며 쓴 작품이라고 한다.

He had his sweater on but it was too large for him.

: 그는 그의 스웨터를 입었다 그러나 그것은 그의 몸집에 비해 너무 컸다.

The native man drew a stone out of his bag and tried to strike it against the big rock to make a fire.

: 그 원주민은 가방으로부터 돌을 하나 꺼냈다 그리고 불을 지피기 위해 그것을 바위에 대어 그었다.

» **원문**

… When she left her home she had slippers on, which were her mother's and too large for her feet. …

… She sat down in a corner of two houses, drawing her little feet close under her. She could not warm them. …

… Her hands were nearly frozen. If she did light a match from her bundle, it would warm her hands and feet. She drew one out, and struck it against the wall. …

» **Note**

☐ have (A) on: (A)를 착용하다.

☐ too (A) for (B): (B)에 비하여 너무 (A)하는

☐ be frozen: 얼어붙다

☐ draw out: 꺼내다

☐ strike (A) against (B): (B)에 대하여 (A)를 그어대다

The Red Shoes

- Hans Christian Andersen

\# **작품 소개:** 카렌은 가난한 소녀이고, 빨간 구두를 갖고 싶어 한다. 같이 사는 아주머니에게 빨간 구두를 얻게 된 카렌은 어른들의 반대에도 교회에 빨간 구두를 신고 가고 무도회에 가서 춤을 춘다. 그런데 이 빨간 구두는 마법에 걸려서 카렌은 춤을 멈출 수가 없다. 결국 다리가 부러진 카렌은 천사의 도움으로 빨간 구두의 마법에서 벗어나게 된다.

Cut the sports section off the rest of the newspaper.

: 그 스포츠 난을 신문의 나머지로부터 도려내라.

Attend the meeting with evening dress on.

: 야회복을 입은 채로 회의에 참석하시오.

» **원문**

> … Then she told him the whole story, and the headman <u>cut off</u> her feet <u>with the red shoes on</u> them. …

» **Note**

- □ cut off: …을 도려[잘라]내다. 여기의 'off'는 '분리', '이탈'의 뜻.
- □ with the red shoes on: 붉은 고무신을 신고
  rf) with 목적어(A)+목적보어(B): (A)가 (B)한 채로('부대상황'의 뜻)

The Three Musketeers(adapted) — Alexandre Dumas

작품 소개; 「삼총사」는 훌륭한 로맨스로 작가는 주엽다 품어다를 바불하며 돌자를 어지러우 여행으로 초대한다. 주인공인 삼총사는 물론 리셸리 외 추기경과 사악한 밀라디에 이르기까 지, 이 소설에 등장하는 인물들은 서양 문화에서 너무나 쉽게 찾아볼 수 있는 전형이기에, 굳 이 강조할 필요조차 없다. 뒤마가 창조한 이 거들먹거리는 가스코뉴 젊은이 역시 끝까지 찬란 하다.

작가 소개: 19세기 프랑스의 극작가, 소설가다. 소설 「삼총사」, 「몬테크리스토 백작」으로 세계 적으로 유명하다. 「앙리 3세와 그 궁정」으로 새로운 로망파극의 선구자 구실을 하였다.

I made a sign to them to stop and wait for me.

: 나는 그들에게 잠깐 멈추고 나를 기다리라고 <u>신호를 보냈다</u>.

The king drew his sword and stuck it into his rival's body

: 왕은 <u>그의 칼을 뽑았다</u> 그리고 적수의 몸을 찔렀다.

Upon my word! I didn't break my promise.

: <u>맹세코!</u> 나는 약속을 어기지 않았습니다.

» **원문**

… But <u>making a sign to him to wait a moment</u>, he stepped to the door and called out in a loud, commanding voice, "Athos! Porthos! Aramis!" …

… Before we had time to <u>draw our swords</u>, they <u>dragged us away by force</u>. That's the whole story." …

… "<u>Upon my word!</u>" replied D'Artagnan, recognizing Arthos. "I did not do intentionally, so I said 'excuse me'. …

I fought her, because she gave me a black look.

: 나는 그녀와 싸웠다. 왜냐하면 그녀가 나에게 빈정대는 시선[무서운 시선]을 주었기 때문이다.

My teacher all the time set a good example for us. Thus as his students, we followed suits.

: 나의 선생님은 늘 우리의 모범이었다. 그러므로 그의 제자로써, 우리는 선례를 따랐다.

The ship was at the wave's mercy.

: 그 배는 파도의 처분대로 있었다.(즉, 파도에 따라 출렁이고 있었다.)

» **원문**

… Aramis gave D'Artgnan a black look, but, quickly collecting himself, he said in his usual calm manner …

… "You swear upon your honour and I upon my word, so there is no doubt that one of us is lying. …

… Then, taking aside the one with whom he was to fight, Athos told him his name in a whisper. Porthos and Aramis followed suit. …

… In an instant D'Artagnan was standing over him pointing his sword at his throat. He had Lord Winter at his mercy. …

- □ black look: 무서운 표정[시선]
- □ collect oneself: 진정하다, 정신을 차리다
- □ swear upon one's honour: 명예를 맹세하다
- □ upon one's word: 맹세코, 이피니
- □ follow suits: (1)같은 짝의 패를 내다 (2)선례를 따르다
- □ at 소유격(A) mercy=at the mercy of 목적격(A): (A)의 처분대로[마음대로]
  ex) The ship was at the mercy of waves.: 그 배는 파도의 처분대로 움직였다.

Wait a minute. I shall not be gone very long.
: 잠깐만 기다리시오. 나는 곧 돌아오겠습니다.

We tried to make away with our enemy.
: 우리는 우리의 적을 제거하고자 노력했다.

I trusted him. He is a man of his word.
: 나는 그를 믿는다. 그는 신의를 지키는 사람이다.

» **원문**

… "My condition is that you go and get the letter which you say is in your companion's pocket." …

… "Good," said the Cardinal. "Please wait for me here. I shall not be gone very long." …

… Only a few minutes ago, in this room, you promised the Cardinal to make away with the Duke of Buckingham. In return the Cardinal will allow you to assassinate D'Artagnan." …

… Milady might have doubted any other man, but not Athos. She knew that he was a man of his word. …

» **Note**

- □ My condition is…that…: 나의 조건은 …하는 것이다
- □ I shall not be very long.: 나는 곧 돌아오겠다.
  ex) I'll be back. 여기의 'shall'은 주어[1인칭]의 의지
- □ make away with…: …을 제거하다
- □ in return: 그 대가로
- □ a man of one's word: 신의를 지키는 사람

084

Peter Pan

- James Matthew Barrie

작품 소개: 네버랜드는 영원히 어른이 되지 않는 나라다. 피터팬, 팅커벨, 웬디, 그리고 웬디의 두 동생 마이클과 존은 네버랜드로의 여행을 시작하게 된다.

작가 소개: 영국의 소설가 겸 극작가(1860~1937)다.

Soon some guests are supposed to visit our house, put away your messy stuff in your room.

: 곧 일부 손님들이 우리 집에 방문할 예정이다. 너의 방에 있는 너의 어질러 진 소지품들을 치워라.

Now he is a touchy boy, be careful lest you should get on his nerves.

: 지금 그는 감정이 예민한 소년이다. 그가 신경에 거슬리지 않도록 조심하라.

» **원문**

… It was quite a common sort of shadow. Mrs. Darling rolled it up carefully and put it away in a drawer. …

… But when he answered, "Peter Pan," she said, "Is that all?" And this rather annoyed him; he was a touchy boy. …

» **Note**

☐ put away: …을 치우다
☐ touchy: 감정이 예민한
　cf) touching=moving: 감동적인

Ivanhoe

- Sir Walter Scott

작품 소개: 1819년에 간행된, 중세기 영국의 색슨족과 노르만족 간의 대립을 배경으로 한 사랑과 무용(武勇)의 이야기다.

작가 소개: 19세기 초 영국의 역사소설가·시인·역사가(1771~1832)다.

I'll try my best <u>in the hope that</u> I can succeed in the future if I struggle to study hard.

: 열심히 공부하면 미래에 성공할 수가 <u>있다는 바람 속에서</u> 나는 최선을 다할 것이다.

<u>Have mercy on me.</u> I didn't mean to burn it.

: <u>저를 한번만 봐주세요.</u> 그것을 불태울 작정은 아니었습니다.

My rival gave me <u>a letter of defiance.</u>

: 나의 경쟁자는 <u>도전장을</u> 나에게 주었다.

Every race <u>should go together</u> in peace and freedom.

: 모든 인종은 평화와 자유 속에서 <u>함께 가야</u>합니다.

» **원문**

… Front-de-Boeuf cast him into a dismal dungeon and treated him very harshly, <u>in the hope that</u> the old Jew would offer money <u>as a ransom</u>. …

… "Do you see the scales? In these very scales shall <u>you weigh me out a thousand pounds of silver</u>." "<u>Have mercy on me</u>, noble knight!" exclaimed Isaac; I am old and poor and helpless. It is a poor deed to crush a worm." …

… "Give it me," said Brian de Bois-Guilbert, who could read and write. "<u>It is a formal letter of defiance</u>." …

… And also King Richard with a train of the noblest Normans, to show how earnestly he desired that <u>the two peoples should go together in friendship and good will</u>. …

» **Note**

□ ransom: 몸값

   ex) hold+사람(A)+to (or for) ransom: 남을 인질로 하여 몸값을 요구하다

□ in the hope of+구(A)=in the hope that+절(A): …라는[하는] 바람으로

□ weigh out…: …을 달아 나누다[가르다], 일정량으로 배분하다. 위 문장의 'shall'은 주어[화자]의 의지를 나타낸다.

□ have mercy on…: …에 자비를 베풀다, 봐주다

□ formal letter of defiance: 공식적인 도전장

   rf) a letter of (A): (A)장

   ex) a letter of recommendation: 추천장

□ go together: 함께 가다, 어울리다

Robinson Crusoe

- Daniel Defoe

작품 소개: 요크 태생인 크루소는 이미지의 민류를 뿌리치고 고힘 힘헤에 니선디. 비디에서 난파해서 홀로 무인도에 표착하여 창의와 연구, 근면과 노력으로 착실한 무인도 생활을 설계해 나간다. 그리고 28년 만에 고국에 돌아온다는 이야기다.

작가 소개: 영국 출신의 소설가다. 인간의 본성을 꿰뚫는 통찰력이 돋보인다.

I didn't carry my umbrella with me in spite of heavy rain, so that <u>I was wet to the skin</u>.

: 폭우가 옴에도 불구하고 나는 우산을 휴대하지 못했다. 그러므로 <u>나는 피부까지 흠뻑 젖었다</u>.

I <u>cut a notch</u> in some pine trees to recognize my path easily on my way back to my home.

: 집으로 돌아오는 길을 좀 더 쉽게 알아보기 위해 나는 약간의 소나무에다가 <u>매듭을 표시해두었다</u>.

» **원문**

… But a huge grey wave came foaming and thundering upon us, turned over the boat, and f<u>lung us all into the water</u>. …

… <u>For I was wet to the skin</u>, with no dry clothes to put on, no food nor water to drink. …

… In this post I <u>cut a notch</u> every day. When it was Sunday, I cut a notch twice as long as the rest every day. …

» **Note**

☐ fling: 내던지다

   cf) fling-flung-flung

☐ wet to the skin: 흠뻑 젖은

☐ cut a notch: 매듭을 새기다

Put your cards up side down before you play the game.
: 게임을 시작하기 전에 너의 카드를 뒤집어 놓아라.

The enemy crept on all fours not to let us see them.
: 적은 우리가 보지 못하도록 엎드려 기었다.

Two members of CID on the criminal's track were shot by him.
: 범인을 추적하고 있었던 두 명의 CID 요원들이 그에 의해 총격 받았다.

Let's take a short cut to save our time.
: 시간을 절약하기 위하여 지름길을 택하자.

» 원문

… When my corn was ripe, the swords I had brought from the ship came in handy, for I used them to reap my crop. …

… Over these I put one of my large clay pots upside down, and round the pot I drew all the fire. …

… Soon it became very low and narrow and I had to creep on all fours. …

… Two of those who were on his track plunged in and followed him, but the third stopped and went back to the others. …

… Then I took a short cut and got behind him and called out to him to stop. …

» **Note**

□ come in handy: 편리하게 쓸 수가 있다, 간편하다
□ upside down: 거꾸로
□ on all fours: 네 발로, 기어
□ on one's track: …을 좇고 있는
□ take a short cut: 지름길을 택하다

I am very cross with my students because they did not obey my words without special reasons.

: 나는 학생들에 대해 매우 기분이 언짢았다, 왜냐하면 그들의 특별한 이유 없이 나의 말을 따르지 않았기 때문이다.

The farmer **scared the harmful birds away** by beating some empty cans.

: 농부는 빈 깡통을 두드림으로써 해로운 새들을 무서워 달아나게 했다.

Some farmers **rose up against** the government to let it accept their claims.

: 일부 농부들이 그들의 주장을 받아들이도록 하기 위해 정부에 대항하여 봉기했다.

» 원문

... "Are you cross with me?" asked he, "What me done?" ...
... "Well," said I, "do not fear. We must fight against them." "Will you stand by me, Friday, and do as I order you?" ...
... "No matter," I said. "Our guns will scare them away." ...
... "And these are my mates. The crew are a bad lot, and when were out at sea they rose up against me and ...

» Note

□ cross: 언짢은, 기분이 상한
□ stand by: (1)대기하다 (2)옆에서다 (3)도와주다
□ scare 목적어(A) away: (A)를 무서워 달아나게 하다[내쫓다]
□ rise up against...: ...에 대해 반기를 들다, 봉기하다

I hit upon a good plan to solve the difficult problem.

: 나는 그 어려운 문제를 해결하기 위한 좋은 생각을 떠올렸다.

I could not contain myself for joy.

: 나는 기뻐 나 자신을 자제할 수가 없었다.

I had a good feast on these fruits.

: 나는 이와 같은 과일들을 마음껏 맛있게 먹었다.

» **원문**

… Then I hit upon a plan by which we could trick them. I told Friday and one of our mates to go to a small hill on the other side of the island, and shout loudly till the seamen answer. …

… I could not contain myself for joy when I saw the fine, big ship which was to take me back to home and friends. The captain had brought me some sweet wine, a prime piece of beef, and some of the best food he had in his ship. I had a right good feast on these things …

… When I had them on, I felt I was not the same man. …

» **Note**

☐ hit upon…: …이 번뜩 생각나다

☐ contain oneself: 억제하다, 자제하다

☐ have a feast on…: …을 맛있게 실컷 먹다

☐ have on: …을 입다

087
Gulliver's Travel(Brobdingnag)
- Jonathan Swift

At last I succeeded in solving the difficult problem, so my mind was free from care.

: 마침내 나는 그 어려운 문제를 해결하는데 성공했다. 그러므로 나의 마음은 근심이 없어졌다.

We have many miles to walk and now we are short of fresh water. Let's hurry up.

: 가야할 많은 마일이 있고 지금 물이 부족하다. 서두르자.

» 원문

… As my mind was thus free from care as to the well-being of my family, I said good-bye to them, and went on board the Adventure bound for Surat on the twentieth of June, 1702. …

… Though we had a sufficient store of food left, we were short of fresh water. …

» Note

□ free from care: 근심이 없는
　cf》 care-free: 근심[걱정]이 없는
□ on board: 승선하여
　ex》 go on board: 승선하여 출항하다
□ be short of...: ...이 부족하다

338

Some rose thorns pierced through my clothes into my flesh.

: 일부 장미 가시들이 나의 옷을 뚫고 살을 찔렀다.

Some opened manholes made me tread short and fall down.

: 일부 열려있는 맨홀들이 내가 발을 헛디디게 해 넘어지게 만들었다.

The scientist put the worm close to his eyes, and gave it a turn or two with the pincers.

: 과학자는 벌레를 그의 눈 가까이에 놓고 핀셋으로 한두 번 그 벌레를 뒤집었다.

» 원문

... But the stalks of corn were so close together that I could but just squeeze through them. ...

... I could not get through here, for the stalks were too close, and the spikes on the ears of corn pierced through my clothes into my flesh. ...

... I gave a cry of fear, which made him tread short. ...

... He took it in the palm of his hand, put it close to his eyes, and gave it a turn or two with the point of pin. ...

» Note

☐ squeeze through...: ...을 헤집고 나아가다
☐ pierce through (A) into (B): (A)를 통과하여 (B)속으로 뚫고 들어가다
☐ make (A) tread short: (A)로 하여금 헛되되게 하다
☐ give a turn or two: ...을 한두 번 뒤집다

The rat in this country was three times the size of an ox in my country.
: 이 나라의 쥐는 우리나라의 황소보다 세 배나 컸다.

Beth drew herself back when she saw the super rat.
: 그 큰 쥐를 보 았을 때 Beth는 몸을 움츠렸다.

Some villagers began to call the mean mayor names.
: 일부 마을 사람들은 그 비열한 시장을 비난하기 시작했다.

» 원문

... This made everyone at table laugh so loud that I was almost deafened with the noise. As I went round it, I happened to stumble against a crust, and went flat on my face, but received no hurt. ...

... I found that this came from a cat, which was three times the size of an ox. ...

... I walked steadily up to the cat's head, and was very glad to find that she drew herself back as if she were more afraid of me. ...

... But all I could do against this was to laugh at him and call him names, because he was so big. ...

» Note

□ be deafened with...: ...으로 귀가 멀다
□ go[fall] flat on one's face: 완전히 코방아를 찧다
□ three times the size of an ox: 황소 크기의 세 배인
  cf) 배수사(A) the size of (B): (B) 크기의 (A) 배
□ draw oneself back: 뒤로 주춤하게 하다[물러나게 하다]
□ call (A) names: ...를 욕하다, 비난하다

The criminals of conscience were pardoned at the president's wish.

: 그 양심수들은 대통령의 소원에 따라 방면되었다.

The drowning man tried to catch the rope but the swift current kept the rope out of his reach.

: 그 물에 빠진 사람이 밧줄을 잡으려고 노력했다 하지만 빠른 물살이 그 밧줄에 도달하지 못하도록 했다.

Stand out of my way. I am in haste now.

: 길을 비켜라. 나는 지금 바쁘다.

He fell into his old ways and he became what he was.

: 그는 다시 옛 방식으로 돌아왔다. 그리고 과거의 그 사람이 되었다.

» **원문**

… The dwarf was pardoned at my wish. …

… At last I crept on my hands and knees till I got under a tree which kept the stones off me. …

… Though I tried to keep out of his reach, he at last caught hold of my coat, and pull me out. …

… I would call to them to stand out of my way, which more than once caused me to get into quarrels. …

… But as time went on, I fell into my old ways, and I was quite like other people. …

» **Note**

☐ pardon: 방면하다
☐ at my wish: 나의 소원에 따라
☐ keep off: 가까이 못 오게 하다
☐ keep out of one's reach: 도달 범위 밖에 있다
☐ catch hold of…: …을 잡다
☐ stand out of one's way: 방해가 되지 않다
☐ fall into…: …을 시작하다, …에 빠지다

Gulliver's Travels(Lilliput)

- Jonathan Swift

‖ 작품 소개‖ 풍자소설 「Gulliver's Travels」에 나오는 소인국이다.

I soon put their minds at rest and cheered them up.

: 나는 그들의 마음을 진정시켰다 그리고 격려했다.

The public clerk made a charge for the tax dodgers.

: 공무원은 탈세자들에게 대금을 청구했다.

» 원문

… I soon put their minds at rest, for I cut the man's bonds and set him on the ground, and off he ran like a hare! …

… And I found out that the King made a charge for those who came twice. …

… The men would get on these and dance and turn head over heels. …

» Note

☐ put one's mind at rest: …의 마음을 안정시키다

☐ make a charge for…: … 에게 대금을 청구하다

☐ turn head over heels: 고개를 젖혀 발아래에 오게 하다. 공중제비하다.

The magician hold out his stick from the box, and held it up and let it down repeatedly.

: 그 마술가는 상자로부터 지팡이를 꺼 내 반복해 들어 올렸다 내렸다 했다.

All troops were drawn up in lines in front of the king.

: 모든 군대들이 왕 앞에 여러 줄로 정렬되었다.

» **원문**

... He would then hold out a stick, and the chief men would creep under, or jump over it, as the King held it up high, or let it down low. They had to be quick at this ...

... The troops with their bands and flags, were then drawn up in lines, and had to march through the arch made by my legs. ...

» **Note**

☐ hold out: 제시하다, 내밀다

☐ creep under...: ... 아래로 기어가다

☐ jump over...: ... 위로 뛰어넘다.

☐ draw up in lines: 여러 줄로 정렬하다

The tailor took the size of my waist and arms to make my school uniform.

: 그 재단사는 나의 교복을 만들기 위해 나의 허리와 팔의 크기를 재었다.

My teacher was cold to me but he is soft on me now.

: 나의 선생님은 나에게 냉혹했었다 하지만 지금은 부드럽게 대해 주신다.

... I took off my coat, <u>lest</u> the tails of it <u>should brush the roofs off the houses</u>, and then I got over the wall. ...

... They let me <u>take the size of my waist and arms</u>, and the rest said that they would <u>work out in sums</u>! ...

... As I told you <u>the King had been cold to me</u> when I would not fight for him once more, and one night a friend of mine brought me some bad news. ...

» **Note**

- □ lest (A) should (B): (A)가 (B)하지 않도록
- □ brush (A) off (B): (A)를 (B)로부터 털어[떼어] 내다
- □ take the size of...: ...재다
- □ work out in sums: (총액을) 계산해 내다
  ex) do(or work) sums: 계산하다, 산수를 풀다
- □ cold to...: ...에게 냉정한

We managed to have the boat upside-down the <u>right side up</u>.

: 우리는 전복된 그 보트를 <u>똑바로</u> 세우는 데 성공했다.

<u>When I got everything ready</u>, I began to paint my picture <u>at full length</u>.

: <u>모든 것을 준비했을 때</u>, 나는 <u>전신 크기로</u> 나의 그림을 그리기 시작했다.

» 원문

... When I had been there three days I saw out on the sea what I thought was a boat upside down. I swam out to it, and found that it was a large boat. By the help of some ships I got it to shore, and in a short time we had it the right side up. ...

... When I had got everything ready, I bade the King and his Court good-bye. As I left him the King gave me some bags of gold coins and his pictures at full length. ...

» Note

- ☐ upside down: 거꾸로
- ☐ the right side up: 똑바로 상태로
- ☐ get ready: 준비되다
- ☐ at full length: 전신으로

The Happy Prince
- Oscar Wilde

작품 소개: 오스카 와일드(Oscar Wilde)의 동화집 「행복한 왕자와 다른 이야기들(The Happy Prince and Other Tales)」을 통해 출간했나. 그의 내표작으로 꼽히는 이 작품은 주변의 소외된 이웃을 돌아보도록 하고, 나눔의 행복을 알려주고자 했다.

작가 소개: 아일랜드 출신의 극작가이자 소설가, 시인이다. 19세기 말 대표적인 유미주의자다. 뛰어난 재기, 쾌락주의와 유미주의, 스캔들 등 주목받는 사교계 인사였으며, 그 때문에 작품보다 사생활이 더욱 유명한 인물이기도 하다.

It is getting darker and darker. Where shall I put up?

: 날씨가 점점 더 어두워지고 있다. <u>어느 장소에서 투숙해야만 하는가?</u>

What's the use of the weapon if it can not keep the enemy off?

: 만약에 적을 막지 못한다면 그 무기는 무슨 소용이 있겠는가?

» 원문

... All day long he flew, and at night-time he arrived at the city. "Where shall I put up?" he said; "I hope the town has made preparations." ...
... Then another drop fell. "What is the use of a statue if it can not keep the rain off?" he said; "I must look for a good chimney-pot," and he determined to fly away. ...

» Note

□ put up=lodge: 투숙하다
□ What's the use of...?: ...은 무슨 소용이 있는가?
□ keep off: 막다

346

She came of a famous musician family.

: 그녀는 유명한 음악가족 출신이다.

The sick king was tossing about on his bed.

: 그 아픈 왕은 침대 위에서 이리저리 몸을 뒤척거리고 있었다.

» **원문**

… I come of a family famous for its agility; but still, it was a mark of disrespect." …

… At last he came to the poor house and looked in. The boy was tossing feverishly on his bed, and the mother had fallen asleep …

… When the moon rose he flew back to the Happy Prince. "Have you any commission for Egypt?" he cried; "I'm just starting." …

» **Note**

☐ come of...: …출신이다
☐ toss (about): 〈잠 못 자고〉뒤척이다
☐ commission: 임무

Hunger and cold made him faint.

: 배고픔과 추위가 그를 졸도하게 만들었다.

The jilted man had his head buried in his hands and began to sob.

: 그 버림받은 남자는 고개를 손에 묻고 흐느끼기 시작했다.

... "There is no fire in the grate, and <u>hunger had made him faint</u>." "I will wait with you one night longer," said the Swallow, who really had a good heart. ...

... <u>The young man had his head buried in his hands</u>, so he did not hear the flutter of the bird's wings ...

... So the Swallow flew over the great city, and <u>saw the rich making merry in their beautiful houses</u>, while the beggars were sitting at the gates. ...

» Note

- □ faint: 실신시키다, 졸도시키다
- □ had his head buried in his hands: 고개를 손에 묻다
- □ make merry: 흥겹게 놀다, 떠들썩하게 놀다

King Alfred and the Cakes(adapted)

- James Baldwin

작품 소개: 영국의 현명한 알프레드 왕은 전쟁 중 피하다가 오두막집에 도착했다. 그리고는 난로에서 케이크를 굽고 있던 부인에게 먹을 것을 구걸한다.

작가 소개: 미국의 소설가다. 흑인들의 종교 체험을 다룬 「산에 올라 고하여라.」로 유명해졌다. 그는 그때까지의 흑인작가와는 달리 백인에 대한 항의로 일관하지 않고, 흑인이기 이전에 한 사람의 미국인이라는 관점에서 문제를 추구하였다.

Let's <u>get our team together</u> again and practice for the championship.

: <u>우리 팀을 다시 모아</u> 우승을 위해 연습합시다.

The master <u>drove</u> his lazy servants <u>out of</u> his castle.

: 주인은 게으른 하인들을 그의 성<u>으로부터 축출했다</u>.

The North army <u>broke up</u> the South army in the Civil War.

: 내란 동안에 북군이 남군을 <u>분쇄했다</u>.

» **원문**

… <u>How can I get my army together again</u>? And how can the I <u>drive</u> the Danes <u>out of</u> this country?" he thought. He forgot his hunger. …

… The king <u>laughed to himself</u>, but he said nothing. He was afraid of the loss of the cakes. …

… But before long, he got his army together again, and <u>broke up</u> the Danes in a great battle. …

Androclus and the Lion(adapted)

- James Baldwin

작품 소개: 안드로클레스가 잔인한 주인을 피해 아프리카의 한 동굴에 몸을 숨기고 있을 때 사자 1마리가 들어와 퉁퉁 부은 앞발을 들어 보이자 그는 커다란 가시를 뽑아주었다. 훗날 안 드로클레스는 체포되어 원형극장 속의 맹수들에게 내던져졌는데, 은혜를 입었던 사자가 그를 알아보고 공격하는 대신 핥아주자 이에 놀란 관중들은 노예 신분에서 그를 풀어주었다.

After a long absence, his wife <u>put her arms around his husband's neck</u> and shed her tears.

: 오랫동안 보지 못한 후에, 그의 아내는 <u>남편의 목을 얼싸 안았다.</u> 그리고 눈물을 흘렸다.

» **원문**

… After a while they asked Androclus to tell them about it. He stood up before them and <u>put his arms around the lion's neck</u>. Then he told about the life with the lion. …

» **Note**

☐ put (A) around (B): (A)를 (B)주위로 놓다[껴안다]

351

The King and His Hawk(adapted)

- James Baldwin

작품 소개: 전쟁을 끝내고 고국에 돌아와 있던 어느 날 아침, 왕은 사냥하기 위해 친구들과 말을 타고 숲으로 갔다. 그들은 활과 화살을 가지고 갔으며, 그 뒤를 몇몇 시종들과 사냥개가 따랐다. 그것은 유쾌한 사냥 모임이었다. 그들은 웃으며 서로 즐겁게 이야기를 나누었다. 그들은 성공적인 사냥이 되기를 기대했다.

I owed my success to an unknown old man. How can I make a return to him?

: 나는 나의 성공을 미지의 한 노인에게 힘입었다. 어떻게 내가 그에게 보답을 할 수가 있겠는가?

» **원문**

… "The hawk saved my life!" he cried, and how did I make a return to him? He was my best friend …

» **Note**

□ make a return to…: …에게 보답하다

Grace Darling(adapted)

- James Baldwin

작품 소개: 스코틀랜드에서 출발한 증기선 Forfarshire은 얼마 못 가 심한 풍랑을 만난다. 그
들에게 있는 것은 작은 보트뿐이었다. 배에 타고 있던 사람들은 과연 살아날 수 있을까. 난파
선에서 사람들을 구한 Grace Darling이라는 용감한 한 여성의 실제 이야기가 실려 있다.

I stepped out from under the cave and began to search for the food.

: 나는 동굴아래로부터 나왔다. 그리고 음식을 찾기 시작했다.

We were going to marry yesterday but the event was postponed by next month.

: 우리는 어제 결혼하기로 되어있었다 그러나 그 행사는 다음 달까지 연기되
었다.

When I failed in the final exam, my heart was broken.

: 기말시험을 낙제했을 때 나의 가슴은 아팠다.

» 원문

… Then Robin Hood stepped out from under the tree, and said, - "I
say, young man! Have you any money to spare for my merry men
and me?" "I have nothing at all," said the young man, "But five
shillings and a ring." …

… We were going to be married yesterday. But her father has
promised her to a rich old man whom she never saw. And now my
heart is broken." …

- □ from under the tree: 나무 아래로부터
- □ was(or were) going to+동원: ...할 예정이었다
- □ heart is broken: 가슴이 아프다

The fierce waves broke against the rock.

: 맹렬한 파도가 바위에 부서졌다.

Had it not been for the water, we would have had some difficulties in returning home.

: 물이 없었더라면 우리는 집으로 돌아오는 데 어려움들을 가졌을 것이다.

... At last they were close to the rock, and now they were in greater danger than before. The fierce waves broke against the boat, and it would have been dashed in pieces, had it not been for the strength and skill of the brave girl. ...

» **Note**

- □ break against...: ...대항하여 부서지다
- □ dash in pieces.: 부딪쳐 산산조각 나다
- □ Had it not been for...=If it had not been for...=but for...=without...: ...이 없었다면('가정법 과거완료'의 '조건절')

The Story of William Tell(adapted)

- James Baldwin

작품 소개: 14세기 스위스 독립 전쟁에서 활약하였다는 영웅이자 활의 명수인 빌헬름 텔이 악독한 대관의 강요를 받아 아들의 머리 위에 사과를 올려놓고 활로 쏘아 떨어뜨렸다는 전설을 제재로 쓴 작품이다.

<u>What if</u> the sun <u>should disappear</u>?

: 태양이 사라진다면 어떤 일이 발생할까?

The hunter <u>fitted his arrow to his bow</u> and let the arrow go.

: 그 사냥꾼은 <u>그의 화살을 활에 재었다.</u> 그리고 화살을 놓았다.

Please <u>set me free</u> for I don't love you anymore.

: <u>나를 해방시켜주오.</u> 나는 당신을 더 이상 사랑하지 않기 때문이요.

» **원문**

> … <u>What if the boy should move?</u> What if the bowman's hand should tremble? What if the arrow should not carry true? …
>
> … Then, without another word, <u>Tell fitted the arrow to his bow</u>. He took aim, and let it fly. The boy <u>stood firm and still</u>. He was not afraid, for he <u>had all faith in</u> his father's skiil. …
>
> … And there is an old story, that, not long after this, Tell did shoot the tyrant with one of his arrows; and thus <u>he set his country free</u>. …

» **Note**

☐ what (should) 동사의 원형 if…?=만약에…한다면 어떤 일이 발생할까?

☐ fit (A) to (B): (A)를 (B)에 재다

☐ have a faith in…: …을 믿다

☐ set (A) free=release (A): (A)를 석방시키다

355

The bell of Atri(adapted)

- James Baldwin

> \# **작품 소개:** 아트리는 옛날에 피체눔이라는 도시였으며 그리스 사루니카만 아이이나섬에서 온 그리스인들이 세웠다. 힘없는 사람들의 억울함이나 한을 풀어주는 정의의 아트리의 종 얘기를 다룬 전래동화 「아트리의 종」이 이곳에서 나왔다.

Our church was built halfway up the side of a gentle hill.

: 우리 교회는 완만한 경사의 언덕 측면으로 반쯤 위에 지어졌다.

The referees called the players together and made a decision about the penalty.

: 그 심판들은 선수들을 소집했다 그리고 그 벌칙에 관해 결정을 내렸다.

This will do for a pencil, go get some board to write on.

: 이것은 연필로 충분히 쓸모가 있을 것이다. 가서 (위에다) 글씨 쓸 어떤 판자를 가져오너라.

Let the burnt skin be as it is.

: 있는 그대로 화상 입은 피부를 내버려 두어라.

Some bad friends did me wrong.

: 일부 나쁜 친구들이 나를 학대했어요.

She has been wronged, so she left for an unknown country.

: 그녀는 잘못 대우받아왔다, 그러므로 그녀는 미지의 나라로 떠나 버렸다.

» 원문

… Atri is the name of a little town in Italy. It is a very old town, and is built halfway up the side of a steep hill. …

… Many years passed by after this. Many times did the bell in the market place ring out to call the judges together. Many wrongs were righted, many ill-doers were punished. At last the hempen rope was almost worn out. …

… "This will do for a rope," he said; and he climbed, and fastened it to the bell. The slender vine, with its leaves and tendrils still upon it, trailed to the ground. "Yes," said the judges, "it is a very good rope. Let it be as it is." …

… "Some one had done me wrong! Oh! come and judge my case! For I've been wronged!" …

» Note

□ halfway up the side of…: …쪽으로 반쯤 위에

□ call (A) together: (A)를 소집하다

□ right some wrongs: 그릇된 일을 시정하다

□ This'll do for…: …를 위해 쓸모가 있을 것이다[충분할 것이다]

□ let (A) be as (A) is: (A)를 있는 상태로 내버려두다

□ do (A) wrong: (A)를 학대하다

□ be wronged: 부당하게 대우받다

Cornelia's Jewels(adapted)

- James Baldwin

작품 소개: 고전적인 건물을 배경으로 어린 딸의 손을 잡고 우아하게 서 있는 여인은 기원전 2세기 고대 로마 공화국에서 농지 개혁을 이끌었던 정치가 그라쿠스 형제의 어머니, 코넬리아다. 코넬리아의 보석 같은 두 아들은 미래의 영웅답게 당당하고 기품 있게 그려졌다.

Our family <u>are worth more than</u> all the gems.

: 우리의 가족은 모든 보석 <u>이상으로</u> 가치가 있다.

» **원문**

… "No, I am not poor," answered Cornelia, and as she spoke <u>she drew her two boys to her side</u>; "for here are my jewels. <u>They are worth more than all your gems.</u>" …

» **Note**

  □ draw (A) to 소유격(B) side: (A)를 (B)의 옆구리로 끌어오다
  □ be worth more than...: ...이상의 가치가 있다

Story of Frankenstein

- Mary Shelley

\# **작품 소개:** 주인공 프랑켄슈테인은 대학 생활을 하면서 2년째 괴물 만드는 작업을 하고 있다. 어느 날 그는 실험에 성공하게 되었고, 노랗고 검은 머리의 괴물을 만들어냈다. 그는 그 실험을 위해 모든 걸 투자했기 때문에 기뻐서 잠도 못 들었다. 이제 그는 여자 친구와 놀 생각에 잠도 못 이뤘지만, 곧 잠이 들고 악몽을 꾼다. 괴물이 자신을 공격하고 겨우 탈출해서 밑층으로 도망 다니는 꿈을 꿨다. 그렇게 밤중에 깨고 그는 불행한 밤을 보냈다.

\# **작가 소개:** 영국의 소설가(1797~1851)다. 오늘날 SF 소설의 선구가 된 괴기소설 「프랑켄슈타인」으로 유명하다.

The exciting atmosphere of having won the game succeeded to a big party.

: 경기의 우승에 대한 흥분된 분위기는 커다란 파티로 이어졌다.

Contrary to my first intention, I changed my mind and gave up my trip.

: 나의 첫 번째 의도와는 달리, 나는 나의 마음을 바꾸었다 그리고 나의 여행을 포기했다.

His body were in proportion.

: 그의 몸은 균형 잡혔다.

... I resolved, <u>contrary to my first intention</u>, to make the being of a gigantic stature; that is to say, about eight feet <u>in height</u>, and <u>proportionately large</u>. ...

... How can I describe my emotions at this catastrophe? or how delineate the wretch, whom, with such infinite pains and care? I had endeavored to form? <u>His limbs were in proportion</u>, and I had selected his features as beautiful. His yellow skin scarcely covered the work of muscles and arteries beneath; his hair was of a lustrous black, and flowing ...

... At last lassitude <u>succeeded to</u> the tumult I had before endured; and I threw myself on the bed in my clothes, endeavoring to seek a few moments of forgetfulness. But <u>it was in vain</u>. I slept indeed, but I was disturbed by the wildest dreams. I thought I saw Elizabeth, my love, <u>in the bloom of health</u>. ...

» Note

- □ contrary to...: ...에 반대하여, 반하여
- □ in height: 신장에 있어
- □ in proportion: 균형 속에 있는
- □ succeed to...: ...으로 계승하다
- □ in vain: 헛된, 헛수고의
- □ in the bloom of health: 건강이 넘치는

The rainwater <u>forced its way through</u> the grasses and the trees.

: 빗물이 풀과 나무를 통하여 흘렀다.

If they <u>comply with</u> our condition, we can accept their offer.

: 만약에 그들이 우리의 조건에 응한다면, 우리는 그들의 제의를 받아들일 수가 있다.

» **원문**

... I started from my sleep with horror; a cold dew covered my forehead, my teeth chattered, and every limb became convulsed; when, by the dim and yellow light of the moon, as it forced its way through the window-shutters, I beheld the wretch, the miserable monster, whom I had created. ...

... I had gazed on him while unfinished: he was ugly then; but when those muscles and joints were rendered capable of motion, it became a thing such as even Dante could not have conceived. ...

... How dare you sport thus with life? Do your duty towards me, and I will do mine towards you and the rest of mankind. If you will comply with my conditions, I will leave them and you at peace.' ...

» **Note**

  ☐ start from...: ...로부터 벌떡 일어나다
  ☐ force one's way through...: ...을 통하여 길을 만들어나가다
  ☐ comply with...: ...에 응하다

I don't want to set myself in opposition to them.
: 나는 그들을 적대시하기를 원하지 않는다.

All kinds of bills for the facilities in the condominium are due.
: 콘도미니엄에서의 모든 시설물에 대한 사용료는 지불기간이 되었다.

Money is due to him for his work
: 그의 일에 대해 마땅히 돈이 지불되어야 한다.

… Remember, you have made me more powerful than yourself; my height is superior to yours; my joints more supple. But I will not be tempted to set myself in opposition to you. I am your creature, and I will be even mild and docile to my natural lord and king, if you will also perform your part. Oh, Frankenstein, don't be fair to every other, and even don't trample upon me alone, to whom your justice, and your clemency and affection, is most due. …

… As he said this, he led the way across the ice: I followed. My heart was full, and I did not answer him, but, as I proceed, I weighed the various arguments that he had used, and determined at least to listen to his tale. …

» **Note**

- □ superior to…: …보다 월등한
  - *rf)* inferior to…: …보다 열등한
- □ be tempted to…: …할 기분이 나다
- □ set oneself in opposition to…: …에게 자신을 적대시하다
- □ due: 응당 치러야[지불해야] 할
- □ lead the way: 길을 인도하다

As soon as I happened to see the horrible monster, I started back.

: 무서운 괴물을 우연히 보자마자, 나는 놀라 뒤로 물러섰다.

I allowed myself to fly in the sky.

: 나는 나 자신을 하늘에 날도록 맡겼다.

... At first I started back, unable to believe that it was indeed I who was reflected in the mirror; and when I became fully convinced that I was in reality the monster that I am, I was filled with bitterest sensations of disappointment and mortification. ...

... Half surprised by the novelty of these sensation, I allowed myself to be the novelty of these sensations, I allowed myself to be borne away by them; and, forgetting my solitude and deformity, dared to be happy. ...

» **Note**

☐ start back: 놀라 물러나다
☐ in reality: 실제로
☐ allow oneself to+동원: ...하도록 자신을 맡기다

They worked together in the interchange of their sympathies.

: 그들은 그들의 공감을 주고받으며 함께 일했다.

I was engaged in my project in my laboratory all day long.

: 나는 하루 종일 나의 실험실에서 나의 연구 계획에 열중했다.

I made a solemn vow in my heart to try my best.

: 나는 최선을 다할 것을 마음속에 굳게 맹세했다.

... At length I wandered toward these mountains, and have ranged through their immense recesses, consumed by a burning passion which you alone can gratify. You must create a female for me, with whom I can live in the interchange of those sympathies necessary for my being. ...

... As I sat, a train of reflection occurred to me, which led me to consider the effects of what I was doing. Three years before, I was engaged in the same manner, and had created a fiend whose unparalleled barbarity had desolated my heart, and filled it for ever with the bitterest remorse. ...

... I felt the room, and, locking the door, made a solemn vow in my own heart never to resume my labours; and then, with trembling steps, I sought my own apartment. ...

» **Note**

- ☐ at length: 마침내
- ☐ consume...: ...에 열중하다
- ☐ in the interchange of (A): (A)와의 교환 속에서[(A)와 주고받으며]
- ☐ a train of: 일련의
- ☐ be engaged in...: ...에 열중하다, ...에 종사하다
- ☐ made a solemn vow in my own heart: 마음속으로 엄숙한 맹세를 하다

I was **in a vessel bound for** the island at that time.

: 그 당시에 나는 그 섬으로 가는 배 안에 있었다.

When I didn't help the drowning man, I felt **the stings of remorse.**

: 물에 빠진 사람을 돕지 못했을 때, 나는 양심의 가책을 느꼈다.

» **원문**

... I pursue him for many months. Guided by a slight clew, I followed the windings of the Rhone, but vainly. The blue Mediterranean appeared; and, by a strange chance, I saw the fiend enter by night, and hide himself in a vessel bound for the Black Sea. I took my passage in the same ship; but he escaped. ...

... A gigantic monster, they said, had arrived the night before, armed with a gun and many pistols; putting to fight the inhabitants of a solitary cottage, through fear of his terrible appearance. ...

... The monster continued to utter wild and incoherent self-reproaches. At length I gathered resolution to address him, in a pause of the tempest of his passion: "Your repentance," I said, "is now superfluous. If you had listened to the voice of conscience, and heeded the stings of remorse, before you had urged your diabolical vengeance to this extremity, Frnkenstein would yet have lived." ...

» **Note**

- ☐ windings of...: ...의 굴곡부, ...의 굽이
- ☐ hide oneself: ...을 숨기다[숨다]
- ☐ bound for: ...향하는, ...행의
- ☐ take passage in...: ...를 타고 항해하다
- ☐ armed with...: ...으로 무장한
- ☐ put to flight: 패주시키다
- ☐ gather resolution to 동원: ...하기 위해 결심을 하다
- ☐ a stings of remorse: 양심의 가책

098

The Bride Comes to Yellow Sky

- Stephen Crane

작품 소개: 소설 역시 서부역사가 소재가 되었는데, Jack Potter란 이름을 가진 보안관이 그 주인공이다. 그의 관할은 바로 옐로 스카인데, 그곳에 Scratchy Wilson이라는 못된 놈이 있었다. 그 악당은 평상시에는 멀쩡하다가 술만 먹으면 천하의 폭군으로 변신한다. 마을은 녀석의 동태를 살피면서 놈이 술을 먹고 행패를 부리나 안 부리나 노심초사다.

작가 소개: 미국의 소설가 겸 시인이자 신문 기자(1871~1900)다.

We'll have a big party. Come and get <u>a big lay-out</u>.

: 우리는 성대한 파티를 가질 것이다. 와서 <u>맛있는 음식을</u> 들어라.

Ten dollars worth of meal for breakfast is <u>too much for us</u>.

: 10달러 가격의 식사는 아침을 위해 <u>우리에게는 과분하다</u>.

» 원문

… "Great! And then after a while we'll go forward to the diner, and <u>get a big lay-out</u>. Finest meal in the world. Charge a dollar."

"Oh, do they?" cried the bride. "Charge a dollar? Why, <u>that's too much-for us</u>-ain't it, Jack?" "Not this trip, anyhow," he answered bravely. "<u>We's going to go the whole thing</u>." Later he explained to her about the train. "You see, it's a thousand miles from one end of Texas to the other; and this train runs right across it, and never stops <u>but</u> four times." …

» **Note**

- □ get a big lay-out: 진수성찬을 먹다
  cf) lay-out: (음식 등을)진열하기
- □ that's too much for us: 그것은 우리들에게 비해 너무 많다[비싸다]
- □ go the whole thing=go to any limit=take a bold step: 어떤 일이든 터놓고 해보다, 대담한 행동을 취하다
- □ but...: ...을 제외하고

We are <u>due (to arrive)</u> in LA at 3 o'clock sharp.
: 우리는 3시 정각에 LA에 <u>도착하기로 되어있다</u>.

Wake up everybody. It's <u>seventeen past nine</u> already.
: 전부 일어나라. 이미 <u>9시 17분</u>이다.

» **원문**

... At one end a bronze figure sturdily held a support for a separated chamber, and at convenient places on the ceiling were frescos in olive and silver. ...

... This individual at times surveyed them from afar with an amused and superior grin. <u>On other occasions</u> he bullied them with skill in ways that did not make it exactly plain to them that they were being bullied. ...

... "<u>We are due in Yellow Sky at 3:42</u>," he said, looking tenderly into her eyes. ...

... "<u>It's seventeen minutes past twelve</u>," she said, looking up at him with a shy and clumsy coquetry. ...

... <u>The pair fell to the lot of a waiter</u> who happened <u>to feel</u> pleasure in steering them through their meal. He view them with the manner of a fatherly pilot, his countenance radiant with benevolence. ...

□ on other occasions: 다른 경우에
□ due: (1)...도착 예정인 (2)<응당 값을>치러야할[받아야할] (3)...에 기인한 (4) 적[정]당한
□ seventeen minutes past twelve: 12시 17분
   rf) past...지나
□ It fell to my lot[The lot fell to me] to do...: 생각지도 않았는데 나는 ...하게 됐다

We decided to keep their customs <u>in accordance with</u> their order.

: 우리는 그들의 명령과 <u>일치하여</u> 그들의 관습을 지키기로 결정했다.

<u>To the delight of us</u>, our team won the game in the score of 7 to 20.

: <u>(우리가) 기쁘게도</u>, 우리 팀이 7대 20의 점수로 이겼다.

» **원문**

... Of course people in Yellow Sky married <u>as it pleased them</u>, <u>in accordance with</u> a general custom; but such was Potter's thought of his duty to his friends, or of their idea of his duty, or of an unspoken form which does not control men in these matters, that he felt he was heinous. ...

... Yellow Sky had a kind of brass band, which played painfully, <u>to the delight of the populace</u>. He laughed <u>without heart</u> as he thought of it. ...

... She flushed in comprehension. <u>A sense of mutual guilt</u> invaded their minds and developed a finer tenderness. They looked at each other with eyes softly aglow. But Potter often laughed the same nervous laugh; the flush upon the bride's face seemed quite permanent. ...

- ☐ in accordance with...: ...와 조화[일치]하여
- ☐ as it pleased them=as they pleased: 그들이 기분 내키는 대로, 좋을 대로
- ☐ to the delight of the populace=to the populace's great delight: 사람들이 매우 기쁘게도
- ☐ without heart: 힘없이
- ☐ a sense of mutual guilt: 상호간의 죄의식

Please keep an eye on my baggage, I'll be back soon .

: 나의 짐 좀 지켜봐주세요, 곧 돌아올게요.

What have I got to do with her? I have nothing to do with her.

: 내가 그녀와 무슨 관계가 있단 말이요? 나는 그녀와 아무런 관계가 없어요.

The coach motioned us to fight on.

: 코치는 우리가 계속 싸우라고 동작으로 신호를 보냈다.

» 원문

... Thereafter the drummer kept a strict eye upon the door. The time had not yet been called for him to hug the floor, but, as a minor precaution, he sidled near to the wall. ...

... "Well, who is he? What's he got to do with it?" "Oh, he's the town marshal. He goes out and fights Scratchy when he gets on one of these tears," "Wow!" said the drummer, mopping his brow. "Nice job he's got." ...

... The drummer wished to ask further questions, which were born of an increasing anxiety and bewilderment; but when he attempted them, the men merely looked at him in irritation and motioned him to remain silent. A sense waiting hush was upon them. ...

- keep on eye on...: ...을 지키다, 주시하다
- (A) have(got) (B) to do with (C): (A)는 (C)와 (B)한 관계에 있다
- be born of...: ...으로부터 태동하다, ...출신이다
- motion (A) to 동뷘: (A)에게 ...하도록 동작으로 신호를 보내다
- a sense waiting hush: 긴장을 기다리는 적막
  rf) hush: 쉿, 입막음, 말없음

When I was between jobs, I used to <u>hang out</u> in town.

: 직업이 없을 때, 나는 시내를 <u>배회하</u>곤 했다.

I am <u>kind of</u> hungry.

: 나는 <u>다소</u> 시장 끼가 있다.

<u>He usually swears at himself</u> when things go wrong.

: 일이 그릇 될 때 <u>그는 보통 자기 자신에게 욕지거리를 한다</u>.

» 원문

... He's about the last one of the old gang that <u>used to hang out</u> along the river here. He's terror when he's drunk. When he's sober he's all right-<u>kind of</u> simple-wouldn't hurt a fly-nicest fellow in town. But when he's drunk-whoo!" ...

... He missed it <u>by</u> a half-inch. <u>He swore at himself</u>, and went away. Later he comfortably fusilladed the windows of his most intimate friend. The man was playing with this town; it was a toy for him. ...

... <u>Tried to sneak up on me</u>," he said. "Tried to sneak up on me!" His eyes grew more baleful. As Potter made a slight movement, the man thrust his revolver venomously forward. "No; don't you do it, Jack Potter. ...

» Note

- swear himself: 자신에게 욕하다
- sneak up on...: ...에게 살금살금 다가가다

099

Ali Baba and the Forty Thieves(adapted)

\# **작품 소개:** 가난한 나무꾼 알리바바가 우연한 기회에 도둑의 일당이 보물을 숨겨둔 동굴에 들어가 그 일부를 집으로 가져온다. 그의 돈 많은 형 카심이 그 비밀을 알고 동굴에 들어가지만, 주문을 잊어서 밖으로 나오지 못하고 도둑들에게 살해된다. 40인의 도둑은 알리바바까지 죽이려고 기도하나, 카심의 여종이었던 어질고 착한 마르자나의 지혜로 도둑들을 퇴치할 수 있게 된다. 마르자나는 자유의 몸이 되어 알리바바의 아들과 결혼한다.

\# **작가 소개:** 미상

'Is it time?' the captive said to himself and as soon as the lamp went out suddenly, he fled for his life into the dark woods.

: '지금이 바로 그 시간인가?' 그 포로는 혼잣말로 중얼거렸다 그리고 불이 나가자마자 그는 숲 속으로 온 힘을 다해 도망쳤다.

At last I became fond of her and pay her great honour.

: 결국 나는 그녀를 좋아하게 되었고 경의를 표하게 되었다.

» **원문**

... Meanwhile Morgiana was busily cooking the supper, but was obliged to stop because her lamp went out suddenly, and found there was no oil in the house. ..., but as she came near the first jar a voice whispered, 'Is it time?' ...

... His plan was discovered, and he fled for his life. ...

... The great merchant was so rich and so friendly that Ali Baba's son soon became very fond of him and invited him to his father's house to supper, wishing to pay him great honour. ...

» **Note**

- □ go out: 나가다, 외출하다
- □ Is it time?: 지금이 그 시간인가?
- □ flee for one's life: 온힘을 다하여 도망치다
- □ become fond of...: ...을 좋아하게 되다
- □ pay 목적어(A) great honour: (A)에게 경의를 표하다

No wonder you should take the first prize.

: 당신이 일등상을 타야 하는 것은 당연하다.

» **원문**

... 'No wonder he would not eat salt with the man he means to kiil,' she said. Then she dressed herself as a dancer with a dagger in her hand ...

... 'You shall marry my son,' he cried, 'and become my daughter, for you deserve well the greatest reward that I can give.' ...

» **Note**

- □ No wonder...: ...하는 것은 당연하다
- □ deserve...: ...받을 가치[자격]가 있다

100

Aladdin and the Wonderful Lamp(adapted)

작품 소개: 알라딘은 새 램프와 헌 램프를 교환하는 일을 하는 사람을 위해 일하는 어린 노동자다. 시장을 어슬렁거리는 소년 알라딘을 유심히 지켜보던 한 마법사가 알라딘에게 접근하여 자신을 그의 삼촌이라고 속인다. 본인을 믿도록 만든 후 알라딘을 숲으로 데려간 마법사는 알라딘에게 동굴 속에 있는 낡은 램프를 가져오라고 하며 위험에 처했을 때 쓸 수 있을 반지 하나를 건네준다.

작가 소개: 미상

This very day I am supposed to meet my old friend in the appointed restaurant.

: <u>바로 오늘</u> 나는 나의 옛 친구를 정해진 식당 안에서 만나기로 되어있다.

» **원문**

… I am your long lost uncle!' and he threw his arms round Aladdin's neck and embraced him. …

… 'Tell your dear mother that I will come and see her <u>this very day</u>.' he cried, "and give her this small present." …

… '<u>It must be a mistake</u>,' she said, 'you have no uncle.' …

» **Note**

☐ this very day: 바로 오늘
☐ It must be a mistake.: 실수임에 틀림이 없다.

The guide showed us the beautiful sights.

: 안내원은 우리들에게 그 아름다운 광경들을 보여주었다.

Sprinkle some salt on the grilled steak and eat it.

: 소금을 석쇠로 구워낸 스테이크 위에 뿌려라 그리고 먹어라.

» **원문**

... and took him all over the city to show him the sights. ...

Aladdin quickly did as he was told, and when the stick blazed up merrily, the old man sprinkled some curious powder on the flames, and muttered strange words. ...

... 'Now,' said the old man, 'look in and you will see stone steps leading downwards. ...

» **Note**

□ show 목적어(A) the sights: (A)를 구경시키다

□ sprinkle: ...을 뿌리다

□ mutter: 중얼거리다

□ stone step: 돌계단

□ leading...: ...으로 통하는, 이끄는

Hand the file up to me at once.

: 그 파일을 나에게 즉시 건네주어라.

If you finish your report by tomorrow, slip it under my research room door.

: 당신이 리포트를 다 끝낸다면, 나의 연구실 문 아래로 그것을 살짝 밀어 넣어라.

He clasped his hands together and began to twist the plastic bottle.

: 그는 그의 손을 꼭 쥐었다. 그리고 그 플라스틱 병을 비틀기 시작했다.

» 원문

… 'Hand it up to me at once,' cried the old man angrily. 'Not till I am safely out,' repeated Aladdin. …

… Uttered the same strange words as before and instantly the stone slipped back into its place, the earth closed over it, and Aladdin was left in darkness. …

… He clasped his hands together, and in doing so rubbed the ring, which the Magician had put upon his finger. …

» Note

□ hand up to…: …에게 건네다, 넘겨주다
□ slip back into one's place: …위치 안에 재빨리[살짝] 밀어 넣다[들어가다]
□ clasp (A) together: (A)를 합쳐 쥐다

I almost fainted <u>for want of</u> food, but I came to myself in the help of some natives.

: 나는 거의 음식<u>이 부족하여</u> 졸도했다. 그러나 일부 원주민의 도움으로 <u>제 정신을 갖게</u> 되었다.

Don't make a hasty decision <u>at such a wild idea</u>.

: <u>그러한 막연한[엉뚱한] 생각에</u> 속단을 하지 말라.

The thief <u>was brought forward</u> the people and was beaten by them.

: 그 도둑은 사람들 <u>앞으로 끌려나와졌고</u> 그들에 의해 매질을 당했다

» **원문**

... He was so weak <u>for want of</u> food, and his joy at seeing his mother was so great, that <u>he fainted away</u>, but when <u>he came to himself</u> he promised to tell her all that had happened. ...

... Aladdin's mother stared at her son, and then began to laugh <u>at such a wild idea</u>. ...

... Then the Prime Minister ordered that <u>she should be brought forward</u>, and she came <u>bowing herself to the ground</u>. ...

» **Note**

- □ for want of...: ...의 부족으로
- □ faint away: 졸도하다, 쇠약해지기 시작하다
- □ come to oneself: 제정신이 들다, 활기를 띠다
- □ at such a wild idea: 어떤 엉뚱한[막연한] 생각 때문에
- □ bring forward: 앞으로 나오게 하다
- □ bow oneself to the ground: 고개를 푹 숙이다

376

The servants presented themselves before the master and begged for their wage raise.

: 하인들은 <u>주인 앞에 나타났다</u> 그리고 임금 인상을 간청했다.

He <u>called up</u> his friends to play soccer together.

: 그는 축구를 하기 위하여 그의 친구들을 <u>불러냈다.</u>

All students <u>crowded around</u> the fascinating pop stars and wanted their autographs.

: 모든 학생들이 매력적인 가수들 <u>주위로 움집했다.</u> 그리고 그들의 싸인을 원했다.

» **원문**

... When the three months had passed, <u>Aladdin's mother again presented herself</u> before the Emperor, and reminded him of his promise ...

... Then he returned home, and <u>once more called up the Slave of the Lamp.</u> ...

... As soon as the people heard his cry, <u>they crowded around him,</u> laughing and jeering, for they thought he must be mad to make such an offer. ...

» **Note**

☐ present oneself: 출석[등]하다, 나타나다

☐ call up: 상기하다, 불러내다

☐ crowd around: 떼 지어 모이다

377

The Terrible Iron Bed(adapted)
from Greek Myth

작품 소개: 아테네 왕의 아들 테세우스는 여행하다가 이상한 얘기를 듣는다. 프로크루스테스라는 여관 주인은 머무르는 손님이 잠자리에 들면 기계장치를 한 쇠침대에 손과 발을 묶어 침대보다 크면 잘라서 맞추고 침대보다 작으면 몸을 늘려서 맞추게 하여 죽인다는 얘기였다. 주인공은 미리 알고 있었기에 주인에게 눕는 모습을 보여달라고 속여 오히려 그와 같은 방식으로 그를 해치운다.

작가 소개: 미상

The robber drew his dagger and <u>sprang upon</u> me.

: 강도는 칼을 뽑았다 그리고 <u>나에게 덤벼들었다.</u>

We <u>took the enemy by surprise</u> in the darkness and they gave in.

: 우리는 야음을 틈타 <u>적을 기습했다</u> 그리고 적은 항복했다.

» **원문**

… When Theseus saw this he <u>sprang upon</u> Procrustes, and <u>taking him by surprise</u>, tied his arms and legs to the bed. …

» **Note**

☐ spring at(on)…: … 에게 덤벼들다
☐ take (A) by surprise: (A)를 기습하다

102

The Monster of Crete (adapted)
from Greek Myth

\# **작품 소개:** 약 3,300여 년 전, 그리스 남쪽 크레타섬에 사람 몸에 소의 머리를 한 괴물이 살고 있었다. 아테네 사람들은 이 괴물에게 해마다 선남선녀 열네 명을 제물로 바쳐야 했다. 이때 등장한 인물이 고대 그리스의 영웅 테세우스다. 테세우스는 산 제물로 바쳐지는 사람들 사이에 섞여 섬으로 들어가서 괴물을 처치하고 아테네로 돌아온다.

\# **작가 소개:** 미상

His action <u>was quick for</u> his thought, so he <u>rose to his feet</u> and tried to hit me.

: 그의 행동은 그의 생각에 비해 빨랐다, 그러므로 그는 벌떡 일어났다 그리고 나를 때리고자 했다.

» **원문**

… Then he tried to get up. But the brave youth <u>was quick for</u> him. Before the monster could <u>rise to his feet</u>, the sword of Theseus had struck through his heart. …

» **Note**

☐ be quick for…: …비하여 너무 재빠르다
☐ rise to one's feet: 벌떡 일어나다
☐ strike through…: …을 꿰뚫다

Noncooperation with Nonviolence

- Mohandas Karamchand Gandhi

> \# **작품 소개:** 영국 정부에 협조하지 않는 것이 unconstitutional(반헌법적) 하다는 이야기라고 들리는데 왜 그렇지 않은가에 대한 간디의 생각을 이야기하는 글이다.
>
> \# **작가 소개:** 본명은 모한다스 카람찬드 간디로 인도 독립운동의 정신적 지도자다.

So much for today. Let's go home.
: 오늘은 <u>이만합시다</u>. 집에 갑시다.

I would like to <u>venture to say</u> you are wrong.
: 나는 당신이 틀리다고 <u>감히 말하고</u> 싶다.

She is healthy and wealthy. <u>What's more</u> she is very beautiful.
: 그녀는 건강하고 부자다. <u>더욱이</u> 그녀는 매우 아름답다.

» **원문**

... I believe that a man is the strongest soldier for daring to perishes unarmed with his breast bare before the enemy. <u>So much for</u> the non-violent part of non-cooperation. I therefore, venture to suggest to my learned countrymen that so long as the doctrine of non-cooperation remains non-violent, so long there is nothing unconstitutional in that doctrine. ...

... I hold and <u>I venture to submit</u>, that there is nothing unconstitutional in it. <u>What is more</u>, I have done every one of these things in my life and nobody had questioned the constitutional character of it. ...

» **Note**

□ So much for... =That's what I have to say about...: ...은 이쯤 해두자
  ex) So much for today.: 오늘은 이만 끝냅시다.
□ What's more=Besides=Furthermore=Plus: 게다가

Franklin D. Roosevelt's Declaration of War

- Franklin Delano Roosevelt

작품 소개: 세계 대전 1930년대의 대공황을 타개하기 위해서 뉴딜정책을 도입하여 경제를 되살렸다. 제2차 세계대전에 참전하여 종전을 앞당기는 데 큰 역할을 했다. 이것이 이 대통령의 가장 동요를 일으키는 연설문 내용이다.

작가 소개: 미국의 제32대 대통령이다.

What they were telling a lie at that time speaks for itself.

: 그들이 그 당시 거짓말을 하고 있었다는 것은 자명하다.

All measures should be taken to put out the big fire.

: 그 큰불을 진 화하기 위해 모든 조치들이 취해져야만 했다.

» 원문

… And this morning the Japanese attacked Midway Island. Japan has, therefore, undertaken a surprise offensive extending throughout the Pacific area. The facts of yesterday and today speak for themselves. The people of the United States have already formed their opinions and well understand the implications to the very life and safety of our nation.

… As Commander-in-Chief of the Army and Navy I have directed that all measures should be taken for our defense. But always will our whole nation remember the character of the onslaught against us. …

» Note

□ speak for oneself: 자명하다
□ take measures: 조치를 취하다
    ex) take steps=take actions=do something: 조치를 취하다

105

An Iron Curtain Has Descended

- Winston Churchill

작품 소개: 옆에서 해리 트루먼 미국 대통령이 지켜보는 가운데 행한 연설에서 "유럽에는 '철의 장막'이 드리워졌다(An iron curtain has descended across the Continent)"라고 주장하면서 소련의 팽창주의에 대항하기 위한 '영어 사용 국민 간의 형제애적 단결'을 호소했다.

작가 소개: 영국의 유명한 정치가다.

I can not follow you. Please make it clear.

: 당신 말을 이해하지 못 하겠어요. 분명히 말해주세요.

Forgive me. I spoke only for myself.

: 이해해주세요. 나는 단지 내 입장만 말했을 뿐입니다.

I volunteered to serve in the army just because of the sense of duty.

: 나는 단지 의무감 때문에 군에 자원했습니다.

I had to work hard lest I should fall behind other friends.

: 나는 다른 친구들에게 뒤떨어지지 않기 위해 열심히 공부해야만 했다.

» 원문

… Let me, however, make it clear that I have no official mission or status of any kind and that I speak only for myself. There is nothing here but what you see. I can, therefore, allow my mind, with the experience of a lifetime, to play over the problems which beset us on the morrow of our absolute victory in arms, and to try to make sure, with what strength I have, that what has been gained with so much sacrifice and suffering shall be preserved for the future glory and safety of mankind.

The United States stands at this time at the pinacle of world power. It is a solemn moment for the American democracy. For with this primacy in power is also joined an awe-inspiring accountability to the future. As you look around you, you must feel not only the sense of duty done but also you must feel anxiety lest you fall below the level of achievement. …

» **Note**

- □ make (A) clear: (A)를 분명히 하다
- □ speak for oneself: 〈개인의 입장으로부터〉자신의 의견을 제시하다. 자명하다
- □ play over…: …곰곰이 생각해보다
- □ sense of duty: 의무감
- □ lest you (should) fall: 떨어지지 않도록
  cf) lest+주어(A)+(should)+동원: (A)가 …하지 않도록

The betrayer should be permanently outcast from our society.

: 그 배신자는 우리의 사회로부터 영원히 추방되어야 한다.

Fashion grows up in accordance with the mob psychology.

: 유행은 군중 심리와 조화하여 발전한다.

Korea was between dusk and dawn after Japanese invasion.

: 한국은 일본의 침략 후에 암흑기에 있었다.

... The safety of the world, ladies and gentlemen, requires a unity in Europe from which no nation should <u>be permanently outcast</u>. It is from the strong parent races in Europe that the world wars we have witnessed, or which occurred in former times, have sprung. ...

... But now we all can find any nation, wherever it may dwell, <u>between dusk and dawn</u>. Surely we should work with conscious purpose for a grand pacification of Europe within the structure of the United Nations and <u>in accordance with our charter</u>. ...

» **Note**

　□　be outcast from...: ...으로부터 버림받다

　□　between dusk and dawn: 암흑기에

　□　in accordance with: ...와 일치하여, ...에 따라

106

Against Hunger, Desperation, and Chaos

— George C. Marshall

작품 소개: 전쟁으로 피폐한 유럽의 재건을 위한 유럽 부흥계획을 제안하는 내용이다.

작가 소개: 제2차 세계대전 중에 미국 육군 참모총장을 지내고 그 후 국무장관과 국방장관을 지냈다. 1947년 그가 제안한 유럽 부흥계획은 마셜 플랜으로 알려져 있다.

Let's keep up the work in connection with our technology.

: 우리의 기술과 연계하여 그 일을 매진[계속]합시다.

The people concerned are only allowed to enter the main gate.

: 관계자들만이 그 정문을 출입할 수가 있다.

The treaty was signed by a number.

: 그 조약은 다수에 의해 조인되었다.

385

... Furthermore, the people of this country are distant from the troubled areas of the earth and it is hard for them to comprehend the plight and consequent reactions of the long-suffering peoples, the Europe and the effect of those reactions on their governments <u>in connection with</u> our efforts to promote peace in the world. ...

... Aside from the demoralizing effect on the world at large and the possibilities of disturbances arising as a result of the desperation of <u>the people concerned</u>, the consequences to the economy of the United States should be apparent to all. It is logical that the United States should do whatever it is able to do to assist in the return of normal economic health in the world, without which there can be no political stability and no assured peace. ...

... This is the business of the Europeans. The initiative, I think, must come from Europe. The role of this country should consist of friendly aid in the drafting of a European program and of later support of such a program so far as it may be practical for us to do so. The program should be a joint one, agreed to <u>by a number</u>, if not all European nations. ...

» **Note**

- in connection with...: ...와 관련하여, ...에 관계되어
- concerned: 관계[관예]하고 있는
  ex) the authorities concerned: 관계당국
- by a number: 다수에 의해

I Decline to Accept the End of Man

- **William Faulkner**

\# **작품 소개:** William Faulkner의 노벨상 수상 수락 연설 내용이다.

\# **작가 소개:** 미국의 작가(1897~1962)다. 20세기에 가장 영향력 있는 작가 중 한 사람으로, 1949년 노벨 문학상을 받았다.

The book is <u>worth reading</u>.

: 이 책은 <u>읽을 가치가 있다</u>.

The book is <u>worth three dollars</u>.

: 그 책은 <u>3달러 가치가있다</u>.

» **원문**

… There are no longer problems of the spirit. There is only the question: when I will be blown up! Because of this, the young man or woman writing today has forgotten the problems of the human heart in conflict with itself which alone can make good writing because only that <u>is worth writing about</u>, <u>worth the agony and the sweat</u>. …

» **Note**

☐ be worth …ing: …할 만한 가치가 있다

cf) worth+명사: …할 가치가 있는

I have a Dream

- Martin Luther King

작품 소개: 마틴 루서 킹 주니어가 1963년 8월 28일, 미국 워싱턴 DC에서 행했던 연설에 붙은 별칭이다. 이 연설은 흑인과 백인의 평등과 공존에 대한 요구였다.

작가 소개: 침례교 목사이자 미국 내 흑인 인권운동을 주도했고, 비폭력을 주장했다. 1964년 노벨 평화상을 받았다.

In a sense, they are wrong.

: 어떤 의미에선, 그들이 틀리다.

Please cash this 10-dollar check.

: 이 10달러짜리 수표를 현금으로 바꾸어 주세요.

Our people must fall heir to our land.

: 우리는 우리의 나라를 상속받아야만 한다.

The washing machine is guaranteed for two years.

: 그 세탁기는 2년 동안 보증된다.

» 원문

... In a sense we have come to our nation's Capital to cash a check. When the architects of our republic wrote the magnificent words of the Constitution and the Declaration of Independence, they were signing a promissory note to which every American was to fall heir. This note was a promise that all men would be guaranteed the unalienable rights of life, liberty, and the pursuit of happiness. ...

» Note

☐ cash a check: 수표를 현금으로 바꾸다

388

109

The Speech in the Mass for Peace

- Pope Paul VI

\# **작품 소개:** 평화를 위한 미사에서 로마 교황 6세가 한 연설문이다.

\# **작가 소개:** 재위기간 동안 제2차 바티칸 공의회(1962~65)가 대부분 열렸고, 공의회가 끝난 직후에는 변화하는 교령과 지침을 내렸다. 전도여행, 사회문제와 에큐메니컬 운동에 관심을 보였다.

At last the emigrant <u>set foot on</u> his long-cherished country after a two-month long journey.

: 마침내 그 이주민은 두 달 동안의 긴 여행 후에 그가 마음속에 간직해왔던 나라에 <u>첫 발을 내디뎠다.</u>

» **원문**

… This is this day which the lord has made: let us rejoice and be glad today! This is the day which We have desired for centuries! The day which, for the first times, sees the Pope <u>setting foot on</u> this young and glorious continent! An historic day, for it recalls and crowns the long years of the evangelization of America, and the magnificent development of the Church in the United States! …

» **Note**

□ set foot on…: …에 발을 들여놓다

Nixon's Inaugural Address

- Richard Nixon

\# 작품 소개: 닉슨 대통령의 취임 연설문(닉슨 독트린)이다.

\# 작가 소개: 리처드 닉슨(Richard Nixon)은 미국의 제37대 대통령이다.

After I was selected as a class reader, I took an oath in front of my classmates.

: 학급 실장으로 선출된 후에, 나는 급우들 앞에 나와 선서를 했다.

» **원문**

... I have taken an oath today in the presence of God and my countrymen to uphold and defend the Constitution of the United States. And to that oath, I now add this sacred committment: I shall consecrate my office, my energies and all the wisdom I can summon, to the cause of peace among nations. ...

» **Note**

☐ take[swear/make] an oath: 선서[맹세]하다

Carter's Inaugural Address - Jimmy Carter

\# **작품 소개:** 카터 대통령의 취임 연설문이다

\# **작가 소개:** 미국의 정치가이며 대통령이었다.

The president <u>assumed many responsibilities</u> to rebuild up the stagnated economy.

: 그 대통령은 침체된 경제를 재 보강하기 위한 <u>많은 책임을 떠맡았다.</u>

I will help out all of you <u>to the best of my ability</u>.

: 나는 <u>능력이 닿는 대로</u> 당신 모두를 돕겠습니다.

I <u>took heart</u> from the world famous writer who had endured all his difficulties.

: 나는 모든 어려움을 참아낸 그 세계적으로 유명한 작가로부터 <u>용기를 얻었다.</u>

The result of the football match <u>came short of</u> my expectation.

: 그 축구경기의 결과는 나의 기대<u>에 못 미쳤다.</u>

… As he <u>assumes that responsibility</u>, he will deserve the help and the support of all of us. As we look to the future, the first essential is to begin healing the wounds of this nation, to put the bitterness and divisions of the recent past behind us and to rediscover those shared ideals that lie at the heart of our strength and unity as a great and as a free people. …

… For more than a quarter of century in public life, I have shared in the turbulent history of this era. I have fought for what I believed in. I have tried <u>to the best of my ability</u> to discharge these duties, and meet those responsibilities, that were entrusted to me.

Sometimes I have succeeded. And sometimes I have failed, but always I <u>have taken heart</u> from what Theodore Roosevelt once said about the man in the arena, "whose face is marred by dust and sweat and blood, who strives valiantly, who errs and <u>comes short</u> again and again because there is not effort without error and shortcoming, but who does actually strive to do the deed, who knows the great enthusiasms, the great devotions, who spends himself in a worthy cause, who at the best knows in the end the triumphs of high achievements. And who at the worst, if he fails-at least fails while daring greatly." …

» Note

☐ assume that responsibility: 책임을 지다[떠맡다]
☐ to the best of one's ability: 힘자라는 대로, 가능한
☐ take[gather/pluck up] heart: 용기를 내다
☐ come short: 기대에 어긋나다, 미치지 않다, 그르치다

The witness appeared in the court and <u>attested once again to</u> the innocence of the pop star.
: 그 증인은 법원에 출두하여 그 팝 가수의 무죄를 <u>다시 한번 증언했다</u>.

When a big fire broke out, the fire fighters <u>tore down</u> the big gate and rush into the room to save the people.
: 큰불이 발생했을 때, 소방수들은 정문을 <u>허물고</u> 사람들을 구하기 위해 방 안으로 돌진해 들어갔다.

» **원문**

… For myself and for our nation, I want to thank my predecessor for all he has done to heal our land.

In this outward and physical ceremony we <u>attest once again to</u> the inner and spiritual strength of our nation. As my high school teacher, Miss Julia Coleman, used to say, "We must adjust to changing times and still hold to unchanging principles." …

… That we <u>had torn down</u> the barriers that separated those of different race and region and religion, and where there had been mistrust, built unity, with a respect for diversity. …

» **Note**

☐ attest to…: …을 증언하다

ex) He attested to the genuineness of the signature.: 그는 그 서명의 진짜를 증언했다.

☐ tear down: 무너뜨리다

112

Reagan's 1st Inaugural Address

- Ronald Wilson Reagan

작품 소개: 레이건 대통령의 취임 연설문이다.

작가 소개: 미국 제40대 대통령이었다.

It is **nothing less than** an invasion.
: 그것은 침략행위나 마찬가지다.

It is no coincidence that we met right here after twenty years. We have done our best to see each other so far.
: 20년 후에 우리가 바로 여기서 만난 것은 **결코 우연이 아니다**. 우리는 지금까지 서로를 보기 위해 최선을 다해왔다.

» **원문**

... The orderly transfer of authority as called for in the Constitution takes places as it has for almost two centuries and few of us stop to think how unicue we really are. In the eyes of many in the world, this every-four year ceremony we accept as normal is <u>nothing less than</u> a miracle. ...
... <u>It is no coincidence that</u> our present troubles parallel the proportion of the intervention and intrusion in our lives that have resulted from unnecessary and excessive growth of government ...

» **Note**

☐ nothing less than...: (1)적어도 ...이상, 꼭 ...만큼 (2)다름 아닌 바로 ...인
   cf) nothing more than=only
☐ It is no coincidence that...: ...한 것은 우연의 일치가 아니다

394

113

The Key to Progress is Freedom

-Ronald Wilson Reagan

\# 작품 소개: 레이건 미 대통령이 모스크바에서 행한 연설문이다.

Please repeat that again. I can not figure it out.
: 다시 말씀해주시오. 그것을 이해할 수가 없습니다.

The entertainers are endowed with their talents by the heaven.
: 연예인들은 그들의 재능을 천부적으로 부여받는다.

» 원문

… "There is a folk legend here, where I come from, that when a baby is born, an angel comes down from heaven and kisses it on one part of its body. If the angel kisses him on his hand, he becomes a handyman, if he kisses him on his forehead, he becomes bright and clever. And I've been trying to figure out where the angel kissed you so that you should sit there for so long and do nothing." …

… Go into any schoolroom, and there you will see children being taught the Declaration of Independence, that they are endowed by their creator with certain inalienable rights; among them, life, liberty, and the pursuit of happiness-that no government can justly deny; the guarantees in their constitution for freedom of speech, freedom of assembly, and freedom of religion. …

» Note

☐ figure out: 이해하다, 알아내다, 해결하다
☐ be endowed with…: …을 타고 나다, …을 가지고 태어나다

395

Solzhenitsyn's Speech of Acceptance of His 1970 Nobel Prize

- Alexander Solzhenitsyn

작품 소개: 솔제니친의 1970년 노벨 문학상 수상 수락연설문이다.

작가 소개: 러시아의 소설가, 극작가 및 역사가다.

The president visited the flood-washed area <u>in the flesh</u>.
: 그 대통령은 홍수로 씻겨 내려간 지역을 <u>몸소</u> 방문했다.

His speech <u>was subjected to</u> severe criticism.
: 그의 연설은 심한 <u>혹평을 받았다.</u>

I participated in this meeting <u>on behalf of</u> my father.
: 나는 나의 <u>아버지를 대신하여</u> 이 회의에 참가했습니다.

» **원문**

... Many Nobel Prize Laureates have appeared before you in this hall, but the Swedish Academy and the Nobel Foundation have probably never had as much bother with anyone as they have had with me. On at least one occasion I have already been here, although not in the flesh. ...

... It has prevented me from being crushed in the severe persecution to which I have been subjected. It has helped my voice to be heard in places where my predecessors have not been heard for decades. It has helped me to express things that would otherwise have been impossible. ...

... And I would like to express my heartfelt gratitude to the members of the Swedish Academy for the enormous support their choice in 1970 has given my work as a writer. I venture to thank them on behalf of that vast unofficial Russia which is prohibited from expressing itself aloud, which persecuted both for writing books and even for reading them. ...

» **Note**

☐ in the flesh: 몸소, 직접

  ex) I'm going to see my long-forgotten friend in the flesh: 나는 오랫동안 못 만났던 나의 친구를 직접 만나려고 한다.

☐ be subjected to...: ...을 당하다, ...을 받다 be subject to...: ...을 받기 쉽다, ...을 조건으로 하다

  ex) People's mind are subject to the weather.: 사람들의 마음은 날씨에 영향을 받기 쉽다.

☐ on behalf of...: ...을 대신하여

The Solitude
of Latin America

- Gabriel Garcia Marquez

작품 소개: 1982년 12월 노벨상 수상 수락연설문 내용이다.

작가 소개: 콜롬비아의 소설가이며 1982년 노벨 문학상 수상자다.

I dare to think that all of you are in the wrong.

: 나는 당신 모두가 잘못했다고 <u>감히 생각합니다.</u>

His weird behavior deserved the attention of his fans.

: 그의 특이한 행동은 그의 팬들의 <u>주목을 받을 만했다.</u>

The small boat was at the mercy of the angry waves.

: 그 작은 배는 사나운 <u>파도에 좌우되어</u> 이리저리 움직이고 있었다.

» **원문**

... I <u>dare to think</u> that it is this outsized reality, and not just its literary expression, that <u>has deserved</u> the attention of the Swedish Academy of Letters. ...

... But many European leaders and thinkers have thought so, with the childishness of old-timers who have forgotten the fruitful excesses of their youth as if it were impossible to find another destiny than to live <u>at the mercy of</u> the two great masters of the world. This, my friends, is the very scale of our solitude. ...

> **Note**

- dare to 동원: 감히 … 하다
- deserve+(동)명사: … 받을 만한 가치가 있다
- at the mercy of…: … 에 좌우되어

문학작품 속 실용영어

399